ATTITUDES, PERSONALITY AND BEHAVIOR

MAPPING SOCIAL PSYCHOLOGY

Series Editor: Tony Manstead

Current titles:

Icek Ajzen: *Attitudes, Personality and Behavior (Second Edition)*
Robert S. Baron and Norbert L. Kerr: *Group Process, Group Decision,*
    Group Action (Second Edition)
Marilynn B. Brewer: *Intergroup Relations (Second Edition)*
Steve Duck: *Relating to Others (Second Edition)*
J. Richard Eiser: *Social Judgement*
Russell G. Geen: *Human Aggression (Second Edition)*
Howard Giles and Nikolas Coupland: *Language: Contexts and*
    Consequences
Dean G. Pruitt and Peter J. Carnevale: *Negotiation in Social Conflict*
Wolfgang Stroebe: *Social Psychology and Health (Second Edition)*
John Turner: *Social Influence*
Leslie A. Zebrowitz: *Social Perception*

ATTITUDES, PERSONALITY AND BEHAVIOR

SECOND EDITION

Icek Ajzen

OPEN UNIVERSITY PRESS

Open University Press
McGraw-Hill Education
McGraw-Hill House
Shoppenhangers Road
Maidenhead
Berkshire
England
SL6 2QL

email: enquiries@openup.co.uk
world wide web: www.openup.co.uk

and Two Penn Plaza, New York, NY 10121-2289, USA

First published 2005
Reprinted 2011
Copyright © Icek Ajzen

A catalogue record of this book is available from the British Library

ISBN 10: 0 335 21703 6 (pb)   0 335 21704 4 (hb)
ISBN 13: 9780 335 217038 (pb)   9780 335 217045 (hb)

Library of Congress Cataloging-in-Publication Data
CIP data applied for

Typeset by RefineCatch Limited, Bungay, Suffolk
Printed in the UK by Ashford Colour Press Ltd, Gosport, Hampshire

To Rachela, Ron, and Jonathan

CONTENTS

PREFACE

The first edition of this book was written in a period of consolidation when rapid advances in personality and social psychology allayed concerns that had arisen over the utility of the field's central constructs, traits and attitudes. In it, I tried to highlight the similarities in the ways traits and attitudes are defined and measured, and in the implications of these definitions and measurement procedures for dispositional prediction of behavior. I tried to show how, in light of poor empirical evidence for consistency, enthusiastic acceptance of the trait and attitude concepts gave way, in both domains, to rather pessimistic assessments of the validity and practical utility of the dispositional approach. I traced parallel developments in the two domains that resulted in the adoption of very similar solutions to the consistency dilemma, and in the re-establishment of traits and attitudes as central constructs in personality and social psychology.

Much work in the intervening years has served to confirm these early efforts, to fill in the conceptual gaps, and to apply our newly gained knowledge in a variety of domains. We now have a much more mature understanding of the ways in which attitudes and personality traits affect behavior. In this new edition, I retain much of the original material but also review major new developments in the field. Among other things, I discuss recent innovations in the implicit assessment of attitudes and personality, and the implications of these techniques for the prediction of behavior; the distinction between spontaneous and reasoned processes; accessibility and schematicity; as well as recent work on the relation between intentions and behavior. Whenever appropriate, I discuss the contributions of my own work on the attitudinal prediction of behavior. As I noted in the Preface to the first edition, I have given these contributions undoubtedly more weight than they deserve, and I know that my own biases are felt throughout. In the interest of balance, therefore, I direct the reader to additional sources of relevant information at the end of each chapter.

I would like to express my sincere appreciation to the series editor, Tony

Manstead, for his support and helpful comments in relation to the first edition, and for encouraging me to consider this revision. Without his urging, this project would not have come to fruition.

Icek Ajzen

ONE

ATTITUDES AND PERSONALITY TRAITS

Behavior is a mirror in which everyone shows his image.

(Goethe)

It is common practice for psychologists and laypersons alike to explain human behavior by reference to stable underlying dispositions (Heider 1958; Campbell 1963). When people are caught lying or cheating, they are considered dishonest; when they perform poorly, they are said to lack ability or motivation; when they help a person in need, they are called altruistic or compassionate; and when they discriminate against members of a minority group, they are termed prejudiced.

Dispositional explanations of behavior have a long and distinguished history in personality and social psychology. In the domain of personality psychology the *trait* concept has carried the burden of dispositional explanation. A multitude of personality traits has been identified – among them dominance, sociability, independence, conscientiousness, hostility, helpfulness, self-esteem, emotional stability, ambitiousness – and new trait dimensions continue to join the growing list. In a similar fashion, the concept of *attitude* has been the focus of attention in explanations of human behavior offered by social psychologists. Numerous attitudes have been assessed over the years and, as new social issues emerge, additional attitudinal domains are explored. Examples are attitudes toward the church, toward hospitals and doctors, toward smoking and drinking, toward open education, toward politicians and political parties, toward ethnic groups and nationalities, and toward a host of social issues, such as nuclear power, energy conservation, protection of the environment, and the like.

This book is, at the most general level, concerned with the usefulness of the trait and attitude constructs. Following a brief discussion of the ways in which these dispositions have been conceptualized and measured, we examine the extent to which people in fact act in accordance with their traits and attitudes. We will see that correspondence between measured dispositions and overt actions is not as simple a matter as it might at first appear, and we will discuss some of the factors that have been found to influence the degree of correspondence that can be expected. This review and the integration of the relevant literature in personality and social psychology are followed by a presentation of a theoretical model that offers a general framework for dispositional prediction and explanation of social behavior.

FROM ACTS TO DISPOSITIONS

How do we know that a person is outgoing or reclusive, honest or dishonest, dominant or submissive; that she opposes or favors greater political integration of Europe, approves or disapproves of abortion, likes or dislikes the prime minister? We cannot observe these traits and attitudes, they are not part of a person's physical characteristics, nor do we have direct access to the person's thoughts and feelings. Clearly, personality traits and attitudes are latent, hypothetical characteristics that can only be *inferred* from external, observable cues. The most important such cues are the individual's behavior, verbal or nonverbal, and the context in which the behavior occurs (Heider 1958; Jones and Davis 1965; Kelley 1971).

Inferring personality traits from behavior

A personality trait is defined as a characteristic of an individual that exerts pervasive influence on a broad range of trait-relevant responses. Assumed to be behavioral manifestations of an underlying trait, people's responses are taken as indications of their standing on the trait in question. Table 1.1 shows that trait-relevant information can come from three sources: an observer, the individual him- or herself, or other people familiar with the individual, such as friends, parents, or peers. Many different kinds of responses can be considered manifestations of an underlying personality characteristic. Table 1.1 indicates that the responses used to infer a trait can be overt, i.e. directly observable, or covert, not directly accessible to an outside observer, although some covert responses, such as changes in blood pressure or heart rate, can be assessed by means of appropriate instruments.

Table 1.1   Responses used to infer personality traits

Nature of response	Source of information about responses		
	Observation	*Person*	*Acquaintances*
Overt	Motor acts, nonverbal cues, verbal behavior	Self-reports of motor acts, nonverbal cues	Peer-reports of motor acts, nonverbal cues
Covert	Physiological responses	Self-reports of thoughts, feelings, needs, desires	Peer-reports of thoughts, feelings, needs, desires

Consider, for example, extraversion, or the extent to which a person is outgoing. To infer a person's standing on this trait, we could examine overt behaviors in social situations, such as the number of interactions with others in a given time interval, the number of telephone calls made, the number of conversations with strangers initiated in the course of a week, or the number of words emitted during a 15-minute conversation with another person. In addition, we could consider such nonverbal cues as amount of eye contact with a conversation partner or seating distance from other people. Alternatively, we might direct our attention to internal reactions such as changes in heart rate or blood pressure when addressed by a stranger. Each of these reactions to other people could be taken as an indication of a person's degree of extraversion or introversion.

Of course, observing overt behaviors or internal reactions as they occur in naturalistic settings is costly and time-consuming. Mainly for practical reasons, therefore, personality inventories often rely on self-reports of behavior, or reports provided by others familiar with the individual. Thus, we can ask people about the number of friends they have, how often they initiate conversations with strangers, how many parties they attend, how they feel in the presence of others, and so on. Finally, we can ask a person's acquaintances to provide information about overt or covert responses relevant to sociability: how much the person likes parties, how many close friends she has, the extent to which she is shy in front of others, and so forth. Like observations of overt behaviors or nonverbal cues, self-reports or reports provided by acquaintances can be taken as indications of a person's standing on the underlying sociability trait.

Inferring attitudes from behavior

An attitude is a disposition to respond favorably or unfavorably to an object, person, institution, or event. Although formal definitions of attitude vary, most contemporary social psychologists agree that the characteristic attribute of attitude is its evaluative (pro–con, pleasant–unpleasant) nature (see, e.g., Edwards 1957; Osgood et al. 1957; Bem 1970; Fishbein and Ajzen 1975; Hill 1981; Oskamp 1991; Eagly and Chaiken 1993). This view is strengthened by the fact that, as we shall see below, standard attitude scaling techniques result in a score that locates an individual on an evaluative dimension *vis-à-vis* the attitude object (cf. Green 1954; Fishbein and Ajzen 1975).

Like personality trait, attitude is a hypothetical construct that, being inaccessible to direct observation, must be inferred from measurable responses. Given the nature of the construct, these responses must reflect positive or negative evaluations of the attitude object. Beyond this requirement, however, there is virtually no limitation on the kinds of responses that can be considered. To simplify matters, it is useful to categorize attitude-relevant responses into various subgroups. Thus, we might distinguish between responses directed at others and responses directed at the self, between behaviors performed in public and behaviors performed in private, or between actions and reactions. However, the most popular classification system goes back at least to Plato and distinguishes between three categories of responses: cognition, affect, and conation (see Allport 1954; McGuire 1969, and Hilgard 1980, for general discussions). Within each of these categories, it is also useful to separate verbal from nonverbal responses. Based on Rosenberg and Hovland's (1960) analysis, Table 1.2 shows the different types of responses from which attitudes can thus be inferred.

Cognitive responses

In the first category are responses that reflect perceptions of, and thoughts about, the attitude object. Consider some of the responses we might use to infer attitudes toward the medical profession. Cognitive responses of a verbal nature are expressions of *beliefs* that link the medical profession with certain characteristics or attributes. Beliefs to the effect that physicians are mostly interested in money, that hospitals are overcrowded, that many health professionals are poorly qualified, or that most diseases cannot be cured by traditional methods, might be taken as evidence of a negative attitude toward the medical profession. By way of contrast, a favorable attitude would be implied by expressions of beliefs suggesting that nurses and doctors do their best to help patients, that medicine has made considerable progress over the years, that many physicians work long and inconvenient hours, and the like.

Cognitive responses of a nonverbal kind are more difficult to assess, and the information they provide about attitudes is usually more indirect. For example, we might theorize that people with favorable attitudes toward the medical establishment have relatively low thresholds for the perception of attitude-relevant positive stimuli, while people with unfavorable attitudes have relatively low thresholds for negative stimuli. To infer attitudes toward the medical profession, therefore, we might measure how long it takes a person to appreciate the significance of cartoons depicting doctors, nurses, and hospitals in either a favorable or an unfavorable light.

Affective responses

The second category of responses from which attitudes can be inferred has to do with evaluations of, and feelings toward, the attitude object. Here again, we can distinguish between affective responses of a verbal and of

Table 1.2   Responses used to infer attitudes

Response mode	Response category		
	Cognition	Affect	Conation
Verbal	Expressions of beliefs about attitude object	Expressions of feelings toward attitude object	Expressions of behavioral intentions
Nonverbal	Perceptual reactions to attitude object	Physiological reactions to attitude object	Overt behaviors with respect to attitude object

a nonverbal kind. Verbal affective responses with respect to the medical profession, for example, can be expressions of admiration or disgust, appreciation or disdain. Thus, a person who claims to admire physicians or nurses, or to 'feel good' about available medical care, would seem to hold a favorable attitude toward the medical profession, but a person who indicates that the mere thought of doctors and hospitals is disgusting would seem to hold a negative attitude.

Facial expressions, as well as various physiological and other bodily reactions, are often assumed to reflect affect in a nonverbal mode. Among the bodily reactions considered are the galvanic skin response (electrical conductance of the skin), constriction and dilation of the pupil, heart rate, blood pressure, the reactions of facial muscles, and other reactions of the sympathetic nervous system.

Conative responses

Responses of a conative nature are behavioral inclinations, intentions, commitments, and actions with respect to the attitude object. Starting again with the verbal mode of expression, we can consider what people say they do, plan to do, or would do under appropriate circumstances. Thus, people with negative attitudes toward the medical profession might indicate that they would refuse to be hospitalized, that they see a doctor only when absolutely necessary, or that they discourage their children from going to medical school. Those with positive attitudes, on the other hand, might express intentions to donate money to a fund for a new hospital wing, they might plan to encourage their children to go to medical school, they might indicate a readiness to read about advances in medicine, and so on.

Nonverbal conative responses indicating favorable or unfavorable attitudes toward the medical profession are also easily imagined. Thus, people who actually read books or articles about medicine, who encourage their children to go to medical school, or who accept and follow their physicians' advice would be classified as having positive attitudes, whereas people who refuse to donate money to a medical fund or who write letters to newspapers complaining about the medical profession would be said to have negative attitudes.

In sum, an individual's favorable or unfavorable attitude toward an object, institution, or event can be inferred from verbal or nonverbal responses toward the object, institution, or event in question. These responses can be of a cognitive nature, reflecting perceptions of the object, or beliefs concerning its likely characteristics; they can be of an affective nature, reflecting the person's evaluations and feelings; and they can be of a conative nature, indicating how a person does or would act with respect to the object.

Attitudes versus traits

For the most part, the present book emphasizes the similarities of the trait and attitude concepts. There are, however, also some important differences between traits and attitudes that we should briefly consider. Clearly, both terms refer to latent, hypothetical constructs that manifest themselves in a wide variety of observable responses. In the case of attitudes, these responses are evaluative in nature, and they are directed at a given object or target (a person, institution, policy, or event). Personality traits, by contrast, are not necessarily evaluative. They describe response tendencies in a given domain, such as the tendency to behave in a conscientious manner, to be sociable, to be self-confident, and so forth. The responses that reflect an underlying trait do not focus on any particular external target. Instead, they focus on the individual him- or herself and they can thus be used to differentiate between individuals and to classify them into different personality types. Although attitudes and traits are both assumed to be relatively stable, enduring dispositions, attitudes are typically viewed as more malleable than personality traits. Evaluations can change rapidly as events unfold and new information about a person or issue becomes available, but the configuration of personality traits that characterizes an individual is much more resistant to transformation.

Explicit measures of attitudes and personality traits

The discussion of attitude and personality measurement in this section is not intended to provide a thorough treatment of the subject. Many methods are available, some quite sophisticated in terms of the stimulus situations they create, the ways they assess responses, and the statistical procedures they employ. (Interested readers can consult Green (1954), Edwards (1957), and Fishbein and Ajzen (1975), for the construction of attitude scales; and Kleinmuntz (1967), Jackson (1971), and Wiggins (1973) for personality assessment.) The aim of the present treatment is merely to introduce the reader to some of the basic principles involved in the assessment of dispositions, especially those principles that have some bearing on our discussions in later chapters of attitude–behavior and trait–behavior correspondence.

Most methods used to infer traits or attitudes rely on verbal responses to questionnaire items. Our discussion of trait and attitude measurement in this section will therefore focus on verbal responses, but it should be kept in mind that the same procedures can be applied equally well to observations of nonverbal responses. Furthermore, our discussion will be concerned primarily with self-reports of behavior or of internal states, rather than with reports provided by others familiar with the individual. Again, however, the methods discussed can be applied just as well to peer-reports as to self-reports.

Direct assessment

Single items   The simplest procedure in many ways is to ask respondents to report directly on their own attitudes or personality traits. Many studies in personality and social psychology employ direct probes of this kind. Consider the following examples.

In a study dealing with the effect of vested interest on the attitude–behavior relation (Sivacek and Crano 1982) a 7-point scale was used to assess attitudes of college students toward raising to 21 the legal drinking age in the state of Michigan (where the study was conducted). The scale took the following form:

Michigan's drinking age should be raised to 21

agree :____:____:____:____:____:____:____: disagree

In another study of the attitude–behavior relation (Lord et al. 1984), attitudes toward homosexuals were assessed, among other topics. Respondents were asked to rate, on a 10-point scale, how likable they found the typical homosexual. The investigators did not report the exact details of the scale, but it could have been presented as follows:

Homosexuals are

extremely   not at all
likable :____:____:____:____:____:____:____:____:____: likable

Chaiken and Yates (1985) used two single items, each involving an 11-point scale, to obtain direct measures of attitudes toward capital punishment and toward censorship, as follows:

I favor   I oppose
capital   capital
punishment :____:____:____:____:____:____:____:____:____:____: punishment

I favor   I oppose
censorship :____:____:____:____:____:____:____:____:____:____: censorship

Comparable examples can be found in the personality domain. Thus, in a study that dealt with the introversion–extraversion trait (Monson et al. 1982), undergraduate college students were given the following descriptions of extraverts and introverts:

Extraverts are typically outgoing, sociable, energetic, confident, talkative, and enthusiastic. Generally confident and relaxed in social situations, this type of person rarely has trouble making conversation with others.

Introverts are typically somewhat more shy, timid, reserved, quiet, distant, and retiring. Often this type of person is relatively awkward or ill at ease in social situations, and consequently is not nearly as adept at making good conversation.

As a measure of introversion–extraversion, the participants were asked to indicate which was a better description of themselves.

Buss and Craik (1980) used several methods to assess degree of dominance in a sample of college students, including a 7-point self-rating scale. The scale may have appeared in the questionnaire as follows:

I would describe myself as (check one)
____ extremely dominant
____ quite dominant
____ slightly dominant
____ neither dominant nor submissive

____ slightly submissive
____ quite submissive
____ extremely submissive

In many cases, single-item measures of this kind have proved quite adequate for the assessment of particular attitudes or personality traits. There are, however, potential drawbacks to this method. Some of the problems are shared by other methods and will be considered later, but one issue is particularly troublesome for single-item measures of attitudes or personality traits. This is the question of *reliability*, or the extent to which repeated assessments of the same trait or attitude produce equivalent results. Single responses tend to be quite unreliable, leading to low correlations between repeated observations. Misreading a statement or placing a check mark in the wrong place can produce a response that implies extraversion or a negative attitude toward homosexuals, but on another occasion, the item may be read appropriately, and a different response is given. For this reason, and for other reasons to be discussed below, it is usually preferable to use multi-item measures of attitudes and personality traits.

Multi-item measures   Perhaps the best-known multi-item measure used to obtain a relatively direct indication of attitude is the *semantic differential*, developed by Charles Osgood and his associates (Osgood et al. 1957). Designed originally to measure the meaning of a concept, it is now used in a variety of contexts. As a measure of attitude, the semantic differential consists of a set of bipolar evaluative adjective pairs, such as *good–bad*, *harmful–beneficial*, *pleasant–unpleasant*, *desirable–undesirable*, and *awful–nice*. Each adjective pair is placed on opposite ends of a 7-point scale, and respondents are asked to mark each scale as it best reflects their evaluation of the attitude object. Thus, the following evaluative semantic differential could be used to assess attitudes toward homosexuals:

Homosexuals are

pleasant :___:___:___:___:___:___:___: unpleasant
harmful :___:___:___:___:___:___:___: beneficial
good :___:___:___:___:___:___:___: bad
awful :___:___:___:___:___:___:___: nice

Responses are scored from −3 on the negative side of each scale to +3 on the positive side, and the sum over the four scales is a measure of the respondent's attitude toward homosexuals.

In their study of attitude change mentioned earlier, Chaiken and Yates (1985) used such an evaluative semantic differential as another way of assessing attitudes toward capital punishment and toward censorship. The 4-item semantic differential with respect to capital punishment looked as follows:

Capital punishment is

good :___:___:___:___:___:___:___: bad
foolish :___:___:___:___:___:___:___: wise
sick :___:___:___:___:___:___:___: healthy
harmful :___:___:___:___:___:___:___: beneficial

A simple replacement of 'Capital punishment' by 'Censorship' allowed the investigators to use the same instrument to assess attitudes toward censorship.

Personality researchers have tended to use adjective check-lists, rather than opposite adjective pairs, to obtain self-reports of personality traits. Consider, again, the extraversion–introversion trait mentioned earlier. In the paragraph descriptions of this trait dimension shown above, several specific adjectives were used to illustrate the two extremes: outgoing, sociable, energetic, confident, talkative, and enthusiastic versus shy, timid, reserved, quiet, distant, and retiring. This list of adjectives could be presented to respondents in random order, and they could be asked to indicate, for each adjective, how characteristic it was of them. A frequently used format asks respondents to place a number in front of each adjective, as in the following example:

5 = extremely characteristic of me
4 = quite characteristic of me
3 = neither characteristic nor uncharacteristic of me
2 = quite uncharacteristic of me
1 = extremely uncharacteristic of me

____	outgoing	____	shy
____	energetic	____	sociable
____	reserved	____	confident
____	distant	____	talkative
____	enthusiastic	____	retiring
____	quiet	____	timid

The respondent's degree of extraversion is computed as follows. The scores for the introverted adjectives (reserved, shy, timid, and so forth) are reversed, such that 5 becomes 1, 4 becomes 2, etc., and these scores are added to the scores for the extraverted adjectives. The higher the total score, the more extraverted the respondent's self-report.

Direct measures of dispositions that rely on multiple items have fewer problems of reliability than single-item measures. Clerical mistakes and other incidental factors that affect the score on one item but not on the others will have little systematic impact on the overall score. Different kinds of errors associated with different items will tend to cancel each other, leaving the total score relatively unaffected. The greater the number of items used, therefore, the more reliable the score will tend to be. In fact, it is possible to compute the increment in reliability that is likely to result from an increased number of items. The relationship between the number of items in our measure and its reliability is given by the Spearman-Brown prophecy formula, as shown in the following equation:

$$r_{xx'} = \frac{mr_{xx'}}{1 + (m-1)r_{xx'}}$$

where $r_{xx'}$ is the estimate of reliability for a scale m times as long as the original scale, and $r_{xx'}$ is the assessed reliability of the original scale.[1] According to this formula, when a single-item measure has a relatively low reliability of, say, 0.40, a measure consisting of four items will nevertheless have a respectable reliability of 0.72.

Note that nothing has been said so far about the ways in which the semantic differential adjective pairs were selected to assess attitudes toward homosexuals or toward capital punishment, nor about the ways in which extraversion–introversion adjectives were selected. Each adjective pair on a semantic differential is supposed to reflect evaluation of the attitude object, and each adjective on a checklist should be representative of the personality trait that is being assessed. Procedures for selecting appropriate items to be included in an attitude or personality inventory are taken up next in the discussion of indirect methods for the assessment of behavioral dispositions.

Indirect assessment

Direct dispositional measures of the multi-item kind have proved very useful in attitude and personality research. They are easily developed and, for this reason, are very popular, especially in the context of laboratory studies. For some purposes, however, they are somewhat limited because they may elicit relatively superficial responses. Consider, for example, attitudes toward the military. When asked to rate the military on an evaluative semantic differential, responses may reflect an image that is easily accessible from memory at the time of measurement. Perhaps this image was recently created by television coverage of a demonstration brutally suppressed by military forces. If induced to think more thoroughly about the military, however, respondents might consider its role in the defense of their country, educational opportunities it provides for young people who otherwise would go without this education, and so forth. Similarly, people who, in response to an adjective checklist, indicate that they are relatively conscientious might, if induced to scan their behavior more thoroughly, realize that there are many situations in which they behave less reliably than they initially thought they did. Indirect measures of attitudes and personality traits provide opportunities for respondents to review different aspects of a given domain. The responses they provide to a set of specific questions are then used to infer the disposition under investigation.

Earlier we discussed the different kinds of verbal responses that can be used to infer traits and attitudes (see Tables 1.1 and 1.2). Usually, the items that appear on a questionnaire are statements of beliefs, of behavioral intentions, or of actual behavior, and respondents are asked to indicate their agreement or disagreement with each statement. As an example in the attitude domain, consider the following statements taken from a 22-item scale developed to measure attitudes toward the law (Rundquist and Sletto 1936):

The law protects property rights at the expense of human rights. (–)
On the whole, policemen are honest. (+)
It is all right to evade the law if you do not actually violate it. (–)
Juries seldom understand a case well enough to make a really just decision. (–)
In the courts a poor man will receive as fair treatment as a millionaire. (+)
It is difficult to break the law and keep one's self-respect. (+)

Respondents answer each item by choosing one of five alternatives, a format proposed by Likert (1932) as part of his attitude scaling method:

_____ Strongly agree   (5)
_____ Agree   (4)
_____ Undecided   (3)
_____ Disagree   (2)
_____ Strongly disagree   (1)

The scoring key for each item is shown in parentheses. Positive items are scored from 5 (strongly agree) to 1 (strongly disagree), while reverse scoring is used for negative items. The respondent's total attitude score is computed by summing all item scores; high scores indicate positive attitudes toward the law.

A second example of an attitude scale can be found in a study of religion and humanitarianism (Kirkpatrick 1949). The following statements are a sample of the 69 items on Kirkpatrick's attitude toward religion scale:

No scientific law has yet given a satisfactory explanation of the origin of life.   (+)
The soul is a mere supposition, having no better standing than a myth.   (−)
Belief in God makes life on earth worthwhile.   (+)
Without the church there would be a collapse of morality.   (+)
The findings of modern science leave many mysteries unsolved, but they are still incompatible with a personal God concept.   (+)

The scoring key is again given in parentheses. Respondents are asked to indicate whether they agree or disagree with each statement. Agreement with a positive item is counted as +1 and disagreement as −1. For negative items, agreement is counted as −1 and disagreement as +1. Attitudes toward religion are computed by summing over all 69 items; high scores indicate positive attitudes toward religion.

Similar procedures are adopted in the personality domain to assess various personality traits. Consider, for example, Eysenck's (1956) extraversion scale. Among the 24 items on the scale are the following:

Are you inclined to keep quiet when out in a social group?   (no)
Do you like to have many social engagements?   (yes)
Would you rate yourself as a happy-go-lucky individual?   (yes)
Is it difficult to 'lose yourself' even at a lively party?   (no)
Do you generally prefer to take the lead in group activities?   (yes)
Are you inclined to be shy in the presence of the opposite sex?   (no)

Respondents answer yes, no, or undecided to each question. The scoring key in the direction of extraversion is shown in parentheses after each item. An answer in accordance with the scoring key is given two points, an answer contrary to the key is given zero points, and an undecided response is given one point. The sum over all 24 items on the scale is the measure of a person's extraversion tendency.

As another example in the personality domain, consider the following items taken from a 10-item private self-consciousness scale (Fenigstein et al. 1975). Responses to each item are given on a 5-point scale that ranges from *extremely uncharacteristic* to *extremely characteristic*. The scoring key is shown in parentheses. A plus sign indicates that the item expresses high self-consciousness, a minus sign that it expresses low self-consciousness.

> I am always trying to figure myself out.   (+)
> I reflect about myself a lot.   (+)
> Generally, I'm not very aware of myself.   (−)
> I'm alert to changes in my mood.   (+)

Responses are scored from 1 (extremely uncharacteristic) to 5 (extremely characteristic) for items expressing high self-consciousness, and in reversed fashion for items expressing low self-consciousness. The final private self-consciousness score is obtained by summing over all 10 items on the scale.

Item selection   In the measurement of dispositions, the most important part is the formulation of a large set of statements and selection of appropriate items from which the disposition of interest can be validly inferred. The first step in the selection procedure involves mapping the domain of the attitude or personality trait in question. We need to decide what kinds of responses we want to include in our definition of the disposition before we can formulate appropriate items. For example, if we want to measure attitudes toward the European Union, we could decide to restrict our definition of the domain to economic aspects of cooperation and competition among the nations of Europe who are part of the EU. Alternatively, we could define the attitude object much more broadly as including cultural, political, military, and social relations among member nations. Similarly, before we can construct items for a personality measure of, say, conscientiousness, we must define the concept's domain of application. Among other things, we need to map the situations in which conscientiousness can be observed (at work, at home, with friends, etc.) as well as the different kinds of behaviors in which it can find expression (reliability, punctuality, neatness, honesty, and so on).

Once the domain is clearly defined, we can proceed with the construction of items that explore the various aspects of the domain. Of course, not every item that, on the face of it, appears to be relevant for the disposition of interest will in fact be found appropriate. For this reason the investigator usually constructs a large pool of items, perhaps as many as 150 or 200, from which the final set is selected. It is beyond the scope of this chapter to review the different item selection procedures that have been developed for the measurement of attitudes and personality traits. We will here deal only with the major considerations involved in popular methods.

To understand the logic of item selection we must first explore the nature of attitude and personality trait scores. As we saw in the above examples of attitude scales, a respondent's answer to a given item is, depending on the nature of the item, taken as an indication of a positive or of a negative attitude. The response to one item can imply a positive attitude, the response to another item a negative attitude. Only in their totality do responses to the scale reveal the respondent's overall attitude. A person who agrees with many positive items, and with few negative items, is said to have a relatively favorable attitude; a person who agrees with many negative statements and disagrees with many positive statements is said to have a relatively unfavorable attitude; and a person who agrees with about as many positive as negative items is said to have a relatively neutral attitude. Thus, the attitude score, which is computed by summing the responses to all items on the scale, reflects the *degree* to which the respondent's attitude is favorable or unfavorable.

By the same token, responses to statements on a personality scale indicate high or low standing on the personality trait being assessed. The response to one item on a scale designed to assess dominance may indicate that the person is dominant, while the response to another item may imply submissiveness. As in the case of attitudes, the respondent's location on the trait dimension can be ascertained only by considering responses to all items on the scale. Thus, the trait score on a dominance scale indicates the *degree* to which a person is dominant or submissive.

To select the most appropriate items from the large pool constructed by the investigator, the initial set of items is administered to a sample of respondents. Preliminary attitude or trait scores are computed by summing over all items in the pool. Assuming that the majority of items initially constructed by the investigator do indeed reflect the disposition of interest, the preliminary score will be a reasonably good first approximation and can thus serve as a criterion for item selection.[2] That is, to the extent that a given item is a good representative of the dispositional domain, it should correlate with the total score. For this reason, the item-total correlation is the most important, and most frequently used, criterion in item selection procedures. In attitude measurement, this criterion was first proposed by Likert (1932); it is known as the *criterion of internal consistency*, and it is the critical feature of the Likert scaling method (see Green 1954; Edwards 1957).[3]

The next step, then, in the construction of an attitude or personality scale is the selection of items from the initial pool that have the highest correlations with the total score (i.e., with the preliminary attitude or trait score). These items may be said to represent best the disposition of interest, as it is reflected in the total score. Once this criterion is met and we have a set of items that correlate highly with the total score, other considerations may enter as well. One frequent recommendation is that, in spite of their relatively high correlations with the total score, the items selected should not correlate too strongly with each other. We could obtain high correlations among all items in a pool, and hence between each item and the total score, by simply rewording the same statement in different ways. A set of items constructed in this manner would, however, fail adequately to reflect the general attitude or trait domain under investigation. Instead, it would assess a very narrow response tendency. The requirement that items have low correlations among themselves ensures a relatively heterogeneous set of items that explore the general domain, while the internal consistency criterion ensures that each item is in fact representative of that domain.

The final attitude or personality scale consists of a relatively small set of items that have passed the criteria of internal consistency and heterogeneity. This scale can now be administered to a sample of respondents, and attitude or trait scores are computed by summing over all item scores.

Representativeness and validity The fact that items on an attitude or personality scale are concerned with different aspects of the dispositional domain has important implications for the representativeness and validity of our measures. It suggests that, for several reasons, no single item is likely to capture fully the attitude or personality trait of interest. Obviously, each item only deals with a limited aspect of the disposition's domain of application. Moreover, any single response is influenced by a multitude of factors, some quite unrelated to the attitude or personality trait under study. Consider, for example, the statement, 'No scientific law has yet given a satisfactory explanation of the origin of life,' which was part of the attitude toward religion scale mentioned earlier. Some respondents may disagree with this item not because they hold unfavorable attitudes toward religion but because they have respect for science. Conversely, agreement with the statement may reflect dissatisfaction with the state of modern science rather than rejection of science on the basis of religious belief.

It is for these reasons that responses to single items tend to be unrepresentative and poor measures of broad behavioral dispositions. In fact, even after meeting the criterion of internal consistency, items included on the final attitude or personality scale tend to correlate only moderately with the total score. The typical correlation between responses to any given item on a scale and the overall score tends to be in the 0.30 to 0.40 range. Clearly, then, by themselves single items cannot be considered valid indicators of the underlying disposition. Only in the aggregate can responses to an attitude or personality inventory be said to assess the general behavioral disposition of interest. As we aggregate responses by summing the different item scores, we eliminate the influence of unique factors associated with any given item. These unique factors tend to 'cancel out' and the total score reflects the common core of all items on the scale, namely, the attitude or personality trait that is being inferred.

Overcoming self-presentation biases

Although most investigators agree that verbal response scales often yield reliable and valid measures of attitudes and personality traits, a sense of unease can accompany use of such scales. Investigators have long realized that verbal responses to questionnaire items may be systematically distorted or biased by self-presentational concerns and thus may not reflect a person's true attitude or personality (see, e.g., Campbell 1950; Guilford 1954; Cook and Selltiz 1964). This is of special concern in attempts to assess attitudes toward socially sensitive topics, such as racial or sexual attitudes, or personality traits that have strong social desirability overtones, such as honesty or neuroticism. When responding to inventories designed to measure dispositions of this kind, participants may provide socially desirable answers, i.e. answers that reflect favorably on the participant (Bernreuter 1933; Lenski and Leggett 1960; Paulhus 1991). Numerous attempts have been made over the years to overcome self-presentational biases of this kind, some by disguising the purpose of the inquiry, others by using responses over which participants have limited control.

Disguised techniques

In the attitude domain, investigators have tried to disguise their measures by eliciting non-evaluative judgments to questionnaire items. For example, instead of asking respondents to indicate how strongly they agree or disagree with items on a questionnaire, they can be asked to rate the extent to which the statements are *plausible* (Waly and Cook 1965; Saucier and Miller 2003) or to estimate how others would respond to each item. It is expected that respondents' attitudes bias these judgments, such that participants with positive attitudes judge favorable statements as plausible and agreement with such statements as common, whereas participants with negative attitudes judge them as implausible and agreement as unlikely. If this is indeed the case, then it is possible to infer respondents' attitudes from their plausibility or commonality judgments.

In another method, known as the *error-choice technique* (Hammond 1948), the attitude or personality inventory is presented as an information test. Participants are shown two or more response options for each item and are asked to check the correct one. For example, in an attempt to develop a measure of attitude toward the Americans with Disabilities Act (ADA) (Clarke and Nancy 2000), participants read 25 statements about the Act, such as the following:

> An employer asks whether a job applicant drinks alcohol and/or currently uses illegal drugs. The employer
> A. Has violated the ADA
> B. Has not violated the ADA.

According to the logic of the error-choice technique, because participants are presumably unfamiliar with the legally correct responses, they are likely to choose answers on the basis of their underlying attitudes. Thus, selection of the first alternative would indicate a negative attitude toward the ADA, selection of the second a positive attitude.

The error-choice technique has also been used in attempts to obtain bias-free measures of personality characteristics, including neuroticism and extraversion (Wilde and Fortuin 1969; Wilde and de Wit 1970). Items were taken from a standard personality inventory with known proportions of agreement in the general population. Each item was accompanied by two percentages equidistant from the known proportion. For example, the following were two of the items used to assess neuroticism:

> 1. Do you sometimes gossip?   ____ 89%   ____ 97%.
> 2. Do you often suffer from headaches?   ____ 26% ____ 16%.

The inventory was presented to participants as a test of insight into fellow human beings. They were asked to indicate what proportion of respondents in the general population had answered 'yes' for each question. Actually, neither alternative was correct; the true proportions were 91 percent and 21 percent, respectively. Overestimates were scored as indicating greater neuroticism than underestimates.

Responses over which people have limited control

Autonomous reactions   We noted earlier (see Tables 1.1 and 1.2) that it may be possible to infer attitudes and personality traits from various physiological reactions: the galvanic skin response (electrical conductance of the skin), heart rate, blood pressure, palmar sweat, pupillary dilation and constriction, and so forth. Investigators were attracted to these types of responses early on because – being difficult to control – they were thought to be relatively immune to self-presentation biases. It was soon discovered, however, that measures based on physiological reactions are difficult to interpret and tend to have relatively low reliability and validity (see Kidder and Campbell 1970). For these reasons there is currently little interest in such measures.[4]

Projective tests   Other attempts to overcome social desirability bias in attitude assessment have relied on projective techniques originally developed by clinical psychologists to assess unconscious needs and motives that may account for psychoneurotic symptoms or maladaptive behaviors. Among the better-known examples are human figure drawings, sentence completion tests, and responses to ink blots (the Rorschach method) or ambiguous pictures (the Thematic Apperception Test). Applied to the measurement of personality traits, it was hoped that appropriate analyses of responses to unstructured stimuli could, for example, reveal deep-seated fears of other people or needs to affiliate, information that could provide clues about degree of introversion or extraversion. Similarly, racial attitudes might be inferred from responses to ambiguous interracial stimuli. Unfortunately, attempts to use projective techniques to infer attitudes or personality traits have met with little success. As in the case of physiological measures, projective tests tend to suffer from relatively low reliability and they generally provide no incremental validity over more direct assessment methods (see Lilienfeld et al. 2000, for a review).

Implicit measures of attitudes and personality traits

Much excitement has been generated in recent years by a new approach to overcoming self-presentational biases, an approach stimulated by work on priming of automatic reactions. It has been found that pictures, words, or other stimuli – even when presented only very briefly – tend to activate or prime certain implicit reactions, such as an evaluation of the stimulus in question. These implicit reactions can then facilitate or interfere with responses to other stimuli, thus influencing the speed or latency of responses to these stimuli. Consider, for example, a person who is exposed very briefly to a picture of a snake and is then asked to read out loud, as quickly as possible, the next word to appear on a screen. Most people's implicit reaction to a snake is negative and, if the word on the screen is also negative (e.g. *failure*), the implicit reaction will facilitate recognition and hence speed up pronunciation of the word. However, if the word presented on the screen is positive (e.g. *chocolate*), the negative implicit response to the picture of a snake will tend to interfere with recognition and pronunciation of the positive word. It follows that pronunciation of the negative word should be faster than pronunciation of the positive word.

The priming phenomenon can be used to infer attitudes or personality traits by measuring response latencies in a suitable context. The best-known application of this approach is the Implicit Association Test (Greenwald et al. 1998) developed initially to assess racial prejudice. Investigators observed that the nature of racial prejudice in the United States had changed over the years to become relatively subtle and nuanced, milder than the blatant racism of the past (McConahay 1986). It was suggested that respondents, loath to be viewed as bigots, may now express their prejudice more indirectly and symbolically, for example as opposition to preferential treatment for minorities (Sears 1988). Other theorists proposed that racial attitudes had become ambiguous or aversive, containing explicit egalitarian elements as well as more subtle and unacknowledged negative beliefs and feelings (Gaertner and Dovidio 1986). It was argued that explicit attitude measures failed to capture this new form of prejudice, especially because the prejudicial beliefs and feelings may be outside a person's conscious awareness. Because implicit measures like the Implicit Association Test (IAT) rely on response latencies over which people have limited volitional control, they were seen as having the potential to go beyond explicit measures to provide more valid indicators of prejudice and other sensitive attitudes or personality characteristics.

When the IAT is used to assess attitudes toward, say, African Americans, respondents are seated in front of a computer screen and are usually shown, one at a time, pictures of black or white individuals and positive (e.g. *pleasure, miracle*) or negative (e.g. *evil, bomb*) words. They are asked to respond as quickly as possible by pressing one key if they see either the picture of a black person or a positive word and another key if they see a white person or a negative word. Later the task is reversed such that one key is used for black person or negative word and another key for white person or positive word. By comparing response latencies (the speed with which the keys are pressed) in the two situations it is possible to infer the preference for white over black stimulus persons. Such a preference is indicated if participants respond faster to the white/positive and black/negative combinations than to the white/negative and black/positive combinations.

A simpler implicit attitude measure relies on priming of evaluative reactions in a sequential response paradigm (Fazio et al. 1995). To assess racial prejudice with this method, participants may be shown a picture of a black or a white person, followed by a positive or negative word. The participant's task is to respond as quickly as possible to the second stimulus, for example, by rating it as good or bad, or by reading it out loud. Prejudicial attitudes are inferred when negative words elicit faster responses after a photo of a black than a white person, and when positive words produce faster responses when they follow a photo of a white rather than a black person.

The IAT and sequential evaluative priming techniques have been used to obtain implicit measures of prejudice with respect to African Americans as well as members of other minorities and disadvantaged groups such as women, the elderly, and gays and lesbians (see Fazio and Olson 2003, for a review). They have also been applied to such attitude topics as connection to nature (Schultz et al. 2004) and death (Bassett and Dabbs 2003).

It has similarly proved possible to use the Implicit Association Test to measure personality characteristics such as self-esteem (Greenwald and Farnham 2000; Karpinski 2004), shyness (Asendorpf et al. 2002), and aggressive self-concept (Uhlmann and Swanson 2004). For example, to assess shyness by means of the IAT, participants can be asked to press, as quickly as possible, one key for words related to the self (*I*, *me*, participant's first name) or to shyness (*inhibited, timid, insecure*) and a second key for words related to another person (*he, they, her*) or to not being shy (*secure, daring, candid*). On a later set of trials these combinations are reversed, such that one key is associated with the self and non-shy words, a second key with another person and shy words. The discrepancy in response times between the two types of combinations is used as an implicit measure of shyness. Participants are assumed to be higher on this trait to the extent that they respond faster when words related to the self share a key with shy words than with non-shy words (and when words related to another person share a key with non-shy as compared to shy words).

The promise of implicit measures   People tend to express socially desirable attitudes and to report possessing relatively favorable personality characteristics. These self-reports may, at a conscious level at least, indeed reflect what the respondents truly believes. With respect to some attitudinal issues and personality traits, however, explicit measures may be misleading or tell only part of the story. When it comes to socially sensitive issues or personality characteristics, implicit measures may reveal attitudes or traits that people are reluctant to admit even to themselves.

Empirical research on racial prejudice provides some support for the distinction between explicit and implicit measures. As would be expected if we are dealing with two relatively independent attitudes, several studies have reported low or at best modest correlations between explicit and implicit measures of prejudice (e.g. Cunningham et al. 2001; Karpinski and Hilton 2001). On the other hand, not unlike autonomous reactions and projective tests, implicit measures tend to suffer from relatively low reliability (Kawakami and Dovidio 2001). Moreover, there is little agreement as to what exactly is being measured by the IAT or by the sequential evaluative priming technique (see Fazio and Olson 2003). With respect to prejudice, some theorists (e.g. Devine 1989) have argued that explicit measures assess a person's 'true' attitude whereas implicit measures merely reflect learned associations to members of a minority group, associations that may reflect cultural stereotypes but not necessarily the person's own opinions. Other theorists (Fazio et al. 1995) view implicit measures as 'a bona fide pipeline' to racial attitudes, revealing a person's true feelings. And still others (Wilson et al. 2000) believe that people can hold two incompatible attitudes simultaneously, one explicit and one implicit, and that both are 'true.' Thus, although sequential evaluative priming and the implicit association test represent promising new developments in the search for valid attitude assessment, the jury is still out on their ability to live up to their promise.

FROM DISPOSITIONS TO ACTIONS

Personality traits and attitudes are considered to be more than mere abstractions or hypothetical entities invented for the convenience of psychologists. Most theorists assume that these dispositions have an existence of their own, independent of our efforts to infer them. Indeed, once inferred, traits and attitudes are used to *explain* the person's behavior.

Dimensions of personality

The trait approach to personality assumes that individuals can be described in terms of a perhaps large, but finite, number of personality characteristics. In line with this assumption, much research over the years has attempted to identify the primary or basic traits in human personality (e.g. Cattell 1947; Eysenck 1953; Jackson 1967). The emerging consensus is that five major personality dimensions are sufficient to describe people's standing on the great variety of trait terms found in common language (see Fiske 1949; Norman 1963; Digman and Inouye 1986; McCrae and John 1992). Table 1.3 shows the five general personality factors and lists a few examples of trait pairs that are representative of each. People's personalities are thus described quite well if we can specify how sociable, agreeable, conscientious, emotionally stable, and cultured they are. These personality characteristics are expected to find expression in behavior. For example, people who are extraverted should be talkative rather than silent, adventurous rather than cautious, sociable rather than reclusive, etc. And within each of these behavioral categories we can find still more specific response tendencies. Thus, in comparison to relatively silent individuals,

Table 1.3   Five basic personality factors

Factor 1: Extraversion–Introversion
   Talkative – Silent, Frank – Secretive
   Adventurous – Cautious, Sociable – Reclusive

Factor 2: Agreeableness
   Good-natured – Irritable, Gentle – Headstrong
   Cooperative – Negativistic, Not Jealous – Jealous

Factor 3: Conscientiousness
   Tidy – Careless, Responsible – Undependable
   Scrupulous – Unscrupulous, Persevering – Quitting

Factor 4: Emotional Stability
   Calm – Anxious, Composed – Excitable
   Poised – Nervous, Not Hypochondriacal – Hypochondriacal

Factor 5: Culture
   Artistically sensitive – Insensitive, Imaginative – Simple
   Intellectual – Nonreflective, Refined – Crude

Source: After Norman (1963)

talkative people should make more telephone calls, speak up more frequently in group settings, turn more to other people for assistance, and so
forth. In short, the links from traits to behavior proceed from general personality characteristics to more narrowly defined behavioral tendencies
which, in turn, result in relatively specific response dispositions.

A hierarchical model of attitude

The logic whereby attitudes are linked to behavior is remarkably similar to
the trait approach in personality. Earlier we saw that attitudes can be
inferred from cognitive, affective, and conative responses to the attitude
object. For many theorists, the distinction between cognition, affect, and
conation is more than just a system for classifying responses from which
attitudes can be inferred. These theorists assume that each response
category reflects a different theoretical *component* of attitude (see Smith
1947; Katz and Stotland 1959; McGuire 1985; (Eagly and Chaiken 1998; e.g.).
In this view, attitude is a multidimensional construct consisting of cognition, affect, and conation. Although each of these components varies along
an evaluative continuum, it is assumed that the evaluations expressed in
them can differ (see Ostrom 1969; Breckler 1984). A person might feel
uneasy in a hospital (negative affect with respect to the medical profession)
but, at the same time, believe that most doctors are well qualified (positive
cognitive component) and agree to undergo an operation (favorable conative component).

The tripartite model of attitude offered by Rosenberg and Hovland
(1960), which serves as the starting point of most contemporary analyses,
is a hierarchical model that includes cognition, affect, and conation as
first-order factors and attitude as a single second-order factor. In this model,
the three components are defined independently and yet comprise, at a
higher level of abstraction, the single construct of attitude. To extend this
line of reasoning, recall that each component is made up of verbal and
nonverbal response classes, and that each of these is further comprised
of a large number of very specific response tendencies. Attitudes are thus
always inferred from specific responses to the attitude object. We can
classify these responses into broader categories and assign different labels
to those categories, yet we are still dealing with the same evaluative disposition called attitude.

The shared evaluative character of the cognitive, affective, and conative
attitudinal components has sometimes been a source of confusion. This
is especially apparent in attempts to distinguish empirically between
cognition and affect. In fact, there is considerable disagreement as to the
appropriate means of separating these two components. For example, some
investigators (e.g. Norman 1975) have employed the evaluative semantic
differential as a measure of affect, whereas others (e.g. Breckler 1984) have
used it as a measure of cognition. Examination of the semantic differential's
evaluative factor (see Osgood et al. 1957) actually reveals a mixture of what
appear to be cognitive (e.g. useful–useless) and affective (e.g. pleasant–
unpleasant) adjective scales. The two types of scales are often highly correlated and thus tend to reflect the same factor, but at times they are found to

tap two different underlying constructs (see Ajzen and Timko 1986). It is thus possible, by carefully selecting appropriate scales, to use the semantic differential to assess an attitude's cognitive component or its affective component.

The empirical implications of the hierarchical attitude model can be stated as follows. Given that the three components reflect the same underlying attitude, they should correlate to some degree with each other. Yet, to the extent that the distinction between cognitive, affective, and conative response categories is of psychological significance, measures of the three components should not be completely redundant. In combination, these expectations imply correlations of moderate magnitude among measures of the three components. A number of attempts have been made over the years to confirm the discriminant validity of measures designed to tap the different components (Ostrom 1969; Kothandapani 1971; Bagozzi 1978; Bagozzi and Burnkrant 1979; Breckler 1984; Widaman 1985). Depending on the method used and the assumptions made, the data have variously been interpreted either as supporting a tripartite model or a single-factor model (see the exchange between Dillon and Kumar (1985) and Bagozzi and Burnkrant (1985)). The major issue seems to revolve around whether differences between measures of the cognitive, affective, and conative components are to be interpreted as due to differences in the procedures (scales) used to assess them (i.e. as theoretically uninteresting method variance) or as due to true differences between conceptually independent components. Generally speaking, however, most of the data reported in the literature is quite consistent with the hierarchical model in that a single factor is found to account for much of the variance in attitudinal responses, and the correlations among measures of the three components, although leaving room for some unique variance, are typically of considerable magnitude.

Perhaps the strongest evidence for the discriminant validity of measures assessing cognition, affect, and conation was reported by Breckler (1984). Yet, this study also demonstrates considerable commonality among the components. College students were asked to complete a questionnaire containing measures of cognition, affect, and conation while confronted with a caged, live snake. Agreement or disagreement with such statements as, 'Snakes control the rodent population' and 'Snakes will attack anything that moves,' as well as ratings of snakes on scales labeled *kind–cruel*, *clean–dirty*, etc. were used to assess the cognitive component. A measure of the affective component was based on responses, in the presence of a snake, to such statements as 'I feel anxious' and 'I feel happy,' as well as self-ratings of mood: carefree, elated, pleased, tense, fearful, sad, and so forth. Finally, a measure of each respondent's heart rate in the presence of the snake was also available. To assess the conative component, the investigator obtained responses to such statements as, 'I scream whenever I see a snake' and 'I like to handle snakes.' In addition, the participants' willingness to interact with the snake in various ways was observed, and they were asked to rate how closely they would be willing to approach each of 12 snakes shown in color slides. Statistical analyses showed that the three types of responses could indeed be viewed as representing three different factors. At the same time, however, the correlations among the factors were of considerable magnitude. The cognition–affect correlation was 0.38, the affect–conation correlation was 0.50, and the correlation between cognition and conation was 0.70.

The hierarchical model of attitude, then, offers the following account of the way in which attitudes affect behavior. The actual or symbolic presence of an object elicits a generally favorable or unfavorable evaluative reaction, the attitude toward the object. This attitude, in turn, predisposes cognitive, affective, and conative responses to the object, responses whose evaluative tone is consistent with the overall attitude. It follows that individuals with positive attitudes toward, say, the medical profession should exhibit various favorable responses with respect to hospitals, doctors, nurses, etc., whereas individuals with negative attitudes toward the medical profession should exhibit unfavorable responses toward these objects.

SUMMARY AND CONCLUSIONS

In this chapter we saw that attitudes and personality traits are latent, hypothetical dispositions that are inferred from a variety of observable responses. Information about an individual's responses can be provided by the individual in the form of self-reports, it can be collected from friends or acquaintances, and it can be based on direct observation. Personality research has revealed five general response tendencies that represent robust personality characteristics: sociability, agreeableness, conscientiousness, emotional stability, and culturedness. In the attitude domain it is custom-ary to distinguish between verbal or nonverbal responses that represent beliefs, feelings, and action tendencies. Some theorists have argued that these response classes reflect three separate and qualitatively distinct com-ponents of attitude: cognition, affect, and conation. A hierarchical model appears consistent with the results of empirical research. It encompasses evaluative attitude at the highest level, cognition, affect, and conation at an intermediate level, and specific beliefs, feelings, and action tendencies at the lowest level. Attitudes and personality traits are thus assumed to pre-dispose overt behavior relevant to the trait or attitude under consideration.

NOTES

1 Several assumptions have to be met for the formula to hold, among them that inter-item correlations remain stable and that the new items have the same level of reliability as the original items on the scale.
2 It is also possible to use external criteria, such as the ability of each item to discriminate between groups known to differ in their attitudes or person-ality traits, or their ability to predict attitude or personality scores obtained by other means.
3 Especially in personality assessment, a procedure known as factor analy-sis is often employed to identify items that reflect a given trait. The items thus selected also meet the criterion of internal consistency.

4 More promising for attitude assessment are approaches that rely on electrical activity in facial muscles – the facial electromyogram (Cacioppo et al. 1986) – or on event-related brain potentials (Cacioppo et al. 1993). These methods, however, require sophisticated laboratory equipment and careful training in their use. They are thus not suitable for large-scale attitude surveys. Discussion of these methods is beyond the scope of this book.

SUGGESTIONS FOR FURTHER READING

Aiken, L. R. (1999) *Personality Assessment: Methods and Practices* (3rd edn.). Kirkland, MA: Hogrefe and Huber. A basic introduction to personality assessment, this book reviews self-report as well as a variety of alternative measurement procedures.

Campbell, D. T. (1963) Social attitudes and other acquired behavioral dispositions. In S. Koch (ed.), *Psychology: A Study of a Science* (Vol. 6, pp. 94–172). New York: McGraw-Hill. A thoughtful analysis of dispositional concepts, including traits and attitudes. Difficult but rewarding reading for the serious student.

Edwards, A. L. (1957) *Techniques of Attitude Scale Construction*. New York: Appleton-Century-Crofts. A practical guide to various attitude scaling methods. Chapter 6 on the method of summated ratings (Likert scale) is of particular relevance.

TWO

CONSISTENCY IN HUMAN AFFAIRS

The only completely consistent people are the dead.

(Aldous Huxley)

A dispositional explanation of human behavior presupposes a degree of coherence among thoughts, feelings, and actions. If people's reactions toward a given target were completely inconsistent across time and context, we could not attribute them to such stable underlying dispositions as attitudes or personality traits. In this chapter we examine consistency in human affairs, first from a theoretical point of view and then in light of empirical research.

The historical and largely artificial boundaries between personality and social psychology have resulted in divergent research traditions that have tended to obscure the conceptual similarities and common vicissitudes of the trait and attitude concepts (Ajzen 1982, 1987; Sherman and Fazio 1983; Blass 1984). As we saw in Chapter 1, personality traits and attitudes are typically conceived of as relatively enduring dispositions that exert pervasive influence on a broad range of behaviors. Both concepts gained wide popularity in the 1930s with the development of reliable psychometric techniques for their assessment, followed by a veritable avalanche of basic and applied research. For almost three decades the explanatory values and practical utilities of attitudes and traits went virtually unchallenged. Personality psychologists devoted considerable effort to the description of personality structures in terms of multidimensional trait configurations (Cattell 1946; Eysenck 1953; Jackson 1967; see Matthews et al. 2003) while social psychologists – in addition to collecting descriptive data regarding attitudes toward various social issues – attended to the structure of attitudes in terms of their cognitive, affective, and conative components (see Abelson et al. 1968) and to effective strategies of persuasion and attitude change (see Hovland et al. 1953; Petty and Cacioppo 1981, 1986; McGuire 1985; Stiff and Mongeau 2003). At the same time the new techniques and insights were applied to personnel selection, product design and promotion, political behavior, family planning, and a host of other more or less worthy causes. Traits and attitudes seemed assured of a central, lasting role in the prediction and explanation of human behavior.

To be sure, confidence in the trait and attitude concepts was not universal, but the occasional publication of cautionary notes or negative research findings went largely unnoticed. By the 1960s, however, doubts were being voiced with increasing frequency (see, e.g., De Fleur and Westie 1958; Vernon 1964; Deutscher 1966; Peterson 1968; McGuire 1969). Much of the concern was related to the question of consistency.

PSYCHOLOGICAL FOUNDATIONS OF CONSISTENCY

Consistency and regularity in the physical world are taken for granted. They permit us to make order and coherence out of the multitude of events that impinge on our senses every day. Night follows day and one season consistently follows another. Clouds produce rain, objects fall to the ground, lights throw shadows. Doors open when they are pushed or pulled and chairs generally support our weight. In the physical world the 'laws of nature' generate consistency. Human thoughts and feelings, however, are not physical events. They are malleable and modifiable, not compelled by physical forces but obeying laws of their own. Why should they display consistency with each other or with observable behavior?

Some theorists would claim that consistency in human behavior is more apparent than real: that we attribute to ourselves attitudes, motives, and personality traits consistent with our actions (Bem 1965); that consistency is in the eye of the beholder rather than in observed behavior (e.g. Mischel 1969; Shweder 1975; Nisbett and Ross 1980); that we express attitudes and values consistent with our actions in an effort to make a favorable impression on others (e.g. Tedeschi et al. 1971). Most theorists, however, maintain the position that consistency is a fundamental property of human thoughts, feelings, and actions. Divergence between theorists occurs mainly as a result of different interpretations that are given to observed consistencies.

Preference for consistency

Heider (1944, 1958) was perhaps the first social psychologist to propose a theoretical model based on an assumed preference for consistency over inconsistency. According to Heider's balance theory, people's beliefs and attitudes tend toward a state of balance or consistency. We tend to like people who agree with us, to associate positive properties with objects or people we value, to attribute negative motives to people we despise, to help people we admire, and so on. In balanced configurations of this kind, the elements of the situation fit together harmoniously; there is no stress to bring about change. However, when the configuration is imbalanced (e.g. a person we like commits a crime), tension is created which gives rise to action or cognitive reorganization designed to bring about a balanced state of affairs.

Basing his ideas largely on Heider's balance theory, Festinger (1957) examined the effects of inconsistency among cognitive elements, i.e.

among beliefs or items of knowledge concerning the environment, oneself, or one's behavior. In Festinger's theory of cognitive dissonance, inconsistency between two beliefs exists when holding one belief conflicts with holding the other. For example, the belief that another person is ugly is dissonant with the knowledge that the person in question has won a beauty contest, just as buying a Porsche is dissonant with the belief that the car is overpriced. Inconsistency between cognitive elements is assumed to give rise to dissonance, a psychologically unpleasant state that motivates the individual to change one or more cognitive elements in an attempt to eliminate or reduce the magnitude of the existing dissonance. Thus, when people's overt actions conflict with their private attitudes or values, they are expected to try to reduce the resulting dissonance either by modifying their behaviors or by changing their attitudes.

It can be seen that the theories of balance and dissonance assume a motivation for people to maintain consistency among their beliefs, feelings, and actions. This motivation, however, is not considered to be a compelling force; rather, it resembles a preference or tendency of the cognitive system. As Zajonc (1968, p. 341) pointed out with respect to balance theory:

> the dynamic principle of change proposed by Heider does not involve psychological forces of overwhelming strength. They are more akin to *preferences* than to driving forces. There is no anxiety when structures are imbalanced; imbalanced states are not noxious; a compelling need to strive for balance is not assumed.

Functional consistency

Many theorists go beyond preferences to propose that consistency fulfills important needs in a person's life. Common to the different views is the assumption that maintenance of consistency in beliefs, feelings, and actions is essential for a person's effective functioning in the world.

Need for effective action

It has been argued that consistency between one's beliefs and feelings with respect to an object makes it possible to develop a stable, action-directed orientation toward the object (Rosenberg 1965). Consider, for example, the predicament of voters who are favorably disposed toward the Social Democratic Party but who believe that the party's candidate for prime minister is unqualified for the office. This inconsistency makes it difficult to choose a course of action in the election. If, however, they could convince themselves that the candidate is, after all, qualified to become prime minister, that is, if their beliefs about the candidate were to become consistent with their attitudes toward the candidate's party, then the voting decision would be easy to make.

We may learn the need for consistency by repeatedly experiencing that we can act more effectively when beliefs and feelings are consistent than when they are inconsistent. In this fashion, we are assumed to develop a need to maintain consistency between the affective and cognitive components of our attitudes (Rosenberg 1956; Rosenberg and Hovland 1960). In Rosenberg's theory, the affective component of attitude is the overall positive or negative response to an object, while the cognitive component is made up of beliefs about the potentialities of the attitude object for attaining or blocking the realization of valued states. The assumption of affective–cognitive consistency implies that the more a given object is viewed as instrumental to obtaining positively valued goals and to blocking negative valued events, the more favorable will be the person's affect toward the object. For example, people should have positive feelings toward racial integration if they believe that integration enriches one's social life, reduces interracial conflict, improves educational opportunities, and so on, all favorably valued goals. By way of contrast, negative affect should accompany expectations to the effect that racial integration will produce such unfavorable outcomes as lower property values, interracial conflict, a deterioration in the quality of education, and so forth. Inconsistency is observed when people with positive feelings toward an object believe that it hinders attainment of valued goals and promotes attainment of negatively valued outcomes; or when people with negative feelings toward the object expect it to help them attain positively valued goals and to prevent the occurrence of negatively valued events. When cognition and affect are at odds, the need for consistency is assumed to activate processes that spawn changes in beliefs or feelings and thereby bring the attitude's cognitive and affective components in line with each other.

Need for coherence

Some cognitive theorists postulate an overriding need for individuals to understand their worlds, and themselves within them, to be able to predict and control events (e.g., Kelly 1955; Epstein 1980a). Coherence and consistency are indispensable in our quest for understanding and prediction. Inconsistency between elements that comprise our intuitive theories of the world – be it inconsistency between beliefs, feelings, or actions – necessitates realignments to produce an internally consistent perspective. Once a coherent picture of some aspect of our world is established, it tends to be resistant to change. Of course, gradual shifts in our views occur all the time, but drastic changes must be resisted because they challenge fundamental assumptions and central values. In fact, challenges to our basic views of the world are held responsible for anxieties and other strong emotions that may produce abnormal behavior (cf. Epstein 1983b).

Since the self is just another, albeit crucial, aspect of our worlds, the foregoing applies equally well to perceptions of ourselves. To act in ways that are inconsistent with our past behavior or with our important beliefs, attitudes, or values would undermine fundamental assumptions related to the self concept. Consider, for example, a women who views herself as altruistic. If, on a given occasion, she refused to assist another individual in need of help, she might be able to rationalize her behavior, perhaps attributing it to circumstances, and maintain the image of herself as an altruist. However, repeated performance of trait-inconsistent behavior would make it increasingly difficult to preserve this image. Thus, our need to understand ourselves and to have a coherent picture of our own attitudes and personalities produces behavioral consistency.

Inherent consistency

Some theoretical approaches assume, explicitly or implicitly, that human beings are inherently predisposed to think and act in consistent ways. Consistency, in these views, is not merely a preference, nor does it develop to serve other needs. Instead, it is an almost inevitable consequence of the way the human brain functions.

Neurophysiological dispositions

According to Allport (1935: 810), 'An attitude is a mental and neural state of readiness, organized through experience, exerting a directive or dynamic influence upon the individual's response to all objects and situations with which it is related.' In a similar fashion, Allport (1937, 1961) also speculated about the neurological base of personality traits. Although he had little evidence for it and did not make it a central feature of his theorizing, Allport seemed to assume that the basis for consistency in our thoughts and actions would ultimately be found in neurological mechanisms of the brain.

By way of comparison, Eysenck's (1947, 1967) theory of personality is a much more explicit attempt to tie behavioral consistencies to neurophysiological processes. In his theory, traits – representing consistencies of behavior over time – are organized into constellations or syndromes, called personality types. Empirical investigations led Eysenck to conclude that personalities of the normal population consist of a small number of types which can be described in terms of two broad trait dimensions: extraversion, the extent to which a person is outgoing or reclusive, and neuroticism, the tendency to be excessively emotional and to respond with anxiety to stressful situations. An individual's personality type is thus defined in part by its degree of extraversion and neuroticism.[1]

Extraversion–introversion is assumed to reflect the balance between excitatory potentials and inhibitory potentials in the cerebral cortex (Eysenck 1967). Specifically, the balance of these two potentials is said to be in favor of excitation for extraverted individuals and in favor of inhibition for introverted individuals. As to neuroticism, Eysenck proposed that it is related to the functioning of the brain's hypothalamus. A high level of neuroticism is assumed to be associated with a low threshold for excitation of the hypothalamus, i.e. the hypothalamus of relatively neurotic individuals is more easily stimulated to an excessive degree. In short, according to Eysenck's theory, characteristic brain processes predispose people to behave in a consistently extraverted or introverted manner, and to exhibit a high or low degree of emotionality in their reactions to stress.

Intuitively, it seems reasonable to expect that at least some behavioral dispositions have a strong neurophysiological component. Excitability in the personality domain and attitudes toward such emotionally arousing stimuli as snakes or spiders are perhaps good examples. Most traits and attitudes, however, are much less likely to be tied to specific neurophysiological mechanisms, and to be more a function of socialization and learning. Dependability, preferences for certain fashions, and political attitudes are a few examples that come readily to mind. Although they tend to exhibit some degree of stability over time, behavioral dispositions of this kind are much more likely to change in response to experience than are dispositions that have their base in neurophysiological processes of the brain.

Logical consistency

Some theorists have suggested that we are inherently consistent in our responses because of the way we process information and make decisions. For example, McGuire (1960a, 1960b) proposed a model of logical consistency that combines formal logic and statistical probability theory. The model deals with the situation in which a conclusion follows logically from two related premises, i.e. with logical syllogisms. To illustrate, the premises, 'All citizens of countries that are members of the European Union are permitted to reside and work in the United Kingdom' and 'Pierre B. is a citizen of a member country' logically imply that Pierre B. is permitted to reside and work in the UK. In his research, McGuire found that, by and large, people display a fair amount of logical consistency in their beliefs, although one can also observe certain biases and discrepancies. Perhaps more important, after reviewing their beliefs, people tend to change some of them in the direction of increased logical consistency, a phenomenon McGuire (1960a) termed the 'Socratic effect.' This finding indicates that people can recognize logical inconsistencies among the beliefs they hold and that this recognition is sufficient to bring about increased consistency without any added outside pressure.

The assumption that people think and act in more or less logical ways is also embedded in Fishbein and Ajzen's (1975; Ajzen and Fishbein 1980) theory of reasoned action and its successor, the theory of planned behavior (Ajzen 1985, 1991). Rather than treating cognition, affect, and conation as three components of attitude, these theories treat the three types of response tendencies as independent constructs termed, respectively, belief, attitude, and intention. Attitudes are said to follow reasonably from the beliefs people hold about the object of the attitude, just as intentions and actions follow reasonably from attitudes.

Consider first how formation of beliefs may lead reasonably to the development of attitudes that are consistent with those beliefs. Generally speaking, we form beliefs about an object by associating it with certain attributes, i.e. with other objects, characteristics, or events. Thus, perhaps as a result of watching a television program, we may come to believe that the government of a certain country (the object) is corrupt, imprisons innocent people, and mismanages the economy (attributes). Since the attributes that come to be linked to the object are already valued positively or negatively, we automatically and simultaneously acquire an attitude toward the object. In this fashion, we learn to like objects we believe have largely desirable characteristics, and we form unfavorable attitudes toward objects we associate with mostly undesirable characteristics. Specifically, the subjective value of each attribute contributes to the attitude in direct proportion to the strength of the belief, i.e. the subjective probability that the object has the attribute in question. The way in which beliefs combine to produce an attitude is shown in Equation 2.1. As can be seen, the strength of each belief (*b*) is multiplied by the subjective evaluation (*e*) of the belief's attribute and the resulting products are summed. A person's attitude is expected to be directly proportional ($\propto$) to this summative belief index.

$$A \propto \sum b_i e_i \qquad\qquad (2.1)$$

It may be noted that this expectancy-value model of attitude is structurally similar to Rosenberg's (1956) theory of affective–cognitive consistency. However, in contrast to Rosenberg's theory, the model described here does not make the assumption that people have a *need* for consistency; instead, the connection between beliefs and attitudes is construed in terms of reasonable information processing. In addition, whereas an assumed need for affective–cognitive consistency implies mutual influence between the two types of responses, the present model is concerned mainly with the unidirectional effects of beliefs on attitudes.

In the course of our lives we acquire many different beliefs about a variety of objects, actions, and events. These beliefs may be formed as a result of direct observation, they may be self-generated by way of inference processes, or they may be formed indirectly by accepting information from such outside sources as friends, television, newspapers, books, and so on. Some beliefs persist over time, others weaken or disappear, and new beliefs are formed. People can hold a great many beliefs about any given object, but they can attend to only a relatively small number, perhaps eight or nine, at any given moment (see Miller 1956). These *salient* beliefs, easily *accessible* in memory, are assumed to be the immediate determinants of a person's attitude (Fishbein 1963; Fishbein and Ajzen 1975).

Just as attitudes are said to flow reasonably and spontaneously from beliefs, so intentions and actions are seen to follow reasonably from attitudes. The theories of reasoned action and planned behavior postulate that, as a general rule, we intend to perform a behavior if we hold favorable attitudes toward it and, barring unforeseen events, we translate our plans into actions. In short, a causal sequence of events is posited in which actions with respect to an object follow directly from behavioral intentions, and intentions are evaluatively consistent with attitudes that derive reasonably from accessible beliefs about the behavior. A more detailed discussion and elaboration of the links postulated by the theory of planned behavior is presented in Chapter 6.

EMPIRICAL EVIDENCE

Clearly, there are many good reasons for expecting people to display consistency in their thoughts, feelings, and actions. Among them are the desire to project a favorable image of the self, perceptual and motivational preferences for consistent configurations of elements related to the self, satisfaction of various needs served by consistency, and reasonable links among beliefs, attitudes, intentions, and behaviors. Further, some of these tendencies and needs may be related to inherent biologically based dispositions toward consistency. One might presume, in light of these considerations, that it would be easy to demonstrate consistency in people's responses to an object or situation, consistency between the way they think and feel and the way they act.

Casual observation indeed appears to support the presence of consistency in human affairs. We have the impression that some of our acquaintances are generally friendly and outgoing, while others are more introverted and shy; that some people are honest to a fault, while others cannot be trusted; that some of our coworkers behave in a consistently reliable manner, while others are annoyingly unreliable. By the same token, it would appear that we generally associate with people we like, that we eat foods we consider tasty and nutritious, that we support policies we consider desirable, and that we generally behave in accordance with our attitudes. We thus turn to an examination of empirical research in personality and social psychology that has dealt with the question of consistency.

Behavioral consistency

An important implication of the dispositional view of human behavior is that general response tendencies should manifest themselves across a variety of actions and situations. An individual who has a disposition to act impulsively might be expected not only to leave the scene of a traffic accident but also to purchase even relatively expensive items on the spur of the moment, to strike another person when insulted or angry, to eat at irregular intervals, to quit a job without warning, and so on. Conversely, a person who displays lack of impulsivity in one situation should also act in a deliberate manner in other situations. Or, to take another example, if returning books on time to the library is evidence of a stable disposition, say, conscientiousness, then it should follow that people who perform this behavior will also act conscientiously in other ways. They might be expected to remember birthdays of family members and friends, to prepare assignments diligently, to take good care of their possessions, and so forth. The dispositional view thus implies *behavioral consistency*, that is, consistency among different behaviors, performed in different situations, so long as the behaviors in question are all instances of the same underlying disposition. In fact, Campbell (1963) made it clear that behavioral dispositions are evidenced by, and can only be inferred from, consistency in responses. It follows that without response consistency we have no evidence for the existence of stable traits or attitudes.

This is not to say, however, that behavioral consistency is always to be expected. Inconsistency of behavior from one occasion to another can be introduced by factors related to the person performing the behavior, that is, personal factors other than the attitude or personality trait of interest; by factors related to the situation in which the behavior is performed (the context, the target at which the behavior is directed, etc.); and by factors related to the action selected to represent the behavioral domain. Thus, an individual with a positive attitude toward the blind may on one occasion help a blind person across the street and on another occasion pass without offering help. The difference in behavior could be due to differences in mood or attentiveness on the two occasions, to differences in the age of the blind person or the amount of traffic on the road, or to other personal or contextual factors. Another type of inconsistency across occasions can be observed when the individual with a positive attitude toward the blind helps a blind person across the street on one occasion, but on another occasion refuses to assist a blind person in filling out an application form. Here, the difference in behavior can be due not only to differences in personal or situational factors on the two occasions, but also to differences between the two particular actions chosen to represent the behavioral domain of helping the blind.

Empirical research has uncovered little consistency between single actions, even if both actions are taken from the same behavioral domain. Evidence for behavioral inconsistency was presented as early as 1928 by Hartshorne and May, who showed, for example, that dishonesty of a specific kind in a given context (e.g., copying from another student's test paper) was virtually unrelated to dishonesty of a different kind in a different context (e.g. telling a lie outside the classroom). LaPiere's (1934) well-known investigation of racial discrimination can also be seen as supporting the same argument. In the early 1930s, LaPiere accompanied a young Chinese couple in their travels through the United States. Calling on 251 restaurants, hotels, and other establishments, they were refused service only once. After returning home, LaPiere sent a letter to each establishment they had visited, asking the following question: 'Will you accept members of the Chinese race as guests in your establishment?' Of the 128 establishments that replied, over 90 percent replied in the negative. One single action: accepting a Chinese couple as guests in a restaurant or hotel, was found to be inconsistent with another single action: refusal to accept Chinese guests expressed in response to a written inquiry. Findings of this kind are of course hardly surprising if we recall that any single response tends to be highly unreliable. That is, inconsistency between different actions may be due, at least in part, to unreliability of measurement (see Epstein 1979, 1980b, 1983a).

Of greater interest, therefore, is the relation between two single actions when each is reliably assessed. This can be achieved by summing observations of each action across occasions. An early indication that behavioral consistency is low even under such favorable conditions was provided by Dudycha (1936), who reported correlations among several summative measures of behavior related to punctuality: time of arrival at 8 a.m. classes, at college commons, at appointments, at extracurricular activities, at vesper services, and at entertainments. A correlation of moderate magnitude ($r = 0.44$) was observed between punctuality at commons and at entertainments, but the other correlations were much lower; the average correlation was 0.19.

An example in the attitudinal domain is provided by a study of race relations among black and white coal miners (Minard 1952). Through interviews and observations, Minard discovered a general pattern of integration in the mines but widespread segregation in the community. Black and white miners tended to interact freely and on good terms in the mines, but little contact was maintained or permitted after working hours. Specifically, about 60 percent of the white miners displayed this inconsistent pattern of behavior, while approximately 20 percent discriminated in both settings and another 20 percent discriminated in neither.

Later research also provided little evidence in support of behavioral consistency. For example, Funder, Block, and Block (1983) obtained two scaled resistance-to-temptation measures in children: resisting approach to a present and resisting attractive but 'forbidden' toys. Although the scales' reliabilities were not reported, each was based on more than a single observation and was thus likely to have had at least some degree of reliability. The correlation between them, however, was only 0.20. Similarly, even after summing over several behavioral self-reports, Epstein (1979: Study 3) found only very low and mostly nonsignificant correlations between individual behaviors seemingly tapping the same underlying disposition. Thus, the correlation between number of telephone calls made over a period of time and number of letters written in the same time interval was 0.33; and the correlation between number of absences from class and number of papers not submitted was below 0.30; neither correlation was statistically significant.

In a systematic re-examination of behavioral consistency with reliable measures, Mischel and Peake (1982a, 1982b) presented data in the domain of conscientiousness among college students. Nineteen different action tendencies were observed on repeated occasions, including class attendance, punctuality in handing in assignments, thoroughness of notes taken, and neatness of personal appearance. The average correlation among these different kinds of actions representing conscientiousness was a mere 0.13.

In short, empirical research has shown very little support for consistency between different behaviors presumed to reflect the same underlying disposition. We will return to the problem of behavioral consistency and how it might be increased in Chapter 3. At this point, we must consider one additional source of evidence for inconsistency, namely, research on the relation between global measures of attitudes or personality traits and particular behaviors.

Predictive validity

In addition to the failure of empirical research to confirm behavioral consistency, the problem of inconsistency also arose in a different sense, namely, in the sense of *predictive validity*. Defined as relatively enduring response dispositions, attitudes and personality traits are naturally assumed to direct, and in some way determine, social action. Thus, a hostile personality disposition should produce aggressive behavior, and liberal or conservative attitudes should result in corresponding political actions. As we saw in Chapter 1, attitudes and traits are typically inferred from verbal responses to questionnaire items. If these attitude and personality scales indeed assess enduring response dispositions, the obtained scores should predict how an individual will actually behave in a concrete situation. A person who expresses a favorable attitude toward religion on a questionnaire might be expected to attend weekly worship services, pray before meals, participate in Bible classes, watch religious television programs, and so forth. Conversely, nonreligious individuals, as assessed by means of an attitude scale, might not perform any of these behaviors, although they might engage in premarital sex, disobey their parents, and do other things a religious person would be expected to avoid.

Before continuing the discussion of predictive validity, it is important to realize that attitudes and personality traits can express themselves, and can therefore be inferred from, verbal as well as nonverbal responses. This point is often misunderstood. Many investigators assume that verbal responses reflect a person's attitude or personality trait, whereas nonverbal ('overt') actions are measures of behavior. In point of fact, however, both verbal and nonverbal responses are observable behaviors. Neither is more or less a measure of attitude or personality than the other; both types of behavior can reflect the same underlying disposition (see Upmeyer 1981; Roth and Upmeyer 1985). Moreover, the validity of overt behaviors as indicators of a latent disposition cannot be taken for granted, any more so than can the validity of verbal responses to questionnaire items. Both types of behavior must be submitted to standard scaling procedures, and only some responses – verbal or nonverbal – will be found adequate for the assessment of a given attitude or personality trait (cf. Ajzen and Fishbein 1980; Jackson and Paunonen 1985). Some time ago, Merton (1940: 20) made the same point very succinctly:

> The metaphysical assumption is tacitly introduced that in one sense or another overt behavior is 'more real' than verbal behavior. This assumption is both unwarranted and scientifically meaningless ... It should not be forgotten that overt actions may deceive; that they, just as 'derivations' or 'speech reactions' may be deliberately designed to disguise or to conceal private attitudes.

Strictly speaking, therefore, most tests of the 'attitude-behavior' or 'trait-behavior' relation are better conceptualized as tests of the relation between verbal and nonverbal indicators of the same underlying disposition. However, for the sake of simplicity, and in line with common practice, we will continue to refer to attitude-behavior and trait-behavior relations.

The research on behavioral consistency reviewed earlier showed little relation between two or more actions that were assumed to reflect the same underlying disposition. The approach discussed in the present section attempts to predict performance or nonperformance of a given overt behavior, or a narrow range of overt behaviors, from global dispositional measures, typically obtained by means of a questionnaire.

Global attitudes and specific actions

General attitudes have been assessed with respect to a variety of targets, including organizations and institutions (the church, public housing, student government, one's job or employer), religious or ethnic groups

(African Americans, Jews, Catholics), and particular individuals with whom one might interact (a Black person, a fellow student). Attitudes of this kind are then often used to predict one or more specific acts directed at the attitude object.

A good example is the experiment reported by Himelstein and Moore (1963). A sample of white male college students first completed a scale assessing attitudes toward African Americans and, some time later, reported for a psychology experiment. Upon arrival, the participant found another student (a confederate), either Black or white, already seated in the room. While they were waiting for the experiment to begin, a (white) confederate entered the room carrying a petition to extend the university's library hours on Saturday nights. The Black or white confederate either signed or refused to sign the petition and, following this manipulation, the naïve participant was asked to sign. Conformity or lack of conformity with the response of the confederate served as the measure of behavior. The data revealed virtually no correlation between general attitudes toward African Americans and conformity with the Black confederate. Other investigations of the relation between prejudice and behavior have produced similarly disappointing results (see Duckitt 1992: Chapter 3).

In a review of attitude-behavior research, Ajzen and Fishbein (1977) discovered many studies of this kind. Investigators attempted to predict job performance, absenteeism, and turnover from job satisfaction attitudes (e.g. Bernberg 1952; Vroom 1964); they looked at attitudes toward African Americans in relation to conformity with the judgments made by African Americans (Himelstein and Moore 1963), or in relation to willingness to have a picture taken with an African American (De Fleur and Westie 1958; Linn 1965); they used attitudes toward cheating in attempts to predict cheating behavior (Corey 1937; Freeman and Ataoev 1960), attitudes toward labor unions to predict attendance at labor union meetings (Dean 1958), attitudes toward participating as a subject in psychological research to predict actual participation (Wicker and Pomazal 1971), and so forth. Of the 109 investigations reviewed by Ajzen and Fishbein (1977), 54 assessed general attitudes in attempts to predict specific actions. Of these studies, 25 obtained nonsignificant results and the remainder rarely showed correlations in excess of 0.40. A more recent meta-analysis of this literature (Kraus 1995) revealed similarly low correlations between general attitudes and specific actions.

Implicit versus explicit attitude measures   Virtually all early failures to find strong attitude–behavior correspondence relied on explicit measures of attitude. With the development of implicit measures (see Chapter 1), it became possible to re-examine the relation between general attitudes and specific actions. Much of the theorizing and research has focused on racial attitudes (Devine 1989; Fazio and Dunton 1997; Wilson et al. 2000). Although contemporary models of stereotyping and prejudice differ in detail, they agree in their overall expectations regarding the predictive validity of explicit and implicit attitude measures. Generally speaking, implicit attitudes – being automatically activated – are assumed to guide behavior by default unless they are overridden by controlled processes. Because prejudicial attitudes and discriminatory behavior with respect to racial and ethnic minorities are frowned upon in contemporary American society, many people try to inhibit their expression. It follows that implicit prejudicial attitudes should predict behaviors that are not consciously monitored or that are difficult to control (e.g. facial expressions, eye contact, blushing, and other nonverbal behaviors), as well as behaviors that people do not view as indicative of prejudice and thus are not motivated to control (see Dovidio et al. 1996).

Thus far, only a small number of studies have directly tested this hypothesis, with rather disappointing results. To be sure, implicit measures of prejudice have been found superior to explicit measures for the prediction of such nonverbal behaviors as blinking and eye contact (Dovidio et al. 1997), the number of times whites handed a pen to an African American as opposed to placing it on the table (Wilson et al. 2000), as well as the friendliness of white participants in their interactions with a Black person, judged by the Black person on the basis of the white person's nonverbal behavior (smiling, eye contact, spatial distance, and body language) (Fazio et al. 1995; see Fazio and Olson 2003, for a review). A similar effect was obtained in a study dealing with behavior whose implications for prejudice was ambiguous (Sekaquaptewa et al. 2003). The critical behavior in this study was white males' choice of stereotype-consistent or inconsistent questions in a mock job interview with a Black female applicant. In this situation, an implicit measure of prejudice toward African Americans predicted choice of stereotype-consistent behavior better than did an explicit measure. However, even the implicit attitude measures in these studies did not do very well, with correlations rarely exceeding the 0.30 level observed in earlier research with explicit measures.

Global personality traits and specific actions

Examination of the personality literature reveals a comparable pattern of research findings. Correlations between global personality characteristics and narrowly defined behaviors relevant to the trait in question are often nonsignificant and rarely exceed the 0.30 level. In fact, the search for explanations of narrowly defined behaviors in terms of global personality traits has, as a general rule, turned out to be a frustrating experience (see Mischel and Peake 1982; Mischel 1984), and many an investigator has given up in despair.

One example is provided by the large number of investigations that were designed to identify unique personality characteristics of group leaders. To be sure, leadership behavior is not a single act. It is usually assessed by observing the amount of influence a person exerts in a group, by retrospective judgments of group members, or by nominations for leadership. A measure of leadership thus encompasses a range of different behaviors reflecting influence on others in a group setting. Nevertheless, the behaviors involved are much narrower in scope than the broad personality characteristics usually considered in this context, which include such traits as dominance, responsibility, interpersonal sensitivity, need for power, self-esteem, and so forth. In an extensive review of the literature, Mann (1959) summarized obtained relations between measures of leadership and various personality characteristics. Among his summary results: across different investigations, the median correlation of leadership with the trait of adjustment was about 0.25; with extra–introversion it was about 0.15; and no significant correlations were reported with masculinity–femininity. In a later review of the available research in this area, Gibb concluded that 'numerous studies of the personalities of leaders have failed to find any consistent pattern of traits which characterize leaders' (1969: 227).

Overweight and control of body weight are another area of research in which the search for personality correlates of narrowly defined behaviors has proved rather futile.[2] Although it is well known that there are great individual differences in people's ability to control their body weight, 'Prediction of individual differences in weight loss has not at all been successful. Clinical intuition, MMPI, MPI, weight prior to treatment, general anxiety, situation specific anxiety, PAS, EPQ, I-E scale, body image measures, and the 16 PF questionnaire have all failed to predict success in treatment' (Hall and Hall 1974: 362).[3] Looking more generally at the traits of obese individuals, Leon and Roth summarized their review of the research literature as follows: 'The evidence strongly suggests that there are very few personality characteristics that obese persons share that can be considered causative in the development of obesity' (1977: 136).

Another area of research demonstrating the low predictive validity of personality characteristics has to do with the everyday behavior of driving an automobile. Numerous studies have attempted to relate the personality traits of drivers to errors made while driving, to traffic violations, and to involvement in traffic accidents. In their review of this research, Knapper and Cropley stated that the best predictors of good or poor driving tend to be relatively superficial factors, such as years of driving experience and history of past court appearances. However, 'Disappointingly, this kind of research has failed to yield any definite conclusions about personality syndromes underlying good or bad driving' (1981: 197).

More recent research has explored correlations between the big five personality factors mentioned in the previous chapter (neuroticism, extraversion, openness to experience, agreeableness, conscientiousness) and a variety of specific behaviors. In one recent study of college students (Paunonen 2003), measures of the five personality factors were correlated with 27 behavioral criteria, some quite specific, such as dating, cigarette smoking, alcohol consumption, traffic violations, money spent buying lottery tickets, long-term dieting, prescription medications used regularly, participation in sports, and donating blood. In another study (Markey et al. 2004), investigators observed and coded into 64 categories the behavior of children interacting with their parents and correlated these behaviors with measures of the big five personality characteristics provided by the children's mothers. In both studies, the obtained correlations were disappointing. Many of the correlations failed to reach statistical significance, and those that did rarely exceeded the 0.30 level.

Other illustrations of the same phenomenon abound, but the main point to be made is clear: research in diverse domains paints a discouraging picture of our ability to predict specific or narrowly defined behaviors from knowledge of people's general personality characteristics.

Implications

To summarize briefly, years of research have failed to demonstrate impressive consistency among different behavioral manifestations of the same disposition. It took time for this conclusion to be accepted, but by the late 1960s it had become evident that in contrast to casual observation, empirical research had failed to provide strong support for behavioral consistency or predictive validity of traits and attitudes. People were found neither to behave consistently across situations, nor to act in accordance with their measured attitudes and personality traits. The accumulation of research findings of this kind undermined confidence in the trait approach among personality psychologists and cast doubts on the practices of social psychologists who relied on the attitude concept in their attempts to predict and explain human behavior.

The alarm in the domain of personality psychology was sounded by Mischel who, after reviewing the literature, reached the following conclusions:

> it is evident that the behaviors which are often construed as stable personality trait indicators actually are highly specific and depend on the details of the evoking situations and the response mode employed to measure them ... With the possible exception of intelligence, highly generalized behavioral consistencies have not been demonstrated, and the concept of personality traits as broad response predispositions is thus untenable. (1968: 146)

The greatest challenge to the utility of the attitude concept was posed by Wicker's review of the literature in which he summarized:

> Taken as a whole, these studies suggest that it is considerably more likely that attitudes will be unrelated or only slightly related to overt behaviors than that attitudes will be closely related to actions. Product-moment correlation coefficients relating the two kinds of responses are rarely above .30, and often are near zero. (1969: 65)

And, like Mischel in the personality domain, Wicker concluded, 'The present review provides little evidence to support the postulated existence of stable, underlying attitudes within the individual which influence both his verbal expressions and his actions' (1969: 75).

There is also an interesting parallel between Wicker's conclusion regarding the magnitude of typical attitude–behavior correlations and Mischel's (1968) view with respect to the predictive validity of personality traits. Mischel coined the term 'personality coefficient' to describe 'the correlation between .20 and .30 which is found persistently when virtually any personality dimension inferred from a questionnaire is related to almost any conceivable external criterion involving responses sampled in a *different* medium – that is, not by another questionnaire' (1968: 78). Thus, by the end of the 1960s, personality and social psychologists had lost their faith in the trait and attitude concepts, and had concluded that only a very small proportion of behavioral variance could be explained by reference to these dispositions.

SUMMARY AND CONCLUSIONS

This chapter has reviewed a variety of theoretical approaches that assume consistency in people's beliefs, feelings, and actions, and it has presented some preliminary evidence that seems to contradict this assumption. In theory, consistency in human affairs is preferred because of its perceptual simplicity or because inconsistency is psychologically uncomfortable; it serves the needs for coherence and effective action; and it is inherent in human nature as a result of neurophysiological processes and the capacity for logical reasoning. Yet, despite the many good reasons why people should exhibit consistency, empirical research has uncovered considerable inconsistency of behavior across situations and between verbal measures of a disposition and specific nonverbal behaviors.

Lack of behavioral consistency is an embarrassing problem for personality and social psychologists. A person's behavior on one occasion suggests a friendly disposition and on another an unfriendly disposition, one day it implies that the person opposes nuclear power but on another that she favors it. In a similar fashion, carefully constructed measures of friendliness, honesty, or attitudes toward nuclear power are unrelated to observed behavior in specific contexts. Not only does such lack of consistency call into question the very notions of attitudes and personality traits as stable response dispositions, it also undermines our understanding of personality functioning, it challenges our theories of attitude structure and change, and it denies the possibility of effective social interaction.

The remainder of this book is devoted to discussions of various attempts that have been made to cope with the consistency dilemma. We shall see that initial expectations for the predictive validity of trait and attitude measures may have been unduly optimistic and perhaps a bit naïve; and that we now have a much better understanding of the complexities involved. We shall also see that considerable progress has been made toward a resolution of the consistency dilemma and that the trait and attitude concepts have gradually regained their central positions in personality and social psychology.

NOTES

1 Eysenck's theory includes two other major personality dimensions: intelligence and, mainly in the case of clinical populations, psychoticism.
2 As in the case of leadership, reducing and maintaining weight involve a set of behaviors (dieting, exercising), not a single action (see Ajzen and Fishbein 1980), but their range is much more narrowly defined than is the range of behaviors encompassed by the personality traits used to predict weight control.
3 The MMPI, MPI, PAS, EPQ, I-E scale, and 16 PF questionnaire are multi-item instruments designed to measure a variety of personality traits.

SUGGESTIONS FOR FURTHER READING

Abelson, R. P., Aronson, E., McGuire, W. J., Newcomb, T. M., Rosenberg, M. J., and Tannenbaum, P. H. (eds) (1968) *Theories of Cognitive Consistency: A Sourcebook*. Chicago: Rand-McNally. This book is a collection of articles that provide a thorough discussion of theoretical issues related to consistency in human affairs.

Mischel, W. (1968) *Personality and Assessment*. New York: Wiley. This influential book challenged the utility of the trait concept.

Wicker, A. W. (1969) Attitudes versus actions: The relationship of verbal and overt behavioral responses to attitude objects. *Journal of Social Issues*, 25, 41–78. This article set the stage for the re-examination of the attitude–behavior relation. It presents a review of empirical papers showing little correspondence between verbal attitudes and overt actions.

THREE

FROM DISPOSITIONS TO ACTIONS

I have yet to see any problem, however complicated, which, when you looked at it in the right way, did not become still more complicated.

(Poul Anderson)

In Chapter 2 we saw that enthusiasm for the trait and attitude concepts was followed, in the 1960s, by a period of disenchantment due mainly to failures of research to find evidence for consistency from one instance of behavior to another or for predictive validity of trait and attitude measures. It became clear that broad attitude and personality trait measures correlate very poorly with particular behaviors. Just as infatuation and disappointment with the trait and attitude concepts followed parallel lines, so did the proposed remedies for observed inconsistencies that emerged in the 1970s. One popular solution advanced by personality and social psychologists was to look for moderating variables.

THE MODERATING VARIABLES APPROACH

Behaviors are typically performed in a particular context or situation appropriate for the behavior in question. Thus, cheating on exams occurs mainly in classroom situations whereas shoplifting is, by definition, tied to commercial retail establishments. In other words, different behaviors, even if they belong to a common domain such as honesty–dishonesty, are performed in different situations. In addition to the individual's general predisposition, therefore, various features of the situation can affect performance or nonperformance of a given behavior. Not only can situational variables have an impact on a specific behavior independent of whatever stable dispositions people bring to the situation; they can also *moderate* the effects of attitudes or personality traits. That is, people's characteristic traits or attitudes may influence their behavior in some situations but not in others. Consider, for example, the case of a person who is taken ill while walking in the street. A dispositional approach to human behavior might suggest that passers-by will offer help to the extent that they are altruistic. However, the effect of altruism on helping may depend on a variety of situational factors: whether the need for help is readily apparent, the sex and age of the person who was taken ill, the presence or absence of other people who could help, and so on. Situational characteristics of this kind may serve to 'activate' implicit dispositional tendencies (Staub 1974; Schwartz 1977), and it is perhaps only when such activation occurs that people behave in accordance with their dispositions.

It is possible to generalize the notion of moderating variables to other types of factors, in addition to the situation, that may also have an effect on the relation between general attitudes or personality traits and specific behaviors. According to the moderating variables approach, the extent to which a general disposition is reflected in overt action is subject to various contingencies. Attitudes and personality traits are thus assumed to interact with other variables in their effects on specific behaviors. This *interactionist* or *contingent consistency* position was adopted both in the domain of personality (e.g., Bowers 1973; Ekehammar 1974; Endler and Magnusson 1976) and in the domain of social psychology (e.g., Warner and DeFleur 1969; Fazio and Zanna 1981; Snyder 1982). (See also Sherman and Fazio (1983) for a discussion of moderating variables in personality and social psychology.) The factors that were said to interact with attitudes or personality traits may be grouped into three broad categories: (1) situational circumstances surrounding performance of the behavior; (2) characteristics of the individual; and (3) secondary characteristics of the disposition. In this chapter we examine research related to these types of moderating variables, consider theoretical developments that may help to integrate them into a systematic conceptual framework, and discuss the limitations of this approach.

Situational factors as moderators

While most efforts to identify moderating variables have been directed at individual differences and at a disposition's secondary characteristics, several potential candidates of a situational nature have also been investigated. The general idea here is that different indicators of the same disposition will be more consistent with each other in some situations than in others.

An obvious potential moderating variable related to the behavioral context is *situational constraint*. People should generally be more likely to act in accordance with their attitudes and personality traits in the absence rather than presence of situation constraints. On the basis of self-ratings, Monson, Hesley, and Chernick (1982) selected extraverted and introverted college students for participation in their study. Each student's taped interaction with two confederates was rated for the amount spoken and the degree of extraversion displayed. To manipulate situational constraints, the two confederates either acted neutrally during the interaction, thus permitting expression of the student's personality trait, or they imposed constraints by strongly encouraging or discouraging the student's participation in the discussion. As might be expected, there was significantly less behavioral variance in the two high constraint conditions than in the condition of low constraint. That is, students tended to talk when they were encouraged to do so and to be relatively quiet when they were discouraged from talking. There was much greater variability in behavior when the confederates acted neutrally. The correlations between extraversion–introversion and behavior showed the expected pattern: stronger correlations ($r = 0.56$ and 0.63 for the two measures of behavior) under low constraint than under high constraint ($r = 0.10$ and 0.38).

Another study (Warner and DeFleur 1969), however, reported moderating effects of the situation that appear to be at variance with these findings. A large sample of college students was divided at the median score on a scale designed to assess attitudes toward African Americans. The measure of behavior was each participant's signed indication of willingness or refusal to perform one of eight behaviors, ranging from making a small donation to a charity for African American students to dating an attractive African American student. These commitments were elicited by means of a letter sent to each participant. For half the sample the letter assured anonymity of response whereas for the other half it indicated that the participant's response would be made public in campus newspapers. It stands to reason that the public condition involved greater social constraints than did the private condition. We might thus expect behavior to be more consistent with attitudes in the latter than in the former. Although the results of the study must be interpreted with caution because of a very low response rate, they showed exactly the opposite pattern. The effect of attitude on signed approval or disapproval of the requested behavior was greater in the public condition (a difference of 77.8 percent between respondents with positive and negative attitudes toward African Americans) than in the private condition (a difference of 17.2 percent).

Another situational moderator is more subtle in nature, involving aspects of a situation that can create high or low levels of *self-awareness*. Wicklund and his associates (Duval and Wicklund 1972; Wicklund 1975) have studied the effects of heightened self-awareness in the laboratory, typically by means of confronting the participant with a mirror. Presence of a mirror is expected to raise awareness of private aspects of the self, including attitudes and values, and should therefore increase consistency between general dispositions and specific actions.

To test this hypothesis, Carver (1975) performed two replications of a study in which attitudes toward punishment were assessed by means of several questions concerning its perceived effectiveness and the participant's willingness to use punishment. At a later point in time, the participants had an opportunity to administer shocks of varying intensities on 35 'error' trials in the Buss (1961) aggression paradigm. In this paradigm, participants are led to believe that the study investigates the use of punishment, in the form of electric shocks, to improve performance on a learning task. The naïve participant is to serve as teacher and another student (actually an assistant to the investigator) serves as pupil. Each time the pupil makes a mistake, the teacher is to administer a shock of an intensity selected by the teacher. In reality, of course, no shocks are administered. The pupil goes through a series of learning trials and makes a predetermined number of errors. The average intensity of shocks ostensibly administered is taken as a measure of the aggressiveness of the participant's behavior. Depending on the experimental condition, a mirror was either present or absent during shock administration. In the first study, the two attitude measures predicted mean shock levels with correlations of 0.57 and 0.58 when the mirror was present but the correlations were close to zero when the mirror was absent. A significant interaction between attitude and presence of mirror was also found in the second study, but no correlations were reported.

Similar results were obtained with respect to the relation between personality and overt behavior (Pryor et al. 1977). A mirror was either present or absent during administration of a questionnaire designed to assess sociability. Several days later, the male participants were observed interacting with a female confederate who assumed a passive role. The behavioral measure of sociability was a combination of the number of words emitted by the participants and the confederate's rating of their sociability. There were again two replications of the study, with trait–behavior correlations of 0.55 and 0.73 in the mirror condition and 0.03 and 0.28 in the condition without a mirror.[1]

One final factor related to the situation is its *competency requirements* (Mischel 1984). This factor is actually a combination of situational and personal variables. Mischel (1983, 1984) argued that consistency of behavior across situations may often be reflective of rigidity, maladjustment, and an inability to cope adequately with the requirements of a given situation. Whenever the competency requirements of the situation exceed the level of competence possessed by the individual, behavior will tend to follow well-established patterns. Mischel thus hypothesized that we will find greater consistency in behavior under such conditions. A study conducted by Wright (1983) was designed to test this hypothesis (see Mischel 1984). Emotionally disturbed children in summer camps served as subjects. Behaviors reflecting aggressiveness and withdrawal were of particular interest. Judges rated the situations in which behaviors were observed in terms of their cognitive and self-regulatory requirements, and they also rated the competencies of each child to meet those requirements. Within each behavioral category, correlations were computed among the various specific behaviors involved. These correlations were reported for two replications of the study. When the children's competencies were up to the requirements of the situation, the mean correlations (across behaviors and replications) were 0.35 for aggression and 0.17 for withdrawal. In contrast, when the situational requirements exceeded the competencies of the children, the corresponding correlations were 0.67 and 0.53.

In conclusion, despite the frequent assertion that dispositions interact with situational factors to produce behavior, relatively few studies have submitted this hypothesis to a direct test. The prime situational candidate for an interaction effect, situational constraints, has produced inconclusive results. The experiment by Monson, Hesley, and Chernick (1982) created conditions virtually guaranteeing that the sociability trait would find expression only under low situational constraints. Manipulating constraints in a less blatant fashion, Warner and DeFleur (1969) reported results that were inconsistent with the original interaction hypothesis. Two sets of studies have shown that raising self-awareness by means of a mirror can increase the predictive validity of attitudes and personality traits. As to the moderating effects of a situation's competency requirements, an initial study yielded promising findings but there seems to have been no follow-up research to demonstrate their replicability in other settings.

Individual differences as moderators

The search for individual difference variables as moderators of the relation between dispositions and behavior is based on the assumption that consistency can be expected for some individuals but not for others. Efforts of many investigators have thus centered on identifying the characteristics of individuals that are likely to promote or undermine consistency. These efforts have produced a rather lengthy list of potential moderators, but as we shall see, empirical attempts to verify their operation have met with mixed results.

Personality characteristics

Self-monitoring A number of researchers have attempted to identify stable personality traits that lead certain individuals to exhibit strong consistency between verbal dispositions and actual behavior, and others to exhibit little consistency of this kind, irrespective of the behavioral domain under consideration. A case in point is the tendency toward self-monitoring (Snyder 1974, 1979). People high on this dimension are said to be rather pragmatic, acting in accordance with the requirements of the situation. In contrast, low self-monitoring individuals are assumed to act on the basis of principles, in accordance with their personal values, preferences, and convictions. It follows that we should find stronger attitude–behavior and trait–behavior relations among low than among high self-monitoring individuals.

Although it did not include a measure of overt behavior, a study of mock jury judgments (Snyder and Swann 1976) is often cited as support for the idea that self-monitoring moderates the relation between attitudes and actions. The self-monitoring tendencies of college students were assessed by means of Snyder's (1974) personality scale, and the sample was divided at the median score into subgroups high and low on this trait dimension. A standard scale measuring attitudes toward affirmative action was administered and, two weeks later, participants were asked to reach a verdict in a mock court case involving alleged sex discrimination. The case was brought by a woman who had been rejected for a university faculty position in favor of a male applicant. The materials presented to the respondents included summaries of the applicants' biographies and of the arguments advanced in court on behalf of the plaintiff and of the university. For the total sample of participants, the correlation between attitudes toward affirmative action and the mock jurors' verdicts was a modest 0.22. However, as expected, it was stronger for individuals low in self-monitoring ($r = 0.42$) than for high self-monitoring individuals ($r = 0.03$).

In a subsequent study (Snyder and Kendzierski 1982b), willingness to attend a group discussion on the benefits of affirmative action was found to be greater among participants with positive attitudes toward affirmative action than among participants with negative attitudes. However, this difference was observed only among individuals low in self-monitoring tendency. In this subsample, 50 percent of participants with favorable attitudes toward affirmative action agreed to take part in the group discussion compared to 10 percent with unfavorable attitudes. Among high self-monitoring individuals there was no difference in readiness to attend the group discussion. No measure of actual behavior was obtained.

The parallel expectation that people's self-monitoring tendency influences the predictive validity of personality trait measures has also received some empirical support. In the context of a marketing study (Becherer and Richard 1978), college students expressed their preferences for private brands of eight different products (i.e. brands offered by retailers) as compared to national brands of the same products. The products used were cologne or perfume, mouthwash, complexion aids, alcoholic beverages, vitamins, pocket calculators, coffee, and candy bars. Average preference ratings were correlated with 18 personality traits assessed by means of the California Personality Inventory. Six of the 18 traits were found to make significant contributions to prediction of preference ratings: tolerance, responsibility, socialization, achievement, dominance, and intellectual efficiency. Snyder's scale was again used to divide participants into low and high self-monitoring subgroups. Multiple correlations between personality traits and preference ratings ranged from 0.65 to 0.80 for participants with low scores on the self-monitoring scale and from 0.33 to 0.42 for participants with high self-monitoring scores.

However, studies that looked at actual behavior rather than judgments, readiness to perform a behavior, or preferences, have not always been able to demonstrate the moderating effects of self-monitoring tendency. For example, Kline (1987) reported a trend for attitudes toward cable TV to predict actual cable subscriptions better for consumers low ($r = 0.51$) rather than high ($r = 0.33$) in self-monitoring tendency. However, this difference was not statistically significant. In another study, attitudes toward donating blood at a forthcoming blood drive were used to predict actual blood donations (Zuckerman and Reis 1978). For the total sample of respondents, the attitude–behavior correlation was found to be 0.36, and there was no significant difference between individuals high and low in self-monitoring tendency.

Little evidence for the moderating effects of self-monitoring was also reported in a study of two behaviors among college students (Ajzen et al. 1982). First, voting participation was predicted from several general dispositional measures: social responsibility, liberalism–conservatism, and political involvement. Second, an attempt was made to predict marijuana use from social responsibility. The attitude–behavior and trait–behavior correlations were quite low and self-monitoring failed to have a significant moderating effect on these correlations.

Finally, students' general attitudes toward psychological research were used to predict their volunteering to participate in such research (Snyder and Kendzierski 1982a). The students overheard two confederates express the opinion that volunteering was either a matter of personal choice or that it depended on one's attitude toward psychological research. In neither condition did self-monitoring tendency significantly affect the magnitude of the correlations between attitudes and behavior; these correlations were

0.50 and 0.70 for low and high self-monitoring individuals, respectively, in the attitude-relevant condition, and 0.20 and 0.30 in the personal choice condition.

Private self-consciousness Earlier we examined the moderating effect of self-awareness created by the presence of a mirror in the situation. Instead of manipulating self-awareness experimentally, it is also possible to measure private self-consciousness by means of a personality inventory. This trait refers to people's chronic awareness of private aspects of their selves including, importantly, their feelings, motives, and values (see Buss 1980). Due to their greater awareness of these internal states, people high in private self-consciousness are assumed, across situations, to behave more in accordance with their dispositions than are people low on this dimension.

Empirical support for this hypothesis can be found in a study that dealt with the relation between dispositions toward aggressiveness or hostility and aggressive behavior in the laboratory (Scheier et al. 1978). Dispositional aggressiveness was assessed by means of a multi-item aggressiveness/hostility inventory and Buss's (1961) aggression paradigm, described earlier, was used to observe aggressive behavior. In the present study, there were 25 'error' trials. Private self-consciousness was assessed by means of a personality scale (Fenigstein et al. 1975), and participants were selected from the top and bottom thirds of the distribution. Consistent with expectations, the correlation between the questionnaire measure of aggressiveness and behavior in the aggression paradigm was 0.34 for the total sample, 0.09 for participants low in private self-consciousness, and 0.66 for participants high in private self-consciousness.

A subsequent study (Underwood and Moore 1981) replicated these findings with respect to a different behavioral domain but also obtained some unexpected results. Same-sex pairs of college students talked freely to form an impression of the other person. At the conclusion, each person rated his or her partner on overall sociability and on seven items concerning the extent to which the partner had displayed specific behaviors reflective of sociability. The two sets of ratings were combined to obtain a general measure of sociability during interaction. In addition, participant provided the same ratings for their own behavior. Two behavioral sociability scores were thus available, one based on peer ratings, the other on self-ratings. The dispositional predictor was a personality measure of sociability obtained prior to the interaction, and private self-consciousness was assessed by means of the Fenigstein, Scheier, and Buss (1975) scale. The correlation between the questionnaire measure of sociability and peer ratings of sociable behavior was, as expected, stronger in the case of participants high in private self-consciousness ($r = 0.44$) than for participants low on this dimension ($r = 0.03$). However, when self-ratings of sociability during interaction served as the behavioral dependent variable, the pattern was reversed: $r = 0.27$ and $r = 0.61$, respectively. No convincing explanation for this reversal is readily available.

Need for cognition The final individual difference variable to be discussed as a possible moderator of the relation between general dispositions and specific action tendencies is a person's need for cognition. According to the elaboration likelihood model of persuasion (Petty and Cacioppo 1986), individuals who form their attitudes after carefully scrutinizing available evidence exhibit stronger attitude–behavior correlations than individuals who do little 'central processing' of this kind but instead base their attitudes on relatively superficial external cues. Furthermore, it has been reasoned that people high in need for cognition, i.e. people who have a strong need to understand and make reasonable the world they experience, are more likely to process information carefully than are people with low standing on this dimension (Cacioppo et al. 1986). Taken together, these ideas imply a stronger attitude–behavior correlation among people high as compared to low in need for cognition.

In a study designed to test this hypothesis (Cacioppo et al. 1986: Experiment 2), need for cognition was assessed by means of a personality scale and attitudinal preferences for candidates in a presidential election were used to predict actual voting choice. Consistent with expectations, the attitude–behavior correlation was found to be 0.86 for people high in need for cognition but only 0.41 for people low in need for cognition.

In conclusion, the search for individual differences as moderating variables has produced some interesting effects, but the results are not always consistent across studies. The moderating effect of self-monitoring is found to be quite tenuous; low self-monitoring tendency is sometimes accompanied by greater predictive validity, but at other times there are no differences between high and low self-monitoring individuals. Empirical findings are more encouraging with respect to private self-consciousness. When self-consciousness is high, behavior is more likely to be guided by general attitudes or personality traits than when self-consciousness is low. Finally, need for cognition has been shown to moderate the attitude–behavior relation in one experiment, but more research is needed to establish the generality of this finding.

Secondary characteristics of the disposition

The final class of moderating variables to be considered are secondary characteristics of a disposition. Variables of this kind have been examined primarily with respect to attitudes. In addition to assessing the strength and direction of an attitude, it is also possible to measure its internal structure, a person's involvement in the attitude domain, the confidence with which the attitude is held, the way it was formed, and so on (see Raden 1985, for a review). Each of these factors may influence the magnitude of the relation between general attitudes and specific behavioral tendencies. In the personality domain, the only secondary characteristic to have received more than passing attention is the extent to which a given trait dimension is relevant for a particular individual.

Secondary characteristics of attitudes

Internal structure The multidimensional view of attitude described in Chapter 1 holds that attitudes are composed of cognitive, affective, and conative response tendencies. The question of interest is the degree to which the different components of attitude are evaluatively consistent with each other. Specifically, Rosenberg (1965) postulated that affective–cognitive consistency is a prerequisite for effective action. To test this idea, the moderating effects of consistency between an attitude's affective and cognitive components was examined in a series of three experiments (Norman 1975). It was hypothesized that attitude–behavior correlations are stronger when the two components are consistent rather than inconsistent with each other. The affective component of undergraduates' attitudes toward acting as subjects in psychological research was measured by means of a 9-point favorability scale and, in the third study, also by means of a 16-item evaluative semantic differential. The cognitive component was indexed by an expectancy-value scale (see Chapter 2) based on 12 beliefs regarding the consequences of participating in psychological research. The two measures were each rank-ordered and, following Rosenberg's (1968) suggestion, the absolute difference between the ranks was taken as an index of affective–cognitive inconsistency. A median split partitioned participants into low and high internal consistency subgroups. To obtain measures of behavior, participants in the first two studies were invited to sign up for an experiment (signing up as well as actual attendance were scored), and in the third study they could volunteer for two additional sessions while already participating in an experiment. The results provided partial support for the hypothesis. Across the three studies, the average correlation between behavior and the *affective* measure of attitude was 0.54 under conditions of high affective–cognitive consistency, and significantly lower (mean $r = -0.08$) when affect and cognition were relatively inconsistent with each other. With respect to the correlations between behavior and the *cognitive* measure of attitude, however, a significant difference between the high and low affective–cognitive consistency subgroups was obtained only in the third study (mean $r = 0.47$ and 0.28, respectively).

Moreover, a subsequent replication of Norman's experiment with only minor modifications (Fazio and Zanna 1978a) failed to find any moderating effect of affective–cognitive consistency. To obtain an overall measure of attitude, Fazio and Zanna combined the measures of the affective and cognitive components into a single score. Their analysis resulted in a significant correlation ($r = 0.32$) between the overall attitude and volunteering to serve as a subject in psychological research, but this correlation was not influenced by the degree of affective–cognitive consistency.

A different approach to the question of an attitude's internal consistency was adopted in a study of marijuana use among high school students (Schlegel and DiTecco 1982). On the basis of a 20-item attitude toward marijuana scale, nonusers or initial users were shown to have less differentiated (i.e. more internally consistent) attitudes toward marijuana than occasional or regular users. Attitudes toward smoking marijuana, assessed by means of an evaluative semantic differential, were employed to predict self-reports of actual marijuana use. Consistent with expectations, these attitude–behavior correlations were found to be stronger among relatively undifferentiated (high internal consistency) participants (the average attitude–behavior correlation across different subpopulations was 0.36) than among participants whose attitude structure was relatively complex (mean correlation = 0.18).

Reflection and accessibility   The extent to which attitudes are expressed after sufficient reflection is another secondary characteristic of verbal attitude that is said to affect its relation to overt behavior. It is usually assumed that people are more likely to act in accordance with their attitudes if they 'think before they act' (Snyder 1982). The research on mock juror judgments in a sex discrimination court case (Snyder and Swann 1976) mentioned earlier provided support for this idea. Prior to delivering their verdicts, one-half of the participants were encouraged to reflect upon their attitudes toward affirmative action. In this condition, the correlation between general attitudes toward affirmative action and the verdict was 0.58, as opposed to a correlation of 0.07 in a control group without prior reflection.

It has also been suggested that thinking about an attitudinal issue can make the attitude more readily accessible in memory and thereby influence its predictive validity. Brown (1974) demonstrated the moderating effect of attitude accessibility in a study of compliance with the law. High school students completed several multi-item scales designed to assess attitudes toward the law in general, toward the federal laws of the United States, toward the police, and toward the courts. To assess the accessibility of these attitudes, participants were asked how often they thought about the law in general and about the unlawfulness of such activities as crossing a street against a red light, littering in public places, and speeding in an automobile. Scores on this measure were used to divide participants into low, moderate, and high accessibility subgroups. A scale based on self-reports of compliance with the law on such matters as shoplifting, traffic regulations, and use of narcotics served as the measure of behavior. Consistent with expectations, attitude–behavior correlations were relatively weak when attitude accessibility was low ($r = 0.18$ to 0.33); they increased in magnitude for respondents whose attitudes were moderately accessible ($r = 0.32$ to 0.45); and they were strongest in the high accessibility subgroup ($r = 0.42$ to 0.65).

Vested interest, involvement, and importance   It stands to reason that people with strong vested interest in a behavior are more likely to act on their attitudes than are people with little vested interest in the behavior. Sivacek and Crano (1982) tested this hypothesis in two experiments. The topic of investigation in the first study was a referendum to raise the state's legal drinking age to 21. College students were asked to indicate their positions with respect to this issue on a 7-point scale. As might be expected, most (72 of the 93 participants) were opposed to the proposal. A short time later they were contacted by phone and asked to volunteer to call voters and urge them to vote against the proposal. Age of the respondent was used to operationalize vested interest because younger students would be directly affected by the law whereas older students would not, or would be affected for only a short time. The participants were therefore divided into three groups on the basis of their age. As predicted, the volunteering rate among participants opposed to the proposal increased from 13 percent for students with low vested interest to 47 percent for students with high vested interest. For the total sample, the correlation between attitude toward the proposed change in law and number of calls volunteered was 0.23. When computed separately for the three vested interest groups, the correlation rose from 0.16 in the lowest vested interest group to 0.19 in the moderate vested interest group and to 0.30 in the highest vested interest group.

In the second study (Sivacek and Crano 1982) undergraduate college students completed a scale designed to assess their attitudes toward instituting a comprehensive exam at their university as a prerequisite for graduation. Vested interest in the topic was measured by two questions concerning the likelihood that the respondent would have to take the exam (if instituted) and the extent to which instituting the exam would directly affect the respondent. On the basis of the sum of these two responses, the participants were divided into three vested interest groups. The behavior observed was whether or not participants signed a petition opposing the proposed exam, whether or not they volunteered to help distribute petitions, write letters to newspapers, etc., and the number of hours of help they pledged. In addition, an aggregate measure of behavior was obtained by constructing a scale on the basis of these three actions. For the total sample of participants, attitude–behavior correlations ranged from 0.34 to 0.43 for the three individual actions, while a correlation of 0.60 was obtained in the prediction of the behavioral aggregate. This demonstrates the importance of aggregation to achieve strong attitude–behavior correlations, an issue we will consider in Chapter 4. As to the effect of vested interest, the correlations between attitudes and individual actions ranged from 0.24 to 0.42 in the low vested interest group and from 0.60 to 0.74 in the high vested interest group. Using the behavioral aggregate score, this comparison showed correlations of 0.53 and 0.82, respectively.

A study conducted during a housing shortage at Cornell University (Regan and Fazio 1977) can also be interpreted as demonstrating the moderating effect of vested interest or involvement. As a result of the housing problem, many freshmen were severely inconvenienced by being forced to spend their first few weeks of the fall semester in temporary, uncomfortable accommodations. Attitudes of freshmen toward the housing crisis were assessed by means of five attitudinal items and were found to be quite negative, irrespective of whether the student had been assigned to temporary or to permanent housing. Nevertheless, those assigned to temporary housing had a greater vested interest in remedial action. Six behavioral opportunities were provided to all students in the sample, among them signing a petition addressed to the administration, listing recommendations or suggestions for solving the crisis, and writing a letter to the Housing Office. The correlation between attitudes and an index based on all six behaviors was 0.42 in the high vested interest group and 0.04 in the low vested interest group.

Fazio and Zanna (1978a) used 'latitude of rejection' to operationalize involvement in the topic of psychological research. The number of positions college students judged as objectionable on a 7-point *boring–interesting* scale was taken as an index of latitude of rejection. The greater this latitude, the more involved a person is assumed to be (see Sherif and Hovland 1961). A combination of the affective and cognitive instruments developed by Norman (1975) and described earlier was used to measure attitudes toward serving as a subject in psychological research. Toward the end of the experimental session participants were asked to join a subject pool from which volunteers would be drawn for psychological research. The behavioral criterion was the number of experiments in which a person volunteered to participate. The data showed a significant effect of attitude on behavior ($r = 0.32$) as well as a significant interaction between attitude and involvement. When the sample was divided into high, medium, and low thirds in terms of the involvement measure, the attitude–behavior correlations in the respective subsamples were 0.52, 0.26, and 0.19.

Finally, examining survey data from the 1968, 1980, and 1984 presidential elections in the United States, Krosnick (1988) found a moderating effect of issue importance on the relation between attitudes toward the candidates and voting choice. Prediction of voting choice from attitudes became more accurate as participants assigned greater importance to the issues in the campaign.

Confidence   Several studies have obtained support for the moderating role of a person's degree of confidence in an expressed attitudinal position. Perhaps the first empirical demonstration was provided by Warland and Sample (1973; Sample and Warland 1973). Attitudes of college students toward student government were assessed by means of a 15-item Likert scale developed by Tittle and Hill (1967). After responding to all 15 items, the participants were asked to read each item again and to rate, on a 5-point scale, how certain they were with respect to the response they had given to the item. Based on the sum of these certainty ratings, participants were divided into low and high confidence subgroups. Attitudes toward student government were used to predict participation in undergraduate student elections, ascertained from the voting records. The correlation between attitudes and voting was 0.26 for the total sample, 0.10 for respondents with low confidence in their attitudes, and 0.47 for respondents with high confidence.

A significant moderating effect of attitudinal confidence was also reported in the study by Fazio and Zanna (1978a) described earlier. In addition to expressing their attitudinal positions, the participants rated, on a 9-point scale, how certain they felt about their attitudes toward volunteering to act as subjects in psychology experiments. When the sample was split into three equal subgroups on the basis of these confidence ratings, the attitude–behavior correlation was found to be 0.08 for respondents with low confidence, and about 0.40 for respondents with moderate or high confidence.

Fazio and Zanna (1978b) also demonstrated the moderating effect of confidence by means of an experimental manipulation. As a measure of attitude, college students rated the interest value of each of five types of intellectual puzzles. They were then provided with bogus physiological feedback about the confidence with which they held their attitudes toward the different puzzles. One half of the participants was told that they held their attitudes with a high degree of confidence, the other half that they held their attitudes with little confidence. Three measures of behavior were obtained during a 15-minute free-play situation: the order in which each puzzle type was attempted, the number of puzzles of each type attempted (out of the total available), and the amount of time spent on each type of puzzle. Within-subject correlations (across puzzle-types) were computed between attitudes and each measure of behavior. The average correlation (across the three behaviors and across participants) in the high confidence condition ($r = 0.60$) was significantly greater than the average correlation ($r = 0.44$) in the low confidence condition.

Direct experience It has been suggested that prediction of behavior from attitudes improves to the extent that the attitude is based on direct experience (Fazio and Zanna 1978a, 1978b; Regan and Fazio 1977; see Fazio and Zanna 1981, for a review). Fazio and his associates have demonstrated the moderating effect of direct experience in two settings. In the first (Regan and Fazio 1977), the relation between attitudes and behavior was examined with respect to the five types of intellectual puzzles mentioned above. In the indirect experience condition of the experiment, participants were given a description of each puzzle type and were shown previously solved examples of the puzzles. By way of contrast, in the direct experience condition, participants were given an opportunity actually to work on the same puzzles. As described earlier, expressed interest in each puzzle type served as a measure of attitude, and behavior (order and proportion of each puzzle type attempted) was assessed during a 15-minute free-play period. Correlations between attitudes and the two measures of behavior were 0.51 and 0.54 in the direct experience condition and 0.22 and 0.20 in the indirect experience condition.

A second study demonstrating the moderating effect of direct experience was reported by Fazio and Zanna (1978a). As we saw earlier, this study examined the relation between attitudes toward participating in psychological research and actual participation (by becoming a member of the subject pool and signing up for a certain number of experiments). Amount of direct experience in this situation was defined by the number of experiments in which a person had participated as a subject in the past. The attitude–behavior correlation was 0.42 in the top third of prior experience subsample, 0.36 in the subsample with moderate prior experience, and −0.03 for the least experienced participants.

In conclusion, various lines of research have shown that an attitude's secondary characteristics can moderate the relation between attitudes and behaviors. Thought or reflection, involvement, and confidence have all been found to increase an attitude's predictive validity. The results of experiments on the moderating effects of direct experience have also been generally supportive, although there is at least one discordant note. The Schlegel and DiTecco (1992) study described earlier obtained stronger attitude–behavior correlations among high school students with relatively little direct experience concerning the use of marijuana than among students with a great deal of direct experience, an effect attributed to greater internal consistency of attitudes among the less experienced. However, the moderating effect of an attitude's internal consistency has not been consistently demonstrated.

Relevance of personality traits

Allport (1937) was perhaps the first to suggest that not all trait dimensions are equally relevant to all people. Some individuals can be described as introverts, others as extraverts; but some individuals may not be well described as either consistently introverted or consistently extraverted. For these latter individuals, the introvert–extravert trait dimension is largely irrelevant. Clearly, a measure of this trait should be a better predictor of behavior among people for whom it is relevant rather than among people for whom it is irrelevant.

Variability of behavior across situations   Bem and Allen (1974: 512) argued that the degree to which a trait dimension is relevant for describing a given person can be judged by considering the consistency of the person's trait-related behavior. Specifically, they hypothesized that 'Individuals who identify themselves as consistent on a particular trait dimension will in fact be more consistent cross-situationally than those who identify themselves as highly variable'. However, consistent with Allport's insight, people who are found to behave consistently in one behavioral domain may be inconsistent in another. Thus we can expect to predict behavior only for 'some of the people some of the time.'

To test these ideas, Bem and Allen examined the behavior of college students in the domains of friendliness and conscientiousness. Participants rated the extent to which they thought they *varied* from one situation to another in how friendly and outgoing they were and in how conscientious they were. They were then divided, at the median, into consistent and inconsistent subgroups, separately for each behavioral domain. The participants' standing on the two trait dimensions (friendliness and conscientiousness) was assessed by means of a simple 7-point scale and by means of a multi-item self-report behavioral inventory. With respect to each trait dimension, ratings were provided by the participants themselves, by their parents, and by their peers. In addition, several nonverbal measures of behavior were obtained: friendliness displayed in the course of a group discussion and spontaneously while sitting with a confederate in a waiting room; and conscientiousness indicated by prompt return of course evaluations, completion of course readings, and neatness of personal appearance and of living quarters. Finally, participants also completed an inventory assessing introversion–extraversion, as a possible dispositional predictor of friendliness.

Differences in consistency were explored by comparing the correlations of the high and low variability subgroups.[2] Results in the domain of friendliness supported Bem and Allen's hypothesis. One of the supportive findings had to do with inter-rater reliability of friendliness, i.e. with the correlations among ratings of friendliness provided by the participants themselves, by their parents, and by their peers. These correlations were significantly higher for individuals who considered themselves consistently friendly or unfriendly than for individuals who reported that their friendliness varied from situation to situation. Also, there was evidence that the introversion–extraversion scale was a somewhat better predictor of a person's rated friendliness and of nonverbal behavior in this domain for low variability ($r = 0.25$ to 0.77) than for high variability individuals ($r = -0.12$ to 0.65). Finally, the correlation between friendliness in a group discussion and spontaneous friendliness was stronger in the low ($r = 0.73$) than in the high ($r = 0.30$) variability group.

The results with respect to conscientiousness, however, did not provide as clear a picture. An analysis identical to that performed with respect to friendliness revealed no differences between low and high consistency subgroups. Consequently, Bem and Allen decided to divide participants into consistent versus inconsistent subgroups on the basis of variability in responses to the multi-item self-report behavioral inventory. When this was done, the expected differences in inter-rater reliabilities again emerged, but the correlations among the three objective measures of behavior still failed to show the expected pattern.

In an unsuccessful attempt to replicate the Bem and Allen (1974) findings, Mischel and Peake (1982a) presented data on the correlations among their 19 behaviors in the conscientiousness domain described in Chapter 2. These correlations were computed separately for individuals who had judged themselves low as opposed to high in variability. The expected differences between the subgroups failed to materialize. The mean correlation was 0.15 in the low variability group and 0.10 in the high variability group. Finally, a thorough attempt by Chaplin and Goldberg (1984) to replicate the Bem and Allen findings also resulted in failure. These investigators considered eight personality traits: friendliness, conscientiousness, honesty, sensitivity, assertiveness, activity level, emotional stability, and cultural sophistication. Furthermore, they used three methods to divide respondents into low and high consistency subgroups: Bem and Allen's two methods, as well as a division on the basis of self-rated consistency with respect to various specific behaviors in each of the trait domains. And, like Bem and Allen, they compared the subgroups in terms of inter-rater reliability and in terms of correlations among nonverbal measures of specific actions in each domain. The results revealed few significant differences between high and low consistency subgroups, irrespective of the method used to partition the sample, and there was no systematic pattern to the differences that did emerge.

Schematicity In a closely related line of theorizing, Markus (1977) introduced the concept of *self-schema* as a possible moderator of trait–behavior correlations. Self-schemas are cognitive generalizations about important aspects of the self, conceptions that organize and guide the processing of self-related information. Individuals are assumed to differ in the kinds of traits or behavioral domains that are important or relevant to their self-schemas. People who consider a given trait, say, extraversion, to be highly descriptive of themselves and to be important to their self-concepts are said to be schematic with respect to this trait. Similarly, on the other pole of this personality dimension, if people consider themselves to be highly introverted and this trait is important to their self-concepts, they are said to be schematic introverts. Finally, individuals who view themselves as neither highly extraverted nor highly introverted and consider this trait dimension unimportant to their self-concepts are said to be aschematic in relation to extraversion–introversion. Generally speaking, it is expected that a trait measure will predict behavior better for persons who are schematic with respect to the trait than for persons who are aschematic.

Several investigators (Kendzierski 1988; Estabrooks and Courneya 1997; Yin and Boyd 2000) have tested this hypothesis in relation to exercise schematicity and healthy eating schematicity (Kendzierski and Costello 2004), but the measures obtained have tended to confound schematicity with standing on the trait dimension itself, a practice that results in circular reasoning and makes it impossible to reach unequivocal conclusions regarding the moderating effects of schematicity. Using methods suggested by Markus (1977), participants in one study (Kendzierski 1988) were asked to indicate, on 11-point scales, the extent to which each of three phrases were descriptive of them: *someone who exercises regularly, someone who keeps in shape*, and *physically active*. In addition, they rated, again on an 11-point scale, how important each descriptor phrase was to their self-image. Participants who rated themselves highly on at least two of the three descriptors and indicated that at least two of the three descriptors were important for their self-images were classified as exercise schematics. Conversely, participants who gave themselves low scores on at least two descriptors and rated at least two of them as important for their self-images were classified as non-exercise schematics. To be classified as aschematic, participants had to have rated themselves as moderate on at least two of the descriptors and to have indicated that at least two were not extremely important to their self-images. A measure of behavior was obtained by asking participants a series of questions about how often they engaged in exercise and what kinds of physical activities they performed. Not surprisingly, exercise schematics, i.e. participants who had described themselves as exercising regularly, keeping in shape, and being physically active reported exercising more than aschematics who, in turn, reported exercising more than non-exercise schematics. The possible moderating effect of exercise schematicity on the prediction of behavior from the disposition to exercise could not be tested because the two variables were confounded: exercise schematicity was defined in part by the extent to which a person engages in exercise.

Traitedness   Partly in response to the problematic operational definition of schematicity, Baumeister and Tice (1988) introduced the concept of 'metatrait' to refer to the presence or absence of a trait in an individual's personality. The personalities of *traited* individuals contain the trait dimension under consideration; for these individuals the trait is relevant. Thus, individuals who can be described as either extraverted *or* introverted are traited. In contrast, the personalities of *nontraited* individuals do not contain the introverted–extraverted trait dimension; for them, this trait is irrelevant. Baumeister and Tice hypothesized that a person's standing on a given trait will be a better predictor of behavior for traited as opposed to nontraited individuals. Furthermore, like Bem and Allen, they suggested that traitedness be operationalized in terms of variability of behavior across situations. However, unlike Bem and Allen, they proposed to use as an indicator of variability or traitedness the degree of consistency in responses to different items on a personality inventory designed to assess the trait dimension of interest.

In the first of two studies (Baumeister and Tice 1988), participants completed the locus of control scale (Rotter 1966), a scale designed to assess attribution of life events to internal versus external causes. Variance across responses to the different items on the scale was taken as an indicator of traitedness on the locus of control dimension; participants with variance scores below the median were considered traited whereas participants with variance scores above the median were considered nontraited. The participants were then given an opportunity to practice a video game for as long as they wished in preparation for a final performance test. The game was described as requiring skills and effort (internal factors) more than luck (an external factor). For the total sample of participants, the correlation between locus of control scores and behavior (time spent preparing for the test) was close to zero. However, there was a significant difference between traited and nontraited individuals. As predicted, the correlation for the traited subgroup was quite strong ($r = 0.50$), and significantly higher than the correlation for the nontraited group ($r = -0.30$).

These results could not be replicated, however, in a second study (Baumeister and Tice 1988). In this study, a measure of self-esteem was correlated with the number of hints participants requested in anticipation of solving educational puzzles. Traitedness was defined in terms of the variability of responses across items on the measure of self-esteem. Level of self-esteem did not correlate significantly ($r = -0.21$) with number of hints requested, nor did the magnitude of this correlation vary as a function traitedness.[3]

To summarize briefly, there are indications that certain personality traits are more relevant for some individuals than for others, and that the degree of relevance can influence the predictive validity of a trait measure. However, there is disagreement on how relevance, schematicity, or traitedness is to be defined and measured, and the results concerning moderation by trait relevance are far from conclusive.

THE MODE MODEL: AN INTEGRATIVE THEORETICAL FRAMEWORK

There is an intuitive appeal to the moderating variables approach to the consistency problem. After all, it seems reasonable to argue that some conditions are more conducive than others to a strong association between general dispositions and specific actions. And, indeed, the various moderating variables that have been identified give us a sense of some of the conditions under which we can or cannot expect consistency between general attitudes or personality traits, on the one hand, and specific behaviors, on the other. Thus, the predictive validity of dispositional measures may depend on such situational features as environmental constraints or competency requirements; on such personal factors as the tendency toward self-monitoring, self-awareness, and need for cognition; and on secondary characteristics of the disposition, such as the relevance of a personality trait; or an attitude's internal structure, information and reflection about the attitude object, the attitude's salience, vested interest in the topic, confidence regarding an attitudinal position, and direct experience with the attitude object.

However, the picture that emerges from empirical tests of these ideas is far from clear. Perhaps the strongest and most consistent support for moderating effects has been observed with respect to vested interest or involvement, confidence, and direct experience in relation to an attitudinal issue (see Ajzen and Fishbein, 2005). All these factors tend to increase attitude–behavior correspondence. Among individual difference variables, high self-awareness or private self-consciousness also tend to improve prediction of behavior consistently. Other variables, such as self-monitoring tendency, have produced mixed results; and some factors, such as need for cognition, show promise but require further research. However, if there is one overriding problem with the moderating variables approach to improving correlations between general dispositions and specific behaviors, it is the sheer multitude of moderators that have been identified. Indeed, the number of variables that might moderate the relation between general dispositions and specific actions is potentially unlimited. The steady accumulation of additional moderators over the years, and the recurrent failure to replicate earlier findings regarding the effects of a given moderator, are indicative of the difficulties faced by this approach.

Strength of behavioral dispositions

A concept with the potential to provide an integrative framework for the disparate moderating variables is the strength of the attitudinal or personality disposition. People vary not only in terms of the valence of their attitudes, i.e. the degree to which they evaluate the attitude object positively or negatively, but also in the strength of these evaluations. Individuals with the same position regarding an issue can hold their attitudes with varying degrees of strength or confidence. Similarly, we saw that in addition to a person's standing on a personality dimension, we can consider the extent to which the trait dimension is relevant for the person. Generally speaking, strong attitudes and personality traits are expected to predict behavior better than their weaker counterparts.

Attitude strength

Over the past two decades, the concept of attitude strength has generated a great deal of interest among investigators (see Raden 1985; Krosnick et al. 1993; Petty and Krosnick 1995; Eagly and Chaiken 1998). The properties of attitudes assumed to be indicators of its strength closely resemble some of the attitude's secondary characteristics that are said to moderate the attitude–behavior relation: importance of the attitudinal domain, vested interest, certainty in one's position, direct experience with the attitude object, and information and reflection about the issue (see Petty and Krosnick 1995). Although these different aspects of attitude strength tend to correlate only moderately with each other (Raden 1985; Krosnick et al. 1993), strong attitudes – no matter how operationalized – are assumed to be relatively stable over time, to be resistant to persuasion, and to be good predictors of behavior.

Attitude accessibility   Although intuitively reasonable, it is important to identify the psychological processes responsible for the advantage that strong attitudes may enjoy over weak attitudes. The most detailed and sophisticated account of the processes whereby general attitudes guide behavior can be found in Fazio's (1986, 1990a; Fazio and Towles-Schwen 1999) MODE model. A schematic diagram of the model is shown in Figure 3.1. In this model, attitude is defined as a learned association in memory between an object and a positive or negative evaluation of that object, and attitude strength is equivalent to the strength of this association (Fazio 1990a). Building on past work concerning the effects of attitudes on perceptions and judgments (see Eagly 1998, for a review), the model assumes that strong attitudes influence or bias perception and judgment of information relevant to the attitude object, a bias that is congruent with the valence of the attitude. Thus, people with positive attitudes toward, say, genetically modified food may evaluate new information as favoring this technology whereas people with negative attitudes may evaluate the same information as evidence against the technology.

However, for this bias to occur, the attitude must first be 'activated.' Consistent with the logic of other dual-mode processing theories (see Chaiken and Trope 1999), the MODE model posits that attitudes can be activated in one of two ways: in a controlled or deliberative fashion or in an automatic or spontaneous fashion. The acronym MODE is used to suggest that

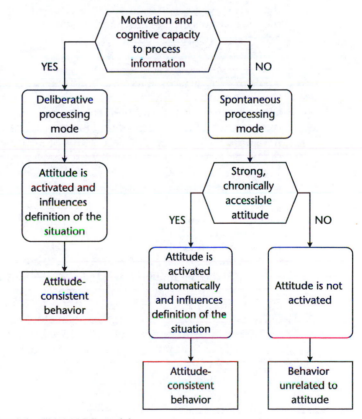

Figure 3.1   The MODE model
Source: After Fazio (1990a)

'*m*otivation and *o*pportunity act as *de*terminants of spontaneous versus deliberative attitude-to-behavior processes' (Fazio 1995: 257). When people are sufficiently motivated and have the cognitive capacity to do so, they can retrieve or construct their attitudes toward an object in an effortful manner. When motivation or cognitive capacity is low, attitudes can become available only if they are automatically activated. However, according to the MODE model, such automatic or spontaneous activation is reserved for strong attitudes. Weak attitudes will usually not be activated in the spontaneous processing mode and will thus not be available to bias the definition of the situation or guide behavior. Instead, behavior will be determined by attitude-irrelevant salient cues associated with the attitude object or the behavioral situation.

Attitude strength thus enters the process at two points. First, whereas weak as well as strong attitudes are activated in the deliberative processing mode, only strong attitudes are accessible when people operate in the spontaneous mode. Second, whether in the deliberative or spontaneous processing mode, only strong attitudes – being chronically accessible – are likely to bias perception of the situation and thus influence behavior. In work with the MODE model, the degree of an attitude's chronic accessibility in memory (i.e. its strength) is usually operationalized by measuring the latency of responses to attitudinal questions: the faster the response, the more accessible the attitude is assumed to be (e.g. Fazio and Williams 1986; see also Fazio 1990b).

Effects of moderating variables   The MODE model suggests that attitude strength – in the form of its accessibility in memory – plays a pivotal role in the link between attitudes and behavior. Generally speaking, relatively accessible attitudes should predict behavior better than less accessible attitudes. Support for this expectation has been obtained in several studies that have compared the predictive validity of attitudes expressed with low as opposed to high response latencies (e.g. Fazio and Williams 1986; Fazio et al. 1989). In a study by Fazio, Powell, and Williams (1989), for example, college students indicated their liking or disliking for each of 100 common products (Star-Kist tuna, Planters peanuts, etc.) and, on the basis of response speed, were divided into high, moderate, and low accessibility subgroups. As a measure of behavior, the participants could choose to take home five products from a set of ten alternatives. The attitude–behavior correlation increased with degree of accessibility, from 0.50 in the low accessibility group to 0.62 in the high accessibility group.

The results of research on moderating variables reviewed earlier in this chapter can now be reinterpreted in terms of attitude strength or accessibility. Attitude strength can account for the moderating effects of many individual difference variables and secondary characteristics of an attitude (Fazio 1995). Thus, with respect to individual difference variables, *self-monitoring tendency* has been found to correlate with latency of responses to attitudinal questions such that low self-monitoring individuals respond faster than high self-monitors (Kardes et al. 1986). This suggests that the former tend to hold stronger attitudes than the latter, and their attitudes are thus expected to predict behavior better. Similarly, *need for cognition* is found to be associated with such defining aspects of attitude strength as persistence over time and resistance to persuasion (Haugtvedt and Petty 1992; see also Shestowsky et al. 1998), which could explain why attitudes predict behavior better for individuals high as compared to low in need for cognition.

The same arguments apply to secondary characteristics of an attitude. Importance of, or vested interest in, an attitudinal issue and confidence in one's position are defining aspects of attitude strength and they also correlate, as would be expected, with the attitude's accessibility in memory (e.g. Kokkinaki and Lunt 1997; Bizer and Krosnick 2001). The moderating effects of these variables on the predictive validity of attitudes can thus be interpreted as due to attitude strength: individuals with high vested interest or confidence hold relatively strong attitudes that are chronically accessible in memory. Evidence for this interpretation comes from a study of consumer behavior (Kokkinaki and Lunt 1997). College students expressed their attitudes toward each of six brands in three product categories: soft drinks, beer, and chocolate bars. The latencies of these responses were also recorded to secure measures of attitude accessibility. In addition, the participants rated the importance they assigned to each product category. Finally, as a measure of behavior, participants were asked to choose three brands from each category. The rated importance of product categories showed a small but significant correlation with attitude accessibility, and both measures moderated the attitude–behavior relation. Although the differences were relatively small, prediction of brand choice was significantly more accurate for high involvement ($r = 0.51$) and for high attitude accessibility ($r = 0.52$) subgroups than for low involvement ($r = 0.43$) and low accessibility ($r = 0.41$) subgroups.

Finally, it has been argued that direct experience with an attitude object produces stronger attitudes than does second-hand information (see Sherman and Fazio 1983; Fazio 1986; Fazio and Williams 1986). As a result, attitudes are more likely to be activated and to guide behavior under direct as opposed to indirect experience conditions. In partial support of this claim, it has been found that, following direct experience with intellectual puzzles, attitudes toward the puzzles are expressed faster than following the receipt of second-hand information about the puzzles (Fazio et al. 1982; Fazio et al. 1983). In a more direct test, the accessibility of attitudes toward five brands of candy bars was found to increase with direct experience and with the number of exposures (one, three, or four) to printed advertisements for the candy bars (Berger and Mitchell 1989). Response latencies to attitudinal questions among participants who were given direct experience tasting the candy bars were found to be at least as low as the latencies of responses after repeated exposures to the ads. Furthermore, as expected, attitudes in the direct experience condition and in the frequent exposure conditions (three or four exposures) predicted subsequent choice of candy bars significantly better ($r \geq 0.70$) than in the single-exposure condition ($r < 0.50$).

Strength of personality dispositions

There is no body of theory and research in the personality domain comparable to that generated by the MODE model in the attitude domain. However, the logic of the MODE model can, with minor modifications, also be applied to personality traits. It can be argued that, like attitudes, strong personality traits are highly accessible in memory and are thus more likely than weak traits to be readily activated and available to bias perception of the situation, influence its definition, and thus guide behavior in accordance with the personality disposition.

Some support for this view is apparent if we define the strength of a personality disposition as its relevance for the individual, i.e. in terms of the individual's schematicity or traitedness in relation to a given personality dimension. Consistent with this perspective, it has been found that trait-schematic individuals respond faster to trait-relevant information about the self than trait-aschematics (Markus 1977). Specifically, participants classified as schematically dependent responded faster when asked to judge the self-relevance of adjectives indicating dependence (e.g. cooperative, tactful, timid) than of adjectives indicating independence (e.g. self-confident, dominating, arrogant). Conversely, independence schematics made faster judgments with respect to independent than with respect to dependent adjectives. There was no significant difference in response latencies among individuals who were aschematic on the dependent–independent dimension.

Similar conclusions have been reached in a study of the association between traitedness and accessibility (Siem 1998). In a sample of military recruits, degree of traitedness was assessed by means of variability in responses to items on a standard personality inventory that assessed each of the big five personality dimensions described in Chapter 1. This measure of traitedness showed some degree of correlation with latency of responses to the items in the personality inventory, i.e. with dispositional strength. These correlations ranged from 0.10 for the openness to experience trait to 0.36 for the agreeableness trait.

Effects of moderating variables   We can now re-examine the variables that have been assumed to moderate the effect of personality characteristics on behavior, primarily self-awareness and private self-consciousness as well as self-monitoring tendency. If the relation between personality and behavior depends on the strength of the personality trait, then the proposed moderators should influence measures of trait strength. Empirical evidence in support of this proposition is scarce. However, at least one line of research (Eichstaedt and Silvia 2003) provides support in relation to private self-consciousness and self-awareness. In this Internet-based study, participants completed the Fenigstein, Scheier, and Buss (1975) self-consciousness scale and were asked to identify, as quickly as possible, target words presented for 400 ms. These target words were either self-relevant (me, myself, self, face, mine) or not self-relevant (up, theory, walk, drop, they). As expected, participants with high scores on the private self-consciousness scale responded faster to the self-relevant words than participants low in private self-consciousness. This finding implies that the self is chronically more accessible among highly self-conscious individuals which could explain why a measure of private self-consciousness predicts behavior better for these individuals than for individuals who are not particularly self-conscious.

In a second study (Eichstaedt and Silvia 2003), self-awareness was manipulated experimentally. In the high self-awareness condition, participants wrote an essay about how they differed from other people whereas in the low self-awareness conditions, participants either wrote an essay about their computers or did not write any essay. This manipulation was followed by the word recognition task used in the first experiment. The results again showed greater accessibility of self-relevant information among highly self-aware individuals. In the high self-awareness condition, participants responded faster to self-relevant words than did participants in the low self-awareness conditions.

MODERATING VARIABLES AND THE QUESTION OF CONSISTENCY

The contingent consistency approach has shed some light on the conditions under which broad attitude and personality dispositions are likely to predict specific behaviors and on the conditions under which a high degree of consistency cannot be expected. Moreover, considerations of attitude strength and strength of personality traits can help to provide an integrated conceptual framework to deal with the large number of moderating variables.

One question that has been raised with respect to this approach (see, for example, Eagly and Chaiken 1993) has to do with the reason for the greater predictive validity of strong attitudes and personality traits. According to Fazio's (1990a) MODE model, strong attitudes are better guides to behavior than weak attitudes because they are more accessible in memory and hence have a greater biasing impact on the definition of the situation. It is the biased definition of the situation that leads to strong attitude–behavior correspondence.

In a study of voting behavior, Fazio and Williams (1986) provided some evidence for this line of reasoning. Voters in the 1984 US presidential election were interviewed several months prior to the election. Among other things, they were asked to express their attitudes toward the two major candidates, Reagan and Mondale, on a 5-point scale, and the latencies of their responses were recorded. On the basis of these response latencies, participants were divided into high and low accessibility subgroups. Immediately following the second of three debates among the presidential and vice-presidential candidates, participants received a questionnaire in which they were asked to rate the extent to which they had been impressed by one as opposed to the other candidate. Finally, following the election, the participants were contacted by telephone and were asked to report whether they had voted in the election and, if so, for whom they had voted. Results showed a clear, though statistically nonsignificant, tendency for an effect of attitude accessibility on the relation between attitudes and ratings of debate performance. Among individuals in the high accessibility subgroup, attitudes toward the candidates correlated more strongly with evaluations of debate performance ($r = 0.72$) than among individuals in the low accessibility subgroup ($r = 0.53$). In terms of voting behavior, the correlation between attitudes toward the candidates and voting choice was quite high, a finding consistent with previous research (see Campbell et al. 1960; Fishbein and Ajzen 1981). More importantly, this correlation was significantly stronger among voters who had relatively easy access to their attitudes ($r = 0.88$) than among voters whose attitudes were less accessible ($r = 0.72$).

Although these findings are consistent with the MODE model analysis, other explanations for the effects of attitude strength can be offered. Thus, it has been suggested that the magnitude of the attitude–behavior relation may be moderated not by attitude accessibility but by other strength-related factors such as confidence, amount of knowledge, or the attitude's temporal stability (see Eagly and Chaiken 1993). One study (Doll and Ajzen 1992) provided an indication that the moderating effect of direct versus indirect experience may be due to the greater stability of attitudes based on direct experience rather than to their greater accessibility. Participants in this study were either allowed to play several different video games for a few minutes (direct experience condition) or they were shown recorded video clips of these games in action (indirect experience condition). At this point, they completed a questionnaire in which they were asked to indicate their attitudes toward each game and the latencies of their responses were also measured. They were then given a period of time to play the games and the amount of time spent with each game was recorded. Finally, at the conclusion of the free-play period, the participants again indicated their attitudes toward the different games. Response latencies served as indicators of attitude accessibility whereas the correlation between initial and final attitudes toward the games served as a measure attitude stability.

Consistent with previous research, attitudes toward the games predicted behavior better in the direct experience condition ($r = 0.57$) than in the indirect experience condition ($r = 0.37$). However, compared to second-hand information, direct experience with the different video games was found to raise not only the accessibility of attitudes toward playing those games but also to increase the temporal stability of the attitudes. Thus, either accessibility or stability could account for the observed superiority of direct experience. To determine which factor provided a better explanation of the moderating effect of type of experience, two analyses of mediation were conducted. One analysis controlled for the effect of attitude accessibility, the other for the effect of temporal stability. These analyses showed conclusively that the effect of direct versus indirect experience could be explained by the greater stability of attitudes formed under direct experience but not by their higher level of accessibility.

Limitations of a moderating variables approach

Fazio's (1990a; Fazio and Towles-Schwen 1999) MODE model has stimulated a great deal of research on the processes whereby general dispositions guide behavior, and it has served to provide a conceptual framework to deal with moderating variables. In the final analysis, however, the MODE model or any other moderating variables approach may fall short in providing a satisfactory solution to the consistency dilemma. First, as we saw in Chapter 2, investigators have tried unsuccessfully to use measures of general attitudes to predict such behaviors as job absence and turnover, various types of interaction with African Americans, participation in civil rights activities, attendance of labor union meetings, and so forth (see Wicker 1969). According to the MODE model, the observed low attitude–behavior correlations imply that participants in these studies held relatively weak attitudes, too weak to influence the definition of the situation and guide behavior – even if these attitudes were activated. Without further evidence, this supposition cannot be completely discounted, but it seems reasonable to assume that people hold fairly strong attitudes toward their jobs, their labor unions, members of minority groups, and civil rights. Strong attitudes of this kind should be chronically accessible and thus available to guide behavior. However, in actuality, even under these ideal conditions from the MODE model perspective, correlations between general attitudes and specific behaviors are found to be disappointing. And the same is true for the relation between broad personality characteristics and observed behavior.

Moreover, whatever information we may have gained by examining moderating variables, it is important to realize that discovery of a factor that moderates attitude–behavior or trait–behavior relations is very much a mixed blessing. 'Though predictions are improved for one subgroup, there remains usually another subgroup for whom predictive efficiency is diminished' (Zedeck 1971: 307). Thus, we may be able to predict, say, tardiness on the job from a personality measure of conscientiousness for employees who are highly self-conscious, but what do we do with employees who possess only a moderate or low degree of self-consciousness? Clearly, it would be preferable if general conscientiousness could predict punctuality on the job for all employees. Unfortunately, the evidence reviewed in Chapter 2 showed that correlations between general dispositions and specific actions of this kind tend to be very low.

The second complicating factor for a contingent consistency approach is the possibility, indeed the likelihood, that the moderating effects of one variable will be found to depend on still other moderators. That is, we can expect higher-order interactions to obscure any systematic lower-order interactions between dispositions and identified moderating factors. The results of several studies illustrate this problem. It was reported, for example, that self-monitoring tendency affected attitude–behavior correlations in the expected manner for some kinds of individuals but not for others (Zanna et al. 1980). The investigators used a self-report of religiosity to predict several measures of religious behavior: a multiple-act index based on 90 self-reported behaviors of a religious nature, an index based on the number of times participants had attended religious services and prayed in private, and an index based on the number of times they had been intoxicated with alcohol and had used illegal drugs. No significant differences were observed in the attitude–behavior correlations of low and high self-monitoring individuals. However, to complicate matters, the study demonstrated a significant second-order interaction such that attitude–behavior correlations depended on a particular combination of self-monitoring tendency and self-reported behavioral variability. Correlations were highest for low self-monitoring individuals who reported that their religious behavior was relatively invariant across situations. All other combinations of self-monitoring and variability resulted in lower correlations of about equal magnitude.

Snyder and Kendzierski (1982a) also reported second-order interactions involving the self-monitoring variable. This study again employed Snyder and Swann's (1976) hypothetical sex discrimination case. With neutral instructions, namely to weigh all relevant evidence before rendering a verdict, the study failed to replicate the original findings; that is, there was no significant difference between low and high self-monitoring individuals in terms of the correlation between attitudes toward affirmative action and the nature of the verdict ($r = 0.18$ and -0.17, respectively). The expected difference emerged, however, when attitudes were made accessible by asking participants to think about their attitudes toward affirmative action before the court case was presented. In this condition of the experiment, the attitude–behavior correlation for low self-monitoring individuals was 0.47, but for high self-monitors it was only 0.18. Finally, attitudes predicted verdicts about equally well for both types of participants ($r = 0.45$ and 0.60) in a third condition which encouraged participants to think about the implications of their verdicts prior to rendering them but after having read the court case.

One study (Miller and Grush 1986) examined the simultaneous moderating effects of self-monitoring and private self-consciousness among college students. The results revealed a complex and unexpected pattern of interactions with respect to the effects of these variables on the relation between attitudes toward spending time on school work and self-reports of academic activities. Self-monitoring tendency had no effect on the attitude–behavior correlation for individuals high in private self-consciousness. Furthermore, and contrary to expectations, for participants low in self-consciousness, attitudes predicted behavior better when the participants had high rather than low scores on the measure of self-monitoring. As to the moderating effect of private self-consciousness, the attitude–behavior correlation was, as expected, stronger for participants high as opposed to low on this trait, but only when they were also low in self-monitoring tendency. A difference in the opposite direction was observed when they were high in self-monitoring tendency.

Earlier we saw that thinking about an attitude object can increase its correlation with a subsequent behavior. However, a series of subsequent studies (Wilson et al. 1984) arrived at contradictory conclusions. The first of three studies employed an intellectual puzzles task, the second dealt with vacation snapshots, and the third with the relationships of dating couples. One half of the participants in each study was asked to list reasons for their attitudes toward the behavioral target: why they found the different puzzles interesting or boring, why they enjoyed or did not enjoy watching the snapshots, and why their dating relationship was good or bad. The behavioral criteria in the three studies were amount of time spent working on each puzzle type, nonverbal expressions of enjoyment while watching the snapshots, and status of the dating relationship about nine months later. In each case, the attitude–behavior correlation was stronger (ranging from 0.53 to 0.57 across studies) when respondents were *not* asked to list reasons for their attitudes than when they were asked to do so (range of correlations: −0.05 to 0.17).

Realizing that their findings appeared to be inconsistent with previous research, Wilson, Dunn, Bybee, Hyman, and Rotondo (1984) argued that whereas self-focused attention involves merely *observing* one's thoughts and feelings, i.e. focusing on them, participants in their studies were asked to *analyze* those thoughts and feelings, i.e. to find reasons for their attitudes. The investigators conjectured that listing reasons may temporarily disrupt an attitude and thus reduce the previously assessed attitude's correlation with behavior. A follow-up study (Wilson and Dunn 1986) again demonstrated reduced attitude–behavior correlations when participants were asked to analyze their attitudes, but failed to corroborate the finding that merely thinking about one's attitude serves to improve behavioral prediction.

To complicate matters further, it has also been reported that listing reasons for an attitude can increase the attitude–behavior correlation if the behavior closely follows attitude measurement, but can decrease the correlation when behavior occurs after a substantial delay (Sengupta and Fitzsimons 2000). Similarly, the effect of thinking about an attitude object can either increase or reduce attitude–behavior correlations, depending on whether the thoughts make salient the cognitive or the affective component of the attitude (Millar and Tesser 1986; Millar and Millar 1998).

Another example of qualifications that must be put on the effects of moderating variables can be found in two studies (Froming et al. 1982) on the relation between attitudes toward punishment and mean shock level administered in the Buss (1961) learning paradigm. The moderating variable of interest in these studies was self-awareness. This investigation showed that manipulation of self-awareness via a mirror and via presence of an audience can produce very different effects. Moreover, the moderating effects were also found to depend on the type of audience. At the beginning of the term, college students completed a 9-item attitude toward punishment scale, once expressing their own opinions and again for the views most people have on the issue. In the first study, the respondents selected for participation had more negative attitudes toward punishment than the attitudes they attributed to others, while the reverse was true in the second study. Shocks on 20 'error' trials were administered without a mirror (control condition), in the presence of a mirror, or in the presence of a two-person audience. In the first study, the audience was said either to merely observe the participants or to evaluate their effectiveness as a teacher; in the second study, the audience consisted either of advanced psychology students (experts) or of classmates. As in previous research, presence of a mirror was found to produce behavior more in accordance with personal attitudes toward punishment, but presence of an evaluative or expert audience induced behavior in accordance not with personal attitudes but with perceived social norms. The nonevaluative and nonexpert audiences had no significant effects on attitude–behavior correspondence. The investigators explained the observed differences between mirror and effective audience conditions by means of Carver and Scheier's (1981) distinction between *private* and *public* self-consciousness. Different environmental cues are assumed to evoke different types of self-consciousness. Specifically, presence of a mirror is assumed to raise private self-consciousness whereas an evaluative audience is said to evoke public self-consciousness. The results of the study are quite consistent with this idea.

Whatever interpretations we manage to offer for such higher-order inter-actions, however, there is no question that they greatly complicate the picture. As Cronbach has noted, 'Once we attend to interactions, we enter a hall of mirrors that extends to infinity. However far we carry our analysis – to third order or fifth order or any other – untested interactions of a still higher order can be envisioned' (1975: 119). Speaking out against the search for person-situation interactions, Nisbett (1977: 235) made the following observations: 'There are serious inherent disadvantages to inter-action hypotheses, notably the difficulty of disconfirming them, their illusory aura of precision, and the disadvantages of complex designs employed to test them.' Beyond pointing to the inherent difficulties of such an approach, these observation raise another troubling issue: whenever an investigation fails to support a hypothesized moderating effect of a given variable, rather than rejecting the hypothesis, we can attribute the failure to as yet undiscovered additional factors upon which the effect of our moderating variable may be contingent in the sense of a higher-order interaction.

However, let us assume for a moment that our research efforts did result in replicable identification of the many moderating factors and their higher-order interactions. Even in such an ideal world we would still be left with a serious problem as far as the prediction of specific actions from general dispositions is concerned. A successful moderating variables approach leads ultimately to the unavoidable conclusion that general dis-positions are, by and large, poor predictors of specific action; they can be expected to predict only some behaviors, for some individuals, in some situations:

> Theoretically, any single instance of behavior can be predicted if all the right moderator variables are included. This is no more than to say that behavior is determined, and that if we knew everything that determined it, we could predict it. However, to do so might require the addition of so many moderator variables that they would generate interactions of such complexity as to make the procedure unfeasible and the results uninterpretable. (Epstein 1983a: 377)

Although we may be able to create in the laboratory the unique set of circumstances required for consistency, the requisite combination of factors is unlikely to obtain under natural conditions. The general lack of consistency between global dispositional measures and specific actions documented in Chapter 2 attests to the fact that in most cases, the prevailing conditions are far from optimal.

SUMMARY AND CONCLUSIONS

The moderating variables approach to the consistency dilemma has provided some useful insights into the relation between general dispositions and specific actions. Strong relations of this kind have been found to depend on a variety of factors that have to do with individual differences among people and with secondary characteristics of the disposition. The moderating effects of some of these variables are better understood than those of others. The present chapter reviewed a number of empirical investigations in detail to show some of the difficulties and complexities involved in the search for contingency effects.

With the exception of an attitude's internal consistency, such secondary characteristics of attitude as the confidence with which it is held, involvement with the attitude object, and the way in which the attitude is acquired all seem to have a systematic impact on accuracy of behavioral prediction. In contrast, research on such individual difference variables as self-monitoring, self-awareness, and private self-consciousness have produced more mixed results. Although it appears that these factors can have a moderating influence on the relation between verbal measures of global dispositions and specific behaviors of a nonverbal kind, obtained moderating effects have not always been replicated and often had to be qualified by higher-order interactions. Recent efforts have turned from constructing an ever-increasing list of moderating variables to the processes whereby attitudes and personality traits guide behavior. The focus on attitude accessibility and trait schematicity or traitedness reduces the number of contingencies that need to be considered and provides an integrative theoretical framework that can help explain how secondary attitude characteristics and individual difference variables exert their moderating effects. However, despite the progress that has been made, the moderating variables approach is unlikely to open the way to dispositional prediction of specific actions. Several interrelated problems lead to this conclusion. While identifying some subset of individuals or conditions for which prediction is possible, the discovery of moderating variables at the same time also identifies another subset for which prediction is not possible. As the number of known moderators increases, and as these moderators are found to interact with still other variables, the latter subset increases at the expense of the former. From a theoretical perspective, moderating variables can enhance our understanding of psychological processes involved in going from general dispositions to specific actions, but from a practical point of view, the contribution of this approach is more problematic. The next chapter, therefore, presents and discusses an alternative approach to the dispositional prediction of behavior.

NOTES

1 Note that in this study the mirror was present or absent during administration of the questionnaire, whereas in the Carver (1975) study the self-awareness manipulation was effected during performance of the behavior.
2 Most tests of moderating effects unfortunately use the procedure of comparing subgroups that differ in terms of the moderating variable. This is not an optimal analytic strategy as it tends to have low statistical power (Cohen 1983) and may confound differences between the subgroup variances with true moderator effects (Tellegen et al. 1982; Baron and Kenny 1986). A preferable approach is to use hierarchical regression analysis to test for interactions between independent and moderator variables (Cohen 1978).
3 In this study, degree of traitedness (i.e. variability in responses to items on the self-esteem scale) correlated significantly with the behavior (number of tips requested). This finding, however, is of no relevance for the present discussion.

SUGGESTIONS FOR FURTHER READING

Cronbach, L. J. (1975) Beyond the two disciplines of scientific psychology. *American Psychologist*, 30: 116–27. This article presents a sophisticated discussion of some of the problems inherent in the interactionist (or moderating variables) approach to the prediction of behavior.

Fazio, R. H., and Towles-Schwen, T. (1999) The MODE model of attitude-behavior processes. In S. Chaiken and Y. Trope (eds), *Dual-Process Theories in Social Psychology* (pp. 97–116). New York: Guilford. This chapter provides a detailed description of the MODE model and its implications for the ways in which general attitudes guide the performance of specific behavior.

Sherman, S. J., and Fazio, R. H. (1983) Parallels between attitudes and traits as predictors of behavior. *Journal of Personality*, 51: 308–45. In this article, the authors review the effects of various moderating variables on the relation between attitudes and behavior and between personality traits and behavior.

Snyder, M. (1982) When believing means doing: Creating links between attitudes and behavior. In M. P. Zanna, E. T. Higgins, and C. P. Herman (eds), *Consistency in Social Behavior: The Ontario Symposium* (Vol. 2, pp. 105–30). Hillsdale, NJ: Erlbaum. This chapter reviews the role of self-monitoring tendency as a moderator of the attitude–behavior relation.

FOUR

THE PRINCIPLE OF COMPATIBILITY

Common sense, which, one would say, means the shortest line between two
points.

(Emerson)

On a foggy evening in February a man is driving his battered van along a
narrow country road. He is returning home after a tiring day of work and
a few drinks in a nearby pub. The road is winding, visibility is poor, and
he is careful to keep within the posted speed limit. Suddenly, as if out of
nowhere, a woman is caught in the headlights. The driver's reaction is
sluggish. He tries to avoid the woman and applies the brakes, but too late.
The van skids and strikes her with a disconcerting thump. The driver is wide
awake now. Within seconds he makes up his mind. He straightens the van
and steps on the accelerator, leaving the scene of the accident and the
victim to her fate.

A deplorable, but not unknown, instance of human behavior. How are we
to explain the driver's failure to assist the woman he has hurt? Certainly, a
great many factors may be involved: fatigue at the end of a long day, the
privacy of a deserted country road in evening fog, the influence of alcohol,
fear of dealing with the police, of facing family and friends, a general
reluctance to get involved in a messy, time-consuming, unpleasant affair.
Every particular instance of human action is, in this way, determined by
a unique set of factors. Any change in circumstances, be it ever so slight,
might produce a different reaction. If the driver had possessed a greater
sense of personal responsibility; if the accident had occurred on a well-
traveled highway; if it had not been a foggy evening; if the driver had not
been under the influence of alcohol; if he had not been so exhausted; if the
victim had been a child; if the driver could have seen the victim's face;
if any of these things had been true, the driver might have stopped his van
and offered assistance.

Many instances of human behavior are 'overdetermined' in the sense
that a multitude of factors combine to produce them. However, it is not
the role of the psychologist to account for unique instances of human
action. Detectives called to investigate the hit-and-run accident might try
to reconstruct the exact circumstances, although they would probably be
more interested in establishing the identity of the driver involved than in

the reasons for his behavior. Perhaps it is the historian who is most concerned with unique events. An individual's behavior on a particular occasion can have momentous consequences, especially if the individual is in a position of power. To understand the unique combination of factors that led up to the behavior is to provide a possible explanation of the events that followed. But psychologists are not historians; they are rarely interested in an individual's action on any particular occasion. Instead, they are engaged in building a science of human behavior, in establishing the general laws of human action. Of concern to the psychologist, therefore, are *regularities* in behavior, consistent *patterns* of action, response *tendencies*. In line with this goal, attitudes and personality traits are concepts designed to capture the dispositional nature of human behavior.

THE LOGIC OF AGGREGATION

Regularities, patterns, or tendencies cannot be discerned in single instances of behavior. Rather, to measure a behavioral tendency, we must aggregate observations made on different occasions. When we compute the average behavioral tendency over repeated occasions, the influence of factors that vary from one occasion to another tends to 'cancel out.' Consider, for example, the act of engaging (or not engaging) in a conversation with a stranger. When observed on particular occasions, this behavior – like the behavior of the driver in the hit-and-run accident – is overdetermined. On one occasion an individual approached by a stranger stops to talk, but on another occasion she hurries past the stranger. A multitude of factors may account for the different reactions: mood states, the press of time, weather conditions, the stranger's appearance, and so on. Factors of this kind tend to intrude in a more or less random fashion. That is to say, they are not present consistently across occasions. The weather varies from one occasion to another, as does one's mood and time schedule, or the physical appearance of different strangers.

Repeated observations of the same action inevitably involve different contexts. Although it is possible in principle to conceive of performing a given behavior under identical conditions on two or more occasions, conditions are rarely, if ever, identical in practice. Given these rather arbitrary variations in the presence or absence of factors that could influence whether or not we engage in a conversation with a stranger, observation of the behavior on a single occasion is a poor measure of the 'typical' reaction, i.e. of the general response tendency. By aggregating over different occasions, however, we eliminate the systematic impact of these arbitrary factors. Averaged over many different occasions, the number of times a person is seen engaging in a conversation with a stranger cannot be attributed to the weather, to temporary moods, or to competing demands on the person's time. Instead, the aggregate measure represents the influence of factors consistently present across different occasions, i.e. the disposition to perform the particular behavior in question. This idea is embedded in the Spearman-Brown prophecy formula described in Chapter 1, and its implications are usually well understood (Mischel 1968; Mischel and Peake 1982a; Mischel and Peake 1982b) if not always heeded in empirical research (see Epstein 1980b).

The logic of aggregation can also be applied to behavioral dispositions that reflect general attitudes or personality traits. We have noted repeatedly that traits and attitudes, as usually defined, represent very broad behavioral dispositions. It stands to reason that such broad dispositions can be validly inferred only from equally broad sets of response tendencies. Consider again the disposition toward extraversion or introversion. Even when aggregated over a large number of occasions, talking to strangers is unrepresentative of a person's general disposition to be sociable. We mean much more by sociability than merely the tendency to engage in conversations with strangers. It also involves maintaining contacts with old friends, making new friends, going to parties, interacting with coworkers on the job, going to the movies with acquaintances, and a hundred-and-one other ways of being outgoing or reclusive. Any single one of these response tendencies is influenced by factors that may be irrelevant for the others. Thus, going to parties is affected not only by one's sociability but perhaps also by availability of baby sitters on weekends, by involvement in such competing social activities on Saturday nights as playing cards or going bowling with friends, etc. Interacting with coworkers on the job, however, is unlikely to be affected by these kinds of factors. Instead, the variables that, besides sociability, may influence the tendency to interact with coworkers include perhaps the nature of one's job, encouragement or discouragement of interaction by management, and so forth.

In short, general behavioral dispositions can be inferred by applying the principle of aggregation to the varied types of specific response tendencies, thus eliminating the contaminating influence of factors other than the disposition of interest. In addition to aggregating repeated observations of a given action to obtain a high degree of consistency across occasions, it is possible to aggregate different actions in a given behavioral domain, observed on various occasions and in diverse contexts. Based on a representative set of responses, such a *multiple-act* index should serve as a valid indicator of the underlying disposition.

Our discussion of aggregation as a means of securing behavioral measures that are stable across occasions or that are representative of broad underlying dispositions is summarized in Table 4.1. The table's rows represent different behaviors and its columns represent observations on different occasions. Each cell in the table contains performance (or nonperformance) of a single behavior on a single occasion, i.e. a *single-act criterion* (S_{11}, S_{12}, ...). By aggregating across the columns within a given row, we obtain, in the row margins, specific *behavioral tendencies*, i.e. tendencies to perform particular behaviors over time (T_1, T_2, ...). In a comparable fashion, we can aggregate rows within a given column and obtain *multiple-act criteria*, as shown in the column margins of Table 4.1 (M_1, M_2, ...). The different behaviors that enter into these measures are each observed on a single occasion. Finally, the broadest multiple-act measure of behavior is obtained when temporally stable action tendencies are aggregated. This multiple-act, repeated occasions criterion is the grand mean which, in Table 4.1, is shown as 'behavioral disposition.' It represents the aggregation of all cells in the table.

Table 4.1 Aggregation of behavior

	Occasions				
Behaviors	*1*	*2*	. . .	*n*	*Behavioral tendencies*
1	S_{11}	S_{12}	. . .	S_{1n}	T_1
2	.				T_2
3	.				T_3
4	.				T_4
.	.				.
.	.				.
.	.				.
.	.				
m	S_{m1}	S_{m2}	. . .	S_{mn}	T_m
Multiple-act criteria	M_1	M_2	. . .	M_n	Behavioral disposition

Source: After Fishbein and Ajzen (1975)

According to the principle of aggregation, neither single-act criteria nor the tendency to perform a specific behavior over time are representative of general traits or attitudes. Only multiple-act criteria are sufficiently general to reflect such broad underlying dispositions. It follows that only multiple-act indices of behavior can be expected to display consistency across situations and to correlate well with verbal measures of general traits and attitudes. By way of comparison, much of the negative research evidence reviewed in Chapter 2 was collected in studies that used tendencies to engage in single actions, or narrowly defined classes of actions, as their behavioral criteria. Behavioral consistency was usually examined by correlating one specific action tendency (e.g. returning books to the library on time) with another specific action tendency (e.g. being on time for appointments); and global measures of traits or attitudes (e.g. dominance, sociability, attitude toward African Americans or toward the church) were used to predict narrow action tendencies deemed relevant for the trait or directed at the attitude object (e.g. using birth control methods, writing letters, conforming with the petition-signing behavior of a Black individual, smiling at a Black research participant). As shown above, the problem with this approach is that single behaviors are typically invalid or poor indicators of an underlying disposition. To claim evidence for inconsistency, the indicators found to be inconsistent with one another must each be based on an appropriate sample of responses from which the latent disposition can be validly inferred. Only when this condition is met can lack of correspondence between observed behaviors be taken as evidence against the existence of a stable behavioral disposition.

Consistency of behavioral aggregates

The question of behavioral consistency has to do with the relation between two behavioral manifestations of the same disposition. Because a single action on a particular occasion is often a poor indicator of the general behavioral tendency, we can at most expect rather low levels of consistency among single actions. Similarly, because single behavioral tendencies (even when aggregated over occasions) are generally unrepresentative of a general behavioral domain, they too cannot be expected to correlate well with each other. Both of these expectations are well borne out by empirical research (see Chapter 2). However, if the logic of aggregation can be applied to the problem of consistency, then two multiple-observation or multiple-act indices, each representative of the same behavioral tendency or disposition, should correlate highly with each other.

Consistency across occasions

The empirical literature provides strong and persuasive evidence for the importance of aggregation to achieve stability of behavior across occasions. In one demonstration (Epstein 1979: Study 4), college students were asked to record, among other things, some of their behaviors on each day of a 14-day period. The behaviors recorded were the number of telephone calls made, the number of letters written, the number of social contacts initiated, the number of hours slept, and the number of hours studied. Consistency of behavior on any two days chosen at random was relatively low, ranging from a reliability coefficient of 0.26 for the number of telephone calls made to 0.63 for the number of social contacts initiated. Behavioral stability increased dramatically when the behavioral indices were aggregated across more than one observation. Comparison of average behavioral scores on the seven odd days with average behavioral scores on the seven even days produced correlations of 0.81 and 0.94 for the number of phone calls and number of social contacts, respectively. Clear evidence for stability of aggregate measures based on repeated observations has also been revealed in a review of research on aggressive behavior (Olweus 1979). Pooling data from a large number of longitudinal studies, the stability of aggregated aggression scores over two points in time was, on the average, found to be 0.68.

Similar results can be found in the domain of conscientiousness. As mentioned in Chapter 2, Mischel and Peake (1982a, 1982b) obtained data concerning repeated performance or nonperformance of 19 different behaviors related to conscientiousness, such as class attendance, punctuality, and thoroughness of note taking. Like Epstein, they found that even though stability of single observations was quite low (the average correlation between observations on two individual occasions was 0.29), it could be greatly increased (to 0.65 on average) by aggregating across observations.

Consistency across situations

The demonstration that high behavioral stability can be established by aggregating observations across occasions is, however, not at the heart of the consistency debate, as Mischel (1983; Mischel and Peake 1982a) has taken pains to point out. Of greater interest than stability of a given behavior across occasions is the degree of consistency among *different* actions assumed to reflect the same disposition. Stability of this kind has usually been termed 'cross-situational consistency' because different actions, even if in the same behavioral domain, almost inevitably are performed in different contexts and at different points in time. Nevertheless, it is important to realize that returning books on time to the library, for example, differs from punctuality in handing in written assignments not only in terms of the context of the behavior (the situation) but also, and perhaps more importantly, in terms of the particular activity involved (cf. Jackson and Paunonen 1985).

According to the principle of aggregation, consistency across different kinds of behaviors and situations can also be obtained by means of aggregation. Evidence in support of this idea has long been available in the convergent validation of attitude scales and personality trait measures. As we saw in Chapter 1, properly constructed attitude and personality scales consist of carefully selected items that assess specific (verbal) responses. Consistent with the principle of aggregation, however, these specific responses are aggregated over all items in the questionnaire to yield the attitude or trait scores. As expected, different multi-item measures of a given attitude or personality characteristic are routinely found to yield comparable results, with convergent validities typically in the 0.60 to 0.80 range. Similar data have been reported in support of the convergent validity of various personality traits measured by different personality inventories (Edwards and Abbott 1973a, 1973b; Lorr et al. 1977). As a specific example, consider the study by Jaccard (1974). Scales taken from the Personality Research Form (Jackson 1967) and from the California Psychological Inventory (Gough 1957) were used to assess dominance in a sample of college students. The correlation between the two multi-item scales was found to be 0.75.

Comparing two different scaling techniques (Likert and Thurstone scaling), Edwards and Kenney (1946) provided evidence for convergent validity of attitude measures. The original pool of items designed by Thurstone and Chave (1929) to assess attitudes toward the church was used to construct a Likert scale and two parallel forms of a Thurstone scale. The two forms of the Thurstone scale were found to correlate 0.72 and 0.92 with the Likert scale. Similarly, and again in the area of attitudes toward religion, Fishbein and Ajzen (1974) reported a high degree of convergent validity among four different types of standard multi-item scales: Thurstone, Likert, Guttman, and the semantic differential. Correlations among the four measures of attitude toward religion ranged from 0.64 to 0.79. This study also provided evidence for consistency among multiple-act indices of *behavior*, although the behaviors in question were self-reports rather than observations of overt actions. The college students who participated in the research were given a list of 100 behaviors dealing with matters of religion and were asked to check the behaviors they had performed. The list of behaviors included praying before or after meals, taking a religious course for credit, and dating a person against parents' wishes. By applying different scaling methods to the behavioral self-reports, three multiple-act indices of religious behavior were constructed. The correlations among these three aggregate measures of behavior ranged from 0.63 to 0.79.

The research reviewed thus far showed behavioral consistency at the aggregate level, but the responses that were aggregated were all obtained by means of questionnaires. Perhaps more convincing, therefore, would be data demonstrating consistency between aggregates based on nonverbal behaviors. Ironically, evidence of this kind was reported very early in investigations of deceit and character (Hartshorne and May 1928; Hartshorne et al. 1929; Hartshorne et al. 1930). In the reports of their findings, the authors focused on the rather low correlations between individual measures, and their research has therefore often been interpreted as demonstrating little behavioral consistency. However, they also found that batteries of tests that aggregated different kinds of cheating in the classroom correlated quite highly with each other. (See Rushton et al. 1983 and Epstein and O'Brien 1985, for discussions of this research.)

Strong evidence for consistency of behavioral aggregates was also reported in a later study of behavior among young people (Small et al. 1983). The investigators joined four small groups of adolescents as counselors on a 30-day wilderness trip and recorded the youngsters' behaviors for two hours each day. The actions recorded fell into two broad categories: eight different kinds of dominance behaviors (e.g. verbal directive, physical assertiveness, verbal or physical threat) and five different kinds of pro-social behaviors (e.g. physical assistance, sharing, verbal support). Moreover, behavioral observations were obtained in three different contexts: setting up and dismantling the camp, activities surrounding meals (including preparation and clean-up), and free time. Multiple-act aggregates were computed for each type of behavior (dominance and pro-social) in each of the three settings, and the data were analyzed separately for each of the four groups of adolescents. Cross-situational consistency of behavioral aggregates was found to be very high. For dominance behavior, correlations between different settings ranged from 0.33 to 0.95, with a mean of 0.73; and for pro-social behavior the range was 0.48 to 0.99, with a mean correlation of 0.79.

Finally, it has been shown that behavioral aggregates are relatively stable over time even when the individual behaviors of which the aggregates are comprised have only low temporal stability (Sroufe and Waters 1977; Waters 1978). Interactions between mothers and their children were observed when the children were 12 months old and again when they were 18 months old. The behavioral category of primary interest were responses on the part of the children indicating attachment as opposed to avoidance. Twenty-eight discrete actions were rated that had to do with smiling and looking at mother, vocalizing, following, and clinging. The stabilities of individual behaviors over the 6-month period were largely nonsignificant, ranging from −0.16 to 0.46. In contrast, the correlations for behavioral aggregates were significant and quite high. Thus, maintaining contact showed a correlation of 0.72 over the 6-month period, avoiding proximity a correlation of 0.62, and resisting contact a correlation of 0.51. Sroufe (1979: 838) described the advantage of aggregation very clearly: 'Individual babies cried less or more, sought more or less contact, showed a toy to mother one time, brought a toy another time, but in some way the overall pattern of behavior indicative of a secure attachment relationship was revealed on both occasions.'

Predictive validity for behavioral aggregates

The aggregation principle also implies that general attitude and trait measures should permit prediction of equally general measures of behavior. That is, we should expect a strong association between multiple-act indices of behavior and standard measures of attitudes or personality traits. The former reflect the general disposition in the form of conative response tendencies while the latter use verbal questionnaire responses, typically falling into the cognitive and affective categories, to infer the same underlying disposition. Several investigations have provided support for the predictive validity of traits and attitudes in relation to behavioral aggregates. Consider, again, the Fishbein and Ajzen (1974) study. Each of the 100 self-reports of religious behavior (representing 100 single-act criteria), the three scaled aggregates as well as the sum over the total set of behaviors (representing four multiple-act behavioral criteria) were correlated with each of the four standard, multi-item measures of attitude toward religion. As is typically found to be the case, prediction of single actions from global attitudes was largely unsuccessful. Although a few attitude–behavior correlations were as high as 0.40, most were rather low and not significant. The average correlation between attitudes toward religion and single behaviors was about 0.14. In marked contrast, the same global measures of attitude correlated highly and significantly with the aggregate indices of religious behavior; these correlations ranged from 0.53 to 0.73, and the mean correlation was 0.63.

Very similar results were reported in the area of activism concerning abortion (Werner 1978). Werner assessed general attitudes toward abortion on demand among male and female respondents. In addition, the respondents were asked to report the extent to which they had performed each of 83 activities related to abortion. Among these activities were 'trying to convince a friend or acquaintance that abortion should be greatly restricted or prohibited,' 'encouraging a woman with an unwanted pregnancy to have an abortion,' and 'circulating an anti-abortion petition.' Consistent with the principle of aggregation, attitude toward abortion was found to be a highly accurate predictor of a multiple-act index based on all 83 activities. For the total sample of respondents, the attitude–behavior correlation was 0.78. Finally, Sjöberg (1982) obtained two measures of attitude toward aid to developing countries among college students in Göteborg (Sweden). These attitude measures were then used to predict a summary index of various self-reported behaviors, including 'participation in Red Cross activities related to developing countries' and 'corresponding with a person in a developing country.' The correlations between the two measures of attitude and the multiple-act criterion in this study were found to be 0.49 and 0.43.

Following closely the procedures employed by Fishbein and Ajzen (1974), Jaccard (1974) examined the relation between the personality trait of dominance and self-reports of dominant behavior. As mentioned earlier, the female undergraduates who participated in Jaccard's study completed two personality scales designed to assess dominance. In addition, they were asked to indicate which of 40 behaviors in the domain of dominance they had performed. Among the behaviors listed were arguing with a teacher, initiating a discussion in class, and intentionally letting your boyfriend beat you at something. A multiple-act measure of dominance behavior was obtained by summing over the 40 actions. Prediction of single behaviors from the general personality trait measures was again rather poor. On average, the correlation between the two personality measures of dominance and the various dominant or submissive behaviors was about 0.20. Much greater success, however, was achieved in predicting the general tendency to behave in a dominant manner; the two personality measures correlated 0.58 and 0.64 with the multiple-act aggregate.

It can be argued as before that the weakness of these investigations is their reliance on self-reports of behavior (see Schuman and Johnson 1976). However, the same pattern of results was reported for observations of non-verbal behavior (Weigel and Newman 1976). The investigators in this study used a multi-item scale designed to measure attitudes toward environmental quality and, three to eight months later, observed 14 behaviors related to the environment. The behaviors involved signing and circulating three different petitions concerning environmental issues, participating in a litter pick-up program, and participating in a recycling program on eight separate occasions. In addition to these 14 single-act, single-observation criteria, Weigel and Newman constructed four behavioral aggregates: one based on petition-signing behaviors, one on litter pick-ups, one on recycling, and one overall index based on all 14 observations. Prediction of each single observation from the general attitude measure was quite weak; the average correlation was 0.29 and not significant. The aggregates over occasions, based on multiple observations of single actions, showed a mean correlation of moderate magnitude with the general attitude ($r = 0.42$), while the multiple-act index over all 14 observations correlated 0.62 with the same attitude measure.

Strong associations between general measures of attitude and an aggregate index of behavior can also be found in a very different domain (Bandura et al. 1969). In this study, the investigators assessed attitudes toward snakes by means of two standard attitude scales. The behavior of undergraduates was then recorded with respect to a graded series of interactions with a snake. These interactions ranged from approaching the snake in an enclosed glass cage to passively permitting the snake to crawl in one's lap. Both attitude measures were found to correlate strongly ($r = 0.73$ and $r = 0.56$) with the multiple-act aggregate behavioral criterion.

As in the case of attitudes, there is evidence for good predictive validity of personality trait measures in relation to aggregates of observed, as opposed to self-reported, behavior (McGowan and Gormly 1976). Undergraduate fraternity members judged each fellow member as being or not being energetic or physically active. The proportion of positive ratings was taken as a measure of each participant's standing on this trait. Five behavioral self-reports (e.g. time spent on sports, longest distance ever walked, longest distance ever run) and five observations of actual behavior (e.g. speed of walking, rate of speed going upstairs, rate of head movements) were available. The correlations between the trait and the ten individual behaviors ranged from 0.13 to 0.64, with an average of 0.42. After aggregation, the five self-reports of behavior had a correlation of 0.65 with the energism trait and the sum of the five observed behaviors correlated 0.70 with the trait.

Finally, the correlation between the trait and an aggregate measure of behavior based on all ten activities (self-reported and observed) was 0.74.

Aggregation and the question of consistency

Chapter 2 reviewed empirical research that showed lack of behavioral consistency and poor predictive validity of attitude and trait measures. Findings of this kind have been interpreted as evidence against the existence of stable behavioral dispositions, but the data reviewed in the present chapter concerning the effects of behavioral aggregation should lay this pessimistic conclusion to rest. Clearly, it is possible to obtain high behavioral (i.e. cross-situational) consistency, as well as impressive predictive validity, so long as the behavioral criteria used are broadly representative of the disposition under consideration.

The issues involved are closely related to questions of measurement reliability and validity. Factors that influence a given behavior, but that are of no particular interest to the investigator, are considered 'error' and are said to contribute to unreliability or invalidity of measurement. To be sure, what is 'error' in one investigation may be the focus of study in another. Variations in mood, ambient temperature, noise level, and other incidental factors are usually of little concern in attempts to predict behavior from attitudes or personality traits, but in other areas of research they constitute legitimate and important topics of investigation (e.g. Dulany 1968; Isen and Levin 1972; Eagly 1974). Nevertheless, the effects of mood, of distracting factors like noise, and so on may be considered irrelevant and may be thought of as introducing unreliability if the investigator's interests lie elsewhere.

It is, of course, not inconceivable that we might be interested in understanding the unique set of circumstances that cause a given action in a specific context, on a given occasion. If so, we may well find that temporary moods, unanticipated distractions, situational demands, and so on account for a large proportion of the behavioral variance. The typical finding of little or no consistency among individual behaviors observed on single occasions, and their low correlations with measures of general attitudes and personality traits, attest to the relative unimportance of stable dispositions in comparison to the effects of incidental factors that are unique to a given occasion. However, with such notable exceptions as voting in an election, we are rarely interested in explaining performance or nonperformance of a single action on a given occasion. Instead, we are usually concerned with relatively stable tendencies to perform (or not to perform) a given behavior: drinking alcohol, rather than drinking a glass of champagne at a New Year's party in the company of friends; using birth control pills, rather than taking the pill on a given day; and so on. Incidental factors uniquely associated with any given occasion are therefore mostly of little concern. Aggregation across a sufficient number of occasions serves the purpose of reducing to an acceptable minimum error variance produced by factors of this kind.

By the same token, variance associated with different actions that are assumed to reflect the same underlying disposition may also be considered a source of error. This is legitimate whenever we are interested in a broad behavioral trend, rather than in understanding the factors that result in a tendency to perform (or not to perform) a given action. Thus, we may want to study aggression rather than administration of electric shocks in a learning situation, or discrimination rather than conformity with a minority group member's judgments. This requires use of multiple-act aggregates that reflect the broad behavioral trend in question. As expected, such broad response dispositions are found to be relatively stable across time and context, and they tend to correlate well with equally broad questionnaire measures of attitudes and personality traits.

The aggregation solution to the consistency problem was anticipated as early as 1931 by Thurstone who pointed out that two persons may hold the same attitude toward some object but that 'their overt actions (may) take quite different forms which have one thing in common, namely, that they are about equally favorable toward the object' (p. 262). It would have come as no surprise to Thurstone that general attitudes are largely unrelated to specific actions, but that they are closely related to multiple-act indices of behavioral trends. As is true of verbal measures of attitudes and personality traits, aggregate measures of behavior provide *quantitative* indicators of the underlying response disposition. Although the intensity of a general attitude or personality trait cannot predict whether or not a particular behavior will be performed, it can predict the strength of the behavioral tendency, as reflected in the aggregate response measure.

Note that not all behaviors can be aggregated with equal effectiveness into a multiple-act measure (see Epstein 1983a; Jackson and Paunonen 1985). It is not sufficient that the behaviors to be combined into an index appear to reflect the same underlying disposition, i.e. that they have face validity. Like items on a personality or attitude scale, they must be shown, by means of acceptable psychometric procedures, to share common variance and thus to be indicative of the same underlying disposition. Fishbein and Ajzen (1974) proposed one possible procedure to estimate the relevance of specific behaviors to a general disposition. It will be recalled that in their study, attitudes toward religion were assessed by means of four standard scales and that the college students who participated in the study indicated whether or not they had performed each of 100 behaviors related to matters of religion. An independent group of judges rated, for each behavior, the likelihood that it would be performed by individuals with positive attitudes toward religion and the likelihood that it would be performed by individuals with negative attitudes toward religion. The absolute difference between these two conditional probabilities was used as a measure of the behavior's relevance to the attitude. This measure of relevance was then compared with the correlation between each behavior and the attitude score. The results show the extent to which the correlation between general attitudes and a specific action can be predicted from the action's judged relevance. These predictions ranged from 0.40 to 0.47 across the four measures of attitude toward religion. We could thus use the relevance index to determine whether a given behavior should or should not be included in a behavioral aggregate.

As mentioned earlier, Sjöberg (1982) replicated the Fishbein and Ajzen (1974) procedures in the domain of attitudes and behaviors with respect to aid to developing countries. In his study, the prediction of attitude–behavior correlations from the behavior's judged relevance to the attitude was 0.28 and 0.36 for two measures of attitude. Sjöberg also demonstrated the utility of a somewhat simpler procedure to identify the relevance of a given behavior, namely, using the correlation between the specific action and the total behavioral score. This index of a behavior's representativeness of the behavioral domain predicted attitude–behavior correlations at the level of 0.48 and 0.45 for the two measures of attitude.

The importance of selecting appropriate behaviors for aggregation is demonstrated in a series of studies by Buss and Craik (1980, 1981, 1984). In one of their investigations, for example, respondents in a pilot study rated each of 100 behaviors in terms of how good an example of dominance they thought it was (Buss and Craik 1980). The average rating served as a measure of the act's prototypicality in relation to the trait of dominance. On the basis of these scores, the behaviors were divided into four categories of 25 behaviors each, from the most to the least prototypically dominant acts. In the main study, respondents completed two personality scales assessing dominance and also provided a self-rating of dominance on a 7-point scale. In addition, they reported the frequency with which they had, in the past, performed each of the 100 dominance behaviors. Four multiple-act indices were constructed by summing over the self-reports in the four prototypicality categories. As is usually the case, correlations between the three standard measures of dominance and each of the 100 single behaviors were very low, averaging between 0.10 and 0.20, depending on the measure used to assess the dominance trait. The correlations with the multiple-act aggregate based on the least prototypically dominant acts, however, were not much better; they ranged from 0.05 to 0.33. Only when the behaviors aggregated were considered very good examples of the dominance trait, i.e. when they appeared clearly relevant to the disposition, did the correlations between assessed dominance and behavioral trends in the dominance domain attain appreciable magnitude, ranging from 0.25 to 0.67.

In short, evidence for consistency and, hence, for the existence of relatively stable response dispositions is obtained when behaviors are appropriately selected and aggregated into multiple-act measures of behavioral tendencies. Mischel and Peake, however, rejected this approach on the grounds that

> cross-situational aggregation also often has the undesirable effect of canceling out some of the most valuable data about a person. It misses the point completely for the psychologist interested in the unique patterning of the individual by treating within-person variance, and indeed the context itself, as if it were 'error.' (1982a: 738).

Although not inconsistent with the view of aggregation described above, this criticism fails to appreciate the fact that, according to the principle of aggregation, broad response dispositions (traits, attitudes) are largely irrelevant to an understanding of specific actions performed in a given context. Lack of consistency between global dispositional measures and specific actions, or between different specific acts, does not constitute evidence that the concept of personality trait as a broad response disposition is untenable

(Mischel 1968) or that there are no stable attitudes within an individual that influence verbal expressions as well as actions (Wicker 1969). Rather, in view of the aggregation principle, such inconsistency reflects poor operationalization of 'behavior.' To have expected strong relations between global measures of personality or attitude and any particular action may have been rather naïve. In fact, such an expectation contradicts our definitions of attitude and personality trait as general behavioral dispositions.

It should be clear at the same time, however, that aggregation has its limitations. Through aggregation across actions and contexts we can demonstrate cross-situational consistency of behavior, as well as consistency between verbal and nonverbal indicators of an underlying disposition. But, obviously, aggregation does not open the way for an understanding of the factors that influence the tendency to perform a particular action. Returning to the hit-and-run accident described at the beginning of this chapter, if we are interested in the determinants of the driver's failure to come to the assistance of the victim, it will serve no useful purpose to treat this behavior as an instance of irresponsibility and to compute a broad index of various actions in the responsibility domain. Such a multiple-act index should, in fact, be stable across situations and correlate well with a questionnaire measure of responsibility, but it adds little to our understanding of the factors involved in hit-and-run incidents. Clearly, we will need to approach this issue in a different manner if we are to deal with the determinants of individual behaviors. In the remainder of this chapter and in Chapters 5 and 6 we examine different ways to deal with the problem of how dispositional variables can be used to predict and explain specific behavioral tendencies.

PREDICTION OF SPECIFIC BEHAVIORAL TENDENCIES

At first glance, the intuitive logic that links a general attitude or personality trait to a specific behavior appears unassailable. After all, it seems reasonable to expect, for example, that people who hold favorable attitudes toward religion are more likely to subscribe to a religious publication than are people who hold unfavorable attitudes toward religion. Likewise, it would appear that in comparison to egotistic individuals, altruists should be more likely to donate money to a fund for the needy or to help an old lady across the street. On closer examination, however, the matter turns out to be more complicated than it appears at first. We noted earlier in the discussion of behavioral aggregates that not all behaviors are equally relevant as indicators of a given attitude or personality trait. By the same token, a given attitude or personality disposition may not be equally relevant for the prediction of all behaviors.

The difficulty encountered in empirical research has to do with the way in which investigators specify behavioral implications of a given attitude or personality trait. To see why this poses a problem, let us examine some absurd possibilities. Consider, for example, an investigation conducted in France which tests the relation between attitudes toward the People's

Republic of China and the number of hamburgers eaten at the McDonald's restaurant on the Champs Élysées in Paris. One would have to go through considerable mental contortions to explain why attitudes should be linked to behavior in this particular case, and the results of empirical research would almost certainly be disappointing. However, what if we tried to relate attitudes toward the People's Republic of China to voting for the communist candidate in the French national elections? Now it might appear that a correlation should emerge. Or, in the domain of personality, imagine a study that examines the relation between dominance and the number of times a person walks to work instead of taking the bus. Here again we would expect little predictive validity, but if we substituted energy level for dominance, a strong relation might appear plausible. In these examples, as in many investigations, a given behavior is considered relevant or irrelevant for a person's attitude or personality trait on the basis of largely intuitive considerations. It follows that, in the absence of a more formal and explicit way of deciding whether or not a given behavior is implied by an attitude or personality trait, many tests of attitude–behavior or trait–behavior relations are little more than tests of the investigator's intuition. From a theoretical point of view they are of rather limited value.

We saw that dispositional prediction of specific behaviors has proved to be a recalcitrant problem. Global attitudes and personality traits are largely unrelated to particular actions; the search for moderating variables ultimately leads to a dead end in that it restricts the predictive validity of global dispositional measures to a small subset of behaviors, individuals, and situations; and aggregation of specific behaviors into multiple-act indices demonstrates the utility of broad dispositions but adds little to our understanding of the factors that determine a *given* behavior. Some of these problems are perhaps inevitable in light of the above observations regarding the intuitive procedures whereby attitudes or traits are considered relevant for specific actions. In the remainder of this chapter we will see that it is, after all, possible to predict specific actions from behavioral dispositions, but that doing so requires going beyond intuition to decide what kinds of attitudes or traits should correlate with a particular behavior. The approach to be described reconceptualizes the nature of behavioral dispositions by turning to attitudes and personality traits that, by their very nature, are closely tied to specific behavioral tendencies.

As we have noted repeatedly, attitudes and personality traits are usually conceptualized as relatively stable dispositions that exert pervasive influence on a broad range of behaviors. In the case of attitudes, the disposition is of an evaluative nature and the behaviors guided by it are directed at the attitude object. Personality traits, on the other hand, are defined in terms of a general class or category of actions that reflect the influence of the same disposition. Yet it is not clear at all how general a trait or attitude must be for it to be considered a behavioral disposition. In Chapter 1 we saw that empirical research has identified five broad personality dimensions: extraversion, agreeableness, conscientiousness, emotional stability, and culturedness. However, each of these dimensions is composed of more narrowly defined personality characteristics, such as talkativeness and caution in the case of extraversion–introversion and tidiness and perseverance in the case of conscientiousness. Perhaps it is possible to reduce a trait's generality still further, thus moving the disposition closer to the behavior that is to be predicted. In a similar vein, the object of an attitude is not necessarily a person, group, institution, or policy; it can also be defined in terms of a particular behavior. People hold attitudes not only toward religion but also toward praying in private; toward democracy and toward voting in a given election; toward the medical establishment and toward maintaining a prescribed medical regimen. In fact, the standard measurement procedures described in Chapter 1 have been used to assess not only very general attitudes but also attitudes toward such specific behaviors as smoking marijuana (Schlegel 1975), using birth control methods (Kothandapani 1971), drinking alcohol (Veevers 1971), and so on.

The principle of compatibility

The above discussion suggests that the behavioral disposition defined by an attitude or personality trait can vary along a dimension of generality, from the very broad and all-inclusive to the specific. The following analysis defines the dimension of generality in a more systematic fashion.

Target, action, context, and time

Any measure of a behavioral disposition, whether verbal or nonverbal, can be defined in terms of four elements: (1) the target at which the disposition is directed; (2) the particular action or actions involved; (3) the context in which the action occurs; and (4) the time of its occurrence (Fishbein and Ajzen 1975; Ajzen and Fishbein 1977). The generality or specificity of each element depends on the measurement procedures employed. A single observation of an action is a highly specific behavioral indicator in that it involves a given behavior, directed at a particular target, and performed in a given context and at a given point in time. By way of contrast, measures of global attitudes toward objects and generalized personality traits specify no particular action, i.e. they are very broadly defined in terms of the action element. Table 4.2 illustrates different levels of generality with respect to

Table 4.2   Levels of generality

Global	*Aggregate index of behavior*			
Behavioral tendency	Attend parties	Talk to friends	Reveal private feelings	Ask for help
Specific context	Attend parties at place of work	Talk to friends by phone	Reveal private feeling to strangers	Ask for help from coworkers
Specific context and time	Attend party at place of work on a given weekend	Phone friends on next Sunday afternoon	Reveal private feelings to strangers on birthday	Ask for help from coworkers on a night shift

the disposition to behave in a sociable manner. Examination of Table 4.2 shows that we can move from a lower level of generality to a higher level by aggregating across one or more elements. Thus, if we record the number of times a person talks to friends on the phone, rather than observing this behavior only next Sunday, we generalize across the time element and obtain a measure of the tendency to talk with friends in a certain context (on the telephone). If we go one step further and record all occasions on which a person talks to friends, rather than merely telephone conversations, we also generalize across the contextual element and thus derive a measure of the general tendency to talk with friends. Finally, as we saw earlier in this chapter, by aggregating over the different behavioral tendencies (talking to friends, attending parties, revealing private feelings, etc.), we reach the highest level of generality, namely the level of the disposition to be sociable.

Returning to the dispositional prediction of specific actions, we noted that we are rarely interested in the lowest level of generality that involves a unique context and specific point in time. As a general rule, we are more concerned with predicting and understanding behavioral tendencies or regularities across occasions. Thus, we may want to predict and explain safe driving over a period of time, rather than on a given afternoon; or we may be interested in the tendency, over time, to discipline children by means of corporal punishment. In behavioral tendencies of this kind, the target and action elements are constant, the context is also relatively stable from one occasion to another in the sense that it is appropriate for the behavior to occur, but the time element is broadly generalized. When referring to dispositional prediction of specific behaviors in the following discussions, we will have in mind these behavioral tendencies over time.

In their review of research on the attitude–behavior relation, Ajzen and Fishbein (1977) formulated a 'principle of compatibility' that can be stated as follows. Two indicators of a given disposition are said to be *compatible* with each other to the extent that their target, action, context, and time elements are assessed at identical levels of generality or specificity. Further, consistency between two indicators of a disposition is a function of the degree to which the indicators are, in this sense, compatible with each other. Thus, according to the principle of compatibility, the more similar the target, action, context, and time elements of one indicator to those of the other, the stronger the statistical relation between them.

The principle of compatibility is very similar to the contiguity hypothesis in Guttman's (1957, 1959) facet theory. Guttman proposed that any variable can be analyzed in terms of an underlying facet structure. The action, target, context, and time elements of behavioral dispositions are examples of facets, and their levels of generality constitute facet elements. Like the principle of compatibility, 'The contiguity hypothesis of facet theory states that the correlation between two variables increases with the similarity between the facet elements defining them' (Guttman 1957: 130).

Weigel, Vernon, and Tognacci (1974) demonstrated the importance of compatibility between the *target* element of the attitude measure and the target at which the behavior is directed. Residents of a community in the western United States participated in this investigation which was conducted with the assistance of the local chapter of the Sierra Club, an organization dedicated to such issues as conservation of natural resources and pollution control. Five months following administration of an initial attitude survey, participants were asked to commit themselves to various activities involving the Sierra Club. Their degree of compliance or refusal was used to compute a 4-step behavioral scale. The lowest level on the scale consisted of refusing to have any further contact with the Sierra Club and the remaining three levels ranged from agreeing to be on the club's mailing list to becoming a club member. It can be seen that this behavioral measure has the Sierra Club as its target and that it represents a generalization across different actions.

Four attitudes, varying in their degree of compatibility with the behavior, were assessed in the initial survey: attitudes toward the Sierra Club, toward conservation of natural resources, toward pollution control, and toward a pure environment in general. Clearly, the target element of the first attitude measure was the same as the target element of the behavior (the Sierra Club). The target elements of the next two attitudes, although not the same as that of the behavior, were issues of importance to the Sierra Club, i.e. conservation of natural resources and pollution control. Finally, the target element of attitude toward environmental protection in general had the lowest degree of compatibility with the target element of the behavior.

The results of the investigation were quite consistent with the principle of compatibility. As the degree of compatibility between target elements increased, so did the attitude–behavior correlation. The behavioral criterion had a correlation of 0.60 with attitudes toward the Sierra Club (high compatibility), correlations of 0.37 and 0.38 with attitudes toward conservation and pollution control (moderate compatibility), and a nonsignificant correlation of 0.16 with attitudes toward a pure environment (low compatibility).

The operation of the compatibility principle has also been demonstrated by experimentally manipulating the similarity between the target elements of attitudes and actions (Lord et al. 1984). In the first of two studies, college students at Princeton University reported their stereotypes of members of a certain 'eating club' (fraternity or sorority) at the university by rating them on a set of 20 personality trait terms. At a later session, the participants expressed their attitudes toward members of the club and toward working with a member of the club on a joint project. They were then given paragraph descriptions of two persons they could work with, one description conforming closely to the stereotype of club members, the other much less in accordance with the stereotype. Finally, participants rated how much they would like to work with each of the two club members. The target element of this behavioral preference measure is the particular person described in the paragraph. This target is clearly more similar to the target of the attitude measures (members of the club in general) when the person described conforms to the stereotype of club members than when it does not. Consistent with the principle of compatibility, the correlations between the two attitude measures and the behavioral preference were stronger under high compatibility in target elements ($r = 0.49$ and 0.69) than under low compatibility ($r = 0.27$ and 0.32). Similar results were obtained in a second study that dealt with the relation between attitudes toward homosexuals and willingness to visit a homosexual individual who was described in accordance with, or not in accordance with, the stereotype of homosexuals.

We are here, however, interested less in compatibility between the target elements of two dispositional measures than in compatibility between their *action* elements. According to the principle of compatibility, we should be able to predict behavior at any level of generality or specificity, so long as the predictor is equally general or specific, i.e. so long as the two measures involve not only the same target, but also the same action, context, and time elements. The principle of aggregation can be recognized as a special case of the compatibility principle. It represents the case of compatibility at relatively high levels of generality. By aggregating over a set of occasions we obtain measures of behavioral trends that correspond in their level of generality to other measures of the same behavioral trends obtained by aggregating over a different set of occasions. Of greater interest, when we aggregate across different behaviors in a given domain or directed at a given object, the resulting multiple-act index corresponds in its level of generality to a properly constructed measure of a general personality trait or attitude. As suggested by the principle of compatibility, aggregated measures of behavior are indeed found to exhibit consistency with each other and to correlate well with questionnaire measures of general attitudes and personality traits. By the same reasoning, the principle of compatibility offers a promising approach to the dispositional prediction of specific action tendencies: according to the principle, we must measure the predictor such that it reflects the specific response tendency of interest. This possibility is examined below, first with respect to personality traits and then with respect to attitudes.

PERSONALITY TRAITS AND SPECIFIC RESPONSE TENDENCIES

We can reduce personality traits to the level of specific response tendencies in a number of different ways. If the principle of compatibility is upheld, behavior-specific trait measures will correlate well with the corresponding action tendencies.

Routines and habits

Human beings are said to be creatures of habit; they tend to persist in doing what they have become accustomed to. It is well known that, with repeated performance, many behaviors become routine to the point where they can be executed with minimal conscious control (Schneider and Shiffrin 1977; Shiffrin and Schneider 1977). For most of us, walking, driving a car, brushing our teeth, getting dressed, and the myriad of other activities we perform every day become routines that do not require much focused attention. It can perhaps be argued that behavioral routines or habits constitute personality traits at the level of specific behaviors. Thus, brushing your teeth in the morning and again at night may be viewed as a behavior-specific response tendency or trait, and if we could measure the strength of this tendency, i.e. the strength of the habit, we should be able to predict future behavior.

Although attempts to develop measures of habit strength are underway (see, for example, Verplanken and Orbell 2003), no good measures are currently available. Instead, investigators tend to rely on frequency of past behavior as a proxy for habit strength under the assumption that frequently performed behaviors are likely to have habituated and become routine. We will examine the role of habit as a determinant of behavior in Chapter 5; at this point, we merely consider the related proposition that frequency of past behavior should predict the likelihood that the behavior will be performed in the future.

Temporal stability of response tendencies

It is often said that the best predictor of future behavior is past behavior. The more frequently a behavior has been performed in the past, the more likely it is to be performed again. In other words, if a person is known to have exhibited a tendency to perform a given behavior, we can assume that, barring unforeseen events, the tendency will continue. Thus, in a random sample of individuals, cigarette smoking in the foreseeable future can be predicted with a high degree of accuracy if we know whether a person has or has not been smoking in the past. Temporal stability of behavioral tendencies will be greater for some behaviors than for others, and it will vary with the amount of time covered in the prediction. The greater the time interval, the more likely it is that intervening events will modify the behavioral tendency. Participation in a smoking cessation program, for example, may reduce or eliminate cigarette consumption in some smokers, while previous nonsmokers may take up use of tobacco in the same time period. Nevertheless, in many instances we would expect sufficient temporal stability to permit fairly accurate prediction from past to future behavior.

A few concrete illustrations may be helpful. In a laboratory experiment (Locke et al. 1984) students' task performance was examined over a series of trials. The task involved finding uses for common objects, such as bricks or clothes hangers, and the measure of behavior was the number of distinct uses listed by a participant. After some initial training, performance on trials 5 and 6 was predicted from performance on trial 4. The correlation between prior and later behavior in this situation was found to be 0.68. In another investigation (Ajzen and Madden 1986), college students' class attendance was recorded on 16 consecutive occasions. The number of times students attended class on the first 8 occasions was found to have a correlation of 0.46 with the number of times they attended class on the second 8 occasions.

The studies by Locke et al. and by Ajzen and Madden involved a relatively short time lag between prior and later behavior. The time lag was much greater in other investigations. For example, in a study of exercise behavior (Norman and Smith 1995), undergraduate college students completed a questionnaire on two occasions, six months apart. Frequency of exercise reported on the second occasion (later behavior) was predicted from exercise frequency reported on the first survey (prior behavior). The correlation between prior and later behavior was found to be 0.68. Similar results were obtained with respect to marijuana use among high school students (Jessor and Jessor 1977). On two occasions, separated by one year, the students in this study replied to four items that assessed the amount of marijuana they were using. Although the two observations of behavior were separated by a considerable period of time, the correlation between later and prior behavior was a respectable 0.53.

The above examples show that prior behavior can permit accurate prediction of later behavior in many situations. Behavior can, however, also be quite variable over time. Some examples concerning temporal instability of behavioral trends can be found in Vinokur and Caplan's (1987; Vinokur et al. 1987) research program concerning job-seeking behaviors of the unemployed. Obviously, job-seeking activities will tend to change once a person has found employment. However, even if we restrict the analysis to only those individuals who, over a period of time, fail to secure employment, we may find that their strategies of looking for a job have changed. In one of their studies, Vinokur and his associates assessed, at three points in time, the reported frequencies with which unemployed men performed each of ten job-seeking activities: read newspapers for job opportunities; checked with employment agencies; talked to friends, family or other people to get information about jobs; used or sent out a résumé to a prospective employer; registered for, or started, a job training program; filled out an application form for a job; telephoned, wrote, or visited potential employers; actually went for a job interview; did things to improve the impression they would make in a job interview (wore the right clothes, got a haircut, etc.); and phoned or went to their union's meeting place. The questionnaire assessing these behavioral tendencies was administered three times at 4-month intervals.

Table 4.3 shows the temporal stability or instability of the different behavioral tendencies.[1] Overall, there were clear individual differences in job-seeking behaviors that remained fairly stable over the time period

Table 4.3   Temporal stability of job-seeking behaviors

	First 4 months	Second 4 months	8 months
Read newspapers	0.45	0.42	0.29
Check with employment agencies	0.38	0.31	0.34
Talk to friends and others	0.47	0.34	0.32
Use or send out a résumé	0.61	0.71	0.57
Job training program	0.20	0.43	0.03*
Apply for a job	0.54	0.35	0.35
Contact potential employers	0.42	0.27	0.29
Go for a job interview	0.47	0.30	0.30
Do things to improve appearance	0.33	0.43	0.31
Go to union	0.51	0.56	0.54

Note: *Not significant; all other correlations $p < 0.05$.
Source: Vinokur and Caplan (1987)

investigated. The average correlation between initial behavioral reports and the reports provided 4 months later was 0.43; for the second 4-month period it was 0.40; and over the total 8-month period an average correlation of 0.33 was obtained.[2] Inspection of the individual behavioral tendencies, however, reveals considerable variation. The number of times people used their résumés, for example, and the number of times they went to their unions remained quite stable throughout. In contrast, checking with employment agencies and taking advantage of job training programs showed only modest degrees of temporal stability.

Clearly, then, behavioral tendencies can be quite stable over time, but they can also have rather low temporal stability when circumstances lead to modification of previous inclinations. In a meta-analysis of 16 different studies (Ouellette and Wood 1998), past behavior was found to have a mean correlation of 0.39 with later behavior, but the fact that behavior can also be quite variable over time was indicated by a highly significant index of heterogeneity in this analysis. A moment's reflection reveals, moreover, that even strong correlations between prior and later behavior are of little explanatory value. It is not very informative to say that people currently behave the way they do because they behaved that way in the past, or because they have a tendency or habit to behave that way. We would still have to explain their past behavior as well as the reasons for the observed temporal stability in behavior. Most likely, temporal stability is the result of stability in the causal antecedents of the behavior under consideration. Certain factors will have led people to perform or not to perform the behavior in the past. To the extent that these factors persist over time, they will continue to exert their influence and thus produce the same behavior later on. If circumstances should change, the behavior will change as well and prior behavior will no longer predict later behavior. Only by identifying the causal antecedents of a behavior, and examining their vicissitudes over time, can we gain a proper understanding of the behavior's temporal stability (or instability). We therefore turn to a different kind of behavioral disposition that, even though tied to the specific response tendency, can still provide useful information about underlying psychological determinants of the behavior.

Perceived behavioral control

Some personality dimensions may be considered dispositions to hold certain beliefs rather than dispositions to act in certain ways. Optimism, idealism, open-mindedness, etc. fall into this category of traits. Of greater interest for present purposes is the concept of internal–external locus of control (Rotter 1954, 1966). This concept refers to the generalized belief that one's outcomes are under the control of one's own behavior as opposed to being under the control of such external factors as powerful others or chance. Much research has attempted to relate perceived locus of control to a broad range of specific actions (see Lefcourt 1981b, 1982, 1983). In view of the poor predictive validity of other general personality traits documented in Chapter 2, it should come as no surprise that, by and large, the results have been disappointing. For example, early work with Rotter's (1966) internal–external (I–E) locus of control scale focused on achievement-related behavior. On the premise that internally oriented individuals are more likely to see a connection between their actions and achievement than externally oriented individuals, it was hypothesized that the former would exert more effort and show greater task persistence than the latter. However, investigations of the relation between locus of control beliefs and academic performance have produced nonsignificant or inconclusive findings (see Warehime 1972).

Another example is provided by the failure of general locus of control measures to predict social or political involvement. Believing that their actions can bring about desired goals, internals should be more likely to participate in the political process. However, as Levenson (1981: 49) stated in her review of this research, 'Perhaps no area of study using the I–E construct has led to more confusing results than that of social and political activism.' While some investigations obtained data in support of the hypothesis (e.g. Gore and Rotter 1963), others found no differences between individuals with internal and external orientations (e.g. Evans and Alexander 1970). Still other studies actually obtained results contrary to prediction, with externals showing greater political involvement than internals (e.g. Sanger and Alker 1972).

Findings of this kind are not unexpected in light of the principle of compatibility. Generalized locus of control beliefs are incompatible with specific behavioral tendencies in terms of target, action, and context; they can thus not be expected to permit accurate prediction. Rotter (1966) was quite aware of the need for more specialized measures of perceived locus of control. Although his I–E scale assesses generalized expectancies, his initial efforts were designed to develop a set of scales or subscales that would measure control expectations with regard to a number of different goal areas, such as achievement, social recognition, and affection (see Lefcourt 1981a).

More specialized locus of control scales were indeed constructed in subsequent years, most notably the Intellectual Achievement Responsibility (IAR) scale (Crandall et al. 1965) and the Health Locus of Control (HLC) scale (Wallston et al. 1976; Wallston et al. 1978). Although dealing with more circumscribed behavioral domains than the original I–E scale, these measures are still quite general and they thus fail to be strictly compatible with any particular action. As might therefore be expected, prediction of specific behavior from the IAR and HLC scales has also met with only very qualified success (see Lefcourt 1982, and Wallston and Wallston 1981, for relevant literature reviews). In the domain of achievement-related behavior, results tend to confirm a positive, if often weak, relation between internality and performance (see Bar-Tal and Bar-Zohar 1977); however, the data also contain 'paradoxical inconsistencies or failures at replication' (Lefcourt 1982: 98). A pattern of weak and inconsistent results is also found in research that has used the HLC scale to predict such health-related behaviors as seeking information about illness, preventive health activities, smoking cessation, weight reduction, dental hygiene, and adherence to medical regimens. In their review of this research area, Wallston and Wallston (1981: 236) reached the following rather pessimistic conclusion: 'Human behavior is complex and multidetermined. It is simplistic to believe that health locus of control beliefs will ever predict very much of the variance in health behavior by itself [*sic*].'

However, in terms of conceptualizing control beliefs that are compatible with a particular behavior of interest, one need not stop at the level of perceived achievement responsibility or health locus of control. Instead, one can consider perceived control over a given behavior or behavioral goal. Along those lines, Bandura (1977, 1982, 1997) introduced the concept of perceived *self-efficacy*, which refers to the subjective probability that one is capable of executing a certain course of action. Several studies have revealed a strong relation between self-efficacy beliefs and behavior (see Bandura 1997, for a review). For example, Bandura, Adams, and Beyer (1977) showed that self-efficacy beliefs correlate strongly with coping behavior. Adult snake phobics received one of two treatments: participant modeling (going through a series of interactions with a snake, assisted by the therapist) or modeling (observation) only. Immediately following treatment, the participants rated the likelihood that they would be capable of performing each of 18 tasks involving a snake (self-efficacy beliefs). During the subsequent performance test, they were asked actually to perform the graded series of behaviors which ranged from looking at, touching, and holding the snake to letting the snake loose in the room and retrieving it. The correlations between perceived self-efficacy and performance were 0.83 and 0.84 in the two treatment conditions, respectively.

The Locke, Frederick, and Bobko (1984) study mentioned earlier also revealed a strong relation between self-efficacy beliefs and behavioral achievement. Remember that the performance criterion in this study was the number of uses for a common object listed in a short period of time. Following a few practice trials, participants expressed their certainty, in percentage points, that they could list varying numbers of uses. This measure of perceived self-efficacy had a correlation of 0.54 with actual number of uses listed.

Closely related to the idea of self-efficacy is Ajzen's (1985, 1991; Schifter and Ajzen 1985; Ajzen and Madden 1986) concept of *perceived behavioral control*. Consistent with the principle of compatibility, it was shown (Ajzen and Timko 1986) that perceived control over specific health-related behaviors is far superior to the more general health locus of control scale in terms of its correlation with corresponding actions. College students reported the frequency with which they performed each of 24 health-related behaviors, such as staying out of smoke-filled rooms, taking vitamin supplements, performing cancer self-examinations, and getting periodic TB tests. Health locus of control was assessed by means of the Wallston, Wallston, and DeVellis (1978) scale, while perceived control with respect to each behavior was measured by asking respondents to rate, on a 7-point scale, how easy or difficult they considered performance of the behavior to be. Internal health locus of control correlated, on average, 0.10 with the 24 individual behaviors. In contrast, the average correlation between perceived behavioral control over a given behavior and performance of the corresponding behavior was 0.77.

Alagna and Reddy (1984) also reported a fairly strong correlation between perceived control and behavioral performance in the health domain. Women completed a questionnaire which, among other things, assessed their beliefs that breast self-examinations can detect lesions, that they were familiar with correct self-examination techniques, and that they could detect lesions in their breasts by means of self-examinations. These three items were summed to yield a measure of perceived control over performing correct breast self-examinations.[3] Following administration of the questionnaire, the women were observed performing a breast examination on a synthetic model, and the proficiency of these examinations was scored by trained observers in terms of the number of correct behaviors performed. The correlation of perceived behavioral control with behavioral proficiency was found to be 0.57.

Over the past 20 years, many studies have examined the relation between perceived behavioral control and behavior with generally favorable results. In a meta-analysis of 60 independent data sets (Armitage and Conner 2001), a mean correlation of 0.37 was obtained between perceived behavioral control and actual behavior.

To summarize briefly, the research described in this section suggests that specific dispositional measures can predict and to some extent account for corresponding behavioral tendencies. Of particular interest in this respect is the concept of perceived behavioral control. When reduced to the level of specific response tendencies, perceived self-efficacy or perceived control over performance of a behavior is found to correlate quite strongly with actual performance. By considering perceived behavioral control we begin to gain an understanding of the factors that influence performance of specific actions. Of course, other factors are also involved and we will consider one other factor below. At this point we merely note that, as a general rule, people attempt to perform a behavior to the extent that they have confidence in their ability to do so. Their attempts are successful if they in fact are capable of performing the behavior in question. We will return to this issue in Chapter 5, where we will examine the concept of perceived behavioral control in greater detail.

ATTITUDES AND SPECIFIC RESPONSE TENDENCIES

Attitude toward a behavior

According to the principle of compatibility, we should be able to predict individual behaviors (directed at a certain target) from measures of attitudes toward those behaviors. By and large, the literature lends support to this expectation. For example, Kothandapani (1971) assessed the attitudes of married women toward personal use of birth control methods by means of 12 standard scales. The self-reported use or nonuse of such methods served as the behavioral criterion. All 12 attitude–behavior correlations were found to be significant, with an average coefficient of 0.69. Similarly, Veevers (1971) used five different instruments to measure attitudes toward drinking alcoholic beverages. Self-reports of actual drinking among residents of two Alberta communities could be predicted from these attitudes, with coefficients ranging from 0.46 to 0.72.

Manstead, Proffitt, and Smart (1983) reported a study on infant feeding practices. Toward the end of their pregnancies, women completed a questionnaire that assessed, among other things, their attitudes toward breast-feeding (as opposed to bottle-feeding) their babies. Six weeks following delivery, a questionnaire sent to each woman ascertained her actual feeding practices during the preceding six weeks. Attitudes toward the behavior of interest were found to have a correlation of 0.67 with the feeding method employed.

In two laboratory experiments, Ajzen (1971; Ajzen and Fishbein 1970) investigated cooperative behavior in different 'Prisoner's Dilemma' games. In these games, two players can each choose between two possible moves, and their joint choices determine how much each player wins or loses (their pay-offs). One option in the game represents a cooperative move, the other a competitive move. The participants in the studies were pairs of same-sex college students who played three Prisoner's Dilemma games that varied in their pay-off matrices. Following a few practice trials, the players were asked to complete a questionnaire that included two semantic differential measures of attitude, each comprised of four or five bipolar evaluative scales. These scales were used to obtain measures of attitude toward choosing the cooperative strategy and of attitude toward the other player. The proportion of cooperative strategy choices following completion of the questionnaire served as the behavioral criterion. Looking at the three games played in the two experiments, actual choice of cooperative moves correlated 0.63, 0.70, and 0.65 with attitude toward choosing the co-operative strategy. By way of comparison, the correlations between attitude toward the other player (a global attitude) and cooperative game behavior were very low and not always significant ($r = 0.26$, 0.09, and 0.27, respectively).

As another example, consider a study conducted during the 1974 general election in the United Kingdom (Fishbein et al. 1976). Voters were inter-viewed prior to the election and their attitudes toward voting for each candidate in their constituencies were assessed by means of an evaluative semantic differential. The average correlation between these attitude measures and actual voting choice was 0.85. More general attitudes toward the candidates themselves also predicted voting behavior, but here the average correlation was only 0.51, significantly lower than the correlation obtained by measuring attitudes toward the act of voting for or against the competing candidates.

In the domain of illicit drug use, attitudes toward using LSD, amphetamines, cannabis, and ecstasy over the next six months were used to predict self-reported frequency of actual use of these drugs during the period in question (McMillan and Conner 2003). Attitude–behavior correlations across the four drugs ranged from 0.35 to 0.58 (all statistically significant). Many studies have examined the relation between attitudes and behavior in the domain of physical exercise. For example, Terry and O'Leary (1995) assessed attitudes toward 'exercising for at least 20 minutes, three times a week for the next fortnight' and two weeks later, participants indicated whether they had exercised for at least 20 minutes, three times per week during the past fortnight. The attitude–behavior correlation was 0.53. In another study (Godin et al. 1987), attitudes toward participating in vigorous physical activities were found to have a correlation of 0.45 with self-reports of the frequency with which participants engaged in such activities.[4]

These findings contrast with the low and often non-significant correlations between general measures of attitude toward an object and single behaviors with respect to the object. Thus, just as behavioral aggregation made it possible to demonstrate strong attitude–behavior correlations at a global level, the shift from general attitudes toward objects to attitudes toward behaviors enables us to apply the attitude construct to the prediction of single behaviors. A narrative review of attitude–behavior research (Ajzen and Fishbein 1977) provided support for the principle of compatibility by showing that correlations between attitudes and behavior were substantial only when these variables were assessed at compatible levels of specificity or generality; when the measures were incompatible, the correlations were very low and usually not significant. The correlation across studies between degree of compatibility and the magnitude of the attitude–behavior relation was found to be 0.83. However, the most compelling support for the importance of compatibility comes from studies that have directly compared the predictive validity of attitudes that were compatible (i.e. attitudes toward behaviors) or incompatible (i.e. attitudes toward general targets) with a single-act criterion. In a meta-analysis of eight studies that manipulated level of compatibility while holding all other variables constant (Kraus 1995), the prediction of behavior from attitude toward the behavior resulted in a correlation of 0.54, whereas the correlation between general attitudes and the single behaviors was only 0.13.

To summarize briefly, in this section we have identified a second determinant of specific response tendencies, namely, attitude toward the behavior in question. Like perceptions of behavioral control, attitudes toward a behavior are found to correlate well with the corresponding behavior, and because they can be assessed ahead of time, they can be used to predict behavioral performance. Beyond permitting prediction, however, the attitude toward behavior concept can also enhance our understanding of the reasons why people exhibit or fail to exhibit a certain behavioral tendency. The studies reviewed above have shown that, as a general rule, people are likely to perform a specific behavior if they view its performance favorably, and they are unlikely to perform it if they view its performance unfavorably. Of course, this is only a first step toward an explanation. We need to know much more about the ways in which favorable or unfavorable attitudes toward behaviors are formed before we can feel confident that we have a good understanding of the factors involved. Chapter 6 deals with these factors in some detail.

SUMMARY AND CONCLUSIONS

The principle of compatibility points the way toward dispositional prediction of specific behavioral tendencies. With varying implications, attitudes and personality traits can be reduced to the level of a particular behavior, and such behavior-specific dispositions are found to correlate well with compatible action tendencies. In the case of traits, reduction to the level of individual response tendencies often involves prediction of behavior from prior behavior and it is accomplished at considerable expense. Prior behavior becomes a poor predictor of later behavior as soon as circumstances change sufficiently to require modification of the behavior; and even when consistency of a given behavioral tendency with prior behavior is observed, such consistency demonstrates merely that the same specific disposition can be assessed at different points in time. It tells us little about the nature of the disposition and it does not add much to our understanding of the underlying causes of the behavior. In fact, it is generally true that personality traits, in and of themselves, have only limited explanatory power. It is not particularly illuminating to say that a person appears on time for appointments because she has a tendency to be punctual, or that she smiles easily because she is friendly. The personality trait itself is inferred from behavior, observed or reported; what explanatory value it does have lies in the fact that it accounts for a specific behavioral tendency (e.g. showing up on time for appointments) in terms of a more general response disposition (e.g. punctuality). However, when – in line with the principle of compatibility – the 'trait' used to predict a behavior is the tendency to perform that very behavior, its explanatory power is lost entirely. One behavior-specific personality trait that can to a large extent escape these limitations is the belief in self-efficacy or control over a given behavior. Perceived behavioral control is found to correlate well with the tendency to perform the behavior and it provides at least a partial explanation for the tendency in question.

Reduction of attitudes to the level of individual behaviors is accomplished without much difficulty. The same methods that are used to assess attitudes toward objects, institutions, or events can be applied directly to the construction of scales that assess attitudes toward a given behavior. Such behavior-specific attitudes correlate well with the corresponding behavior and, like perceived behavioral control, they can help explain why people act the way they do.

NOTES

1 I am grateful to Amiram Vinokur for providing a summary of these data.
2 These correlations contrast with correlations of 0.58, 0.55, and 0.38 for behavioral aggregates computed in accordance with the principle of aggregation.
3 The first of these three items is conceptually different from perceived behavioral control, and it, indeed, had a lower correlation with effective breast self-examination than did the other two items. However, all three items correlated highly with each other, a finding which prompted the investigators to combine them into a single measure.
4 The variability in the magnitude of the reported attitude–behavior correlations in different studies may at least in part be due to the degree of compatibility between the obtained measures of attitude and behavior. For example, attitudes are usually assessed by asking participants how

good or bad it is to perform a given behavior, whereas the measure of behavior often involves the frequency with which it was performed. Respondents who hold very positive attitudes should be very likely to perform the behavior, but there is no expectation that they will necessarily perform the behavior more frequently than respondents who hold less positive attitudes.

SUGGESTIONS FOR FURTHER READING

Ajzen, I. (1982) On behaving in accordance with one's attitudes. In M. P. Zanna, E. T. Higgins and C. P. Herman (eds), *Attitude Structure and Function: The Third Ohio State University Volume on Attitudes and Persuasion* (Vol. 2, pp. 3–15). Hillsdale, NJ: Erlbaum. This chapter summarizes ideas inherent in the principle of compatibility.

Bandura, A. (1997) *Self-Efficacy: The Exercise of Control*. New York: Freeman. In this book, Bandura discusses his theory of self-efficacy and reviews relevant research.

Fishbein, M., and Ajzen, I. (1974) Attitudes toward objects as predictors of single and multiple behavioral criteria. *Psychological Review*, 81: 59–74. This article discusses the principle of aggregation and presents empirical support for the principle in the context of the attitude–behavior relation.

FIVE

FROM INTENTIONS TO ACTIONS

It's a long step from saying to doing.

(Cervantes)

In the previous chapter we began to unravel the mystery surrounding prediction and explanation of specific action tendencies by turning our attention to behavioral dispositions that correspond precisely to the particular action tendency of interest. In the present chapter, we carry this principle of compatibility to its conclusion by examining the immediate antecedents or determinants of behavior.

THE CASE OF WILLFUL BEHAVIOR

Many behaviors in everyday life, often the behaviors of greatest interest to personality and social psychologists, can be thought of as being largely under volitional control. That is to say, people can easily perform these behaviors if they are so inclined, or refrain from performing them if they decide against it. In open, democratic societies most people can, if they so desire, vote in political elections, watch the evening news on television, buy toothpaste at a drugstore, pray at a nearby church, mosque, or synagogue, or donate blood to their local hospitals. If they wish, they may also decide against engaging in any of these activities.

The important point about willful behaviors of this kind is that their occurrence is a direct result of deliberate attempts made by an individual. The process involved can be described as follows. In accordance with deliberations to be taken up in Chapter 6, a person forms an *intention* to engage in a certain behavior. This intention remains a behavioral disposition until, at the appropriate time and opportunity, an attempt is made to translate the intention into action. Assuming that the behavior is in fact under volitional control, the attempt will produce the desired act. Indeed, many theorists agree that the disposition most closely linked to a specific action tendency is the intention to perform the action under consideration (e.g. Fishbein and Ajzen 1975; Triandis 1977; Fisher and Fisher 1992;

Gollwitzer 1993). In other words, barring unforeseen events, people are expected to do what they intend to do.

Predicting behavior from intention

The foregoing discussion implies that we should be able to predict specific behaviors with considerable accuracy from intentions to engage in the behaviors under consideration. Many studies have substantiated the predictive validity of behavioral intentions. When appropriately measured, behavioral intentions account for an appreciable proportion of variance in actual behavior. Meta-analyses covering diverse behavioral domains have reported mean intention–behavior correlations of 0.47 (Notani 1998; Armitage and Conner 2001), 0.53 (Shepherd et al. 1988), 0.45 (Randall and Wolff 1994), and 0.62 (van den Putte 1993). Studies in specific behavioral domains, such as condom use and exercise, have produced similar results, with intention–behavior correlations ranging from 0.44 to 0.56 (Godin and Kok 1996; Hausenblas et al. 1997; Sheeran and Orbell 1998; Albarracín et al. 2001). In a meta-analysis of these and other meta-analyses, Sheeran (2002) reported an overall correlation of 0.53 between intention and behavior.

These meta-analyses include many examples of strong correlations between intentions and volitional behavior. Table 5.1 shows a selective

Table 5.1   Correlations between intentions and volitional behaviors

Behavior	Intention–behavior correlation
Applying for shares in the British Electric Company (East 1993)	0.82
Using birth control pills (see Ajzen and Fishbein 1980: Ch. 11)	0.85
Breast vs. bottle feeding (Manstead et al. 1983)	0.82
Using ecstasy drugs (Orbell et al. 2001)	0.75
Having an abortion (Smetana and Adler 1980)	0.96
Complying with speed limits (Elliott et al. 2003)	0.69
Attending church (King 1975)	0.90
Donating blood (Giles and Cairns 1995)	0.75
Using homeopathic medicine (Furnham and Lovett 2001)	0.75
Voting choice in presidential election (see Ajzen and Fishbein 1980: Ch. 13)	0.80

Note: All correlations are significant ($p < 0.05$).

sample of findings. It can be seen that intentions can accurately predict a variety of corresponding action tendencies, ranging from buying company shares to actions of appreciable personal or social significance, such as using birth control pills, having an abortion, using illicit drugs, donating blood, and choosing among candidates in an election.

Available evidence also supports the idea that intentions are close antecedents of overt actions. If intentions are indeed the immediate determinants of volitional behavior then they should correlate more strongly with the behavior than do other kinds of antecedent factors. Consistent with this argument, the predictive validity of intentions is typically found to be significantly greater than that of attitudes toward the behavior. Consider, for example, the study by Manstead, Proffitt, and Smart (1983) on prediction of breast-feeding versus bottle-feeding of newborn infants. As we saw in Chapter 4, mothers' attitudes toward these alternative feeding practices had a correlation of 0.67 with the feeding method they actually employed. By way of comparison, inspection of Table 5.1 shows that the intention–behavior correlation in this study was 0.82. Very similar results were obtained with respect to cooperation in Prisoner's Dilemma games (Ajzen and Fishbein 1970; Ajzen 1971). In Chapter 4, the correlations between attitudes toward choosing the cooperative alternative and actual game behavior were reported to have ranged from 0.63 to 0.70. When predicted from intentions, correlations with game behavior were found to be in the 0.82 to 0.85 range.

Another example is contained in a study of marijuana use by college students (Ajzen et al. 1982). The students evaluated 'my smoking marijuana in the next 3 or 4 weeks' on a set of semantic differential scales and also indicated, on a 7-point scale, the likelihood that they would perform this behavior. About four weeks later they were contacted by telephone and asked to indicate whether or not they had smoked marijuana during the time that had passed. This self-report of marijuana use correlated 0.72 with intentions; its correlation with attitude toward smoking marijuana was, at 0.53, significantly lower.

Intention–behavior discrepancies

Clearly, research has provided strong evidence that tendencies to perform particular behaviors can indeed be well predicted from corresponding behavioral intentions. At the same time, however, research has also revealed considerable variability in the magnitude of observed correlations, and relatively low intention–behavior correlations are sometimes obtained. Several factors may be responsible for discrepancies between intentions and behavior.

Intention–behavior incompatibility   One possible reason for relatively low intention–behavior correlations is lack of compatibility between measures of these variables. In Chapter 4 we noted the importance of maintaining compatibility to avoid inconsistency between attitudes and actions. General attitudes arguably fail to predict specific behaviors because of a lack of compatibility in the action, context, and time elements. That is, general attitudes identify only the target element whereas a specific behavior involves a particular action directed at the target in a given context and point in time.

Lack of compatibility is usually not a serious problem when it comes to predicting behavior from intentions because the measures of intentions deal not with a general target but with the behavior itself. In fact, the intentions assessed in the studies listed in Table 5.1 were highly compatible with the behaviors in terms of target, action, context, and time elements. For example, in the study reported by King (1975), the behavior of interest was whether or not college students would attend church services in the course of a two-week vacation. This behavior could be predicted with a high degree of accuracy by asking the students, prior to the recess, how likely it was that they would attend church services during that time period.

Nevertheless, incompatibility can arise even when dealing with the prediction of behavior from intention. For example, in a study of managers who were enrolled in a physical exercise program for health reasons (Kerner and Grossman 1998), the frequency with which participants performed a specific prescribed exercise behavior (e.g. climbing stairs or lifting weights) over a 5-month period was only weakly ($r = 0.21$) related to their intentions to exercise in the next 12 months. Just as general attitudes are poor predictors of specific behaviors, intentions with respect to a behavioral category such as exercise are poor predictors of a single instance of the category. A compatible measure of intentions in this study would have asked participants to indicate the extent to which they intended to engage in the particular prescribed exercise behavior in the next 5 months.[1]

Stability of intentions   Clearly, intentions can change over time; the more time passes, the greater the likelihood that unforeseen events will produce changes in intentions. The time interval between measurement of intention and assessment of behavior is therefore often taken as a proxy for stability of intentions. A measure of intention obtained before the changes took place cannot be expected accurately to predict behavior. It follows that accuracy of prediction will usually decline with the amount of time that intervenes between measurement of intention and observation of behavior.

Imagine, for example, a woman who intends to vote for the Democratic candidate in a race for the US Senate. After her intention is assessed, she learns – by watching a television interview with the candidate a few days before the election – that he opposes abortion and equal rights for women. As a result, she 'changes her mind,' decides to vote for the Republican candidate instead, and actually does so in the election. Her actual voting choice corresponds to her most recent intention, but it could not have been predicted from the measure of intention obtained at the earlier point in time.

Several studies have demonstrated the disruptive effects of unforeseen events. For instance, Songer-Nocks (1976) assessed intentions to choose the cooperative alternative at the beginning of a 20-trial, two-person experimental game. One half of the pairs of players were given feedback after each trial which informed them about the choices made by their partners and of the pay-offs to each player. The other pairs were given no such information. Feedback concerning the partner's competitive or cooperative behavior may, of course, influence a player's own intentions regarding future moves in the game. Consistent with this argument, Songer-Nocks reported that providing feedback significantly reduced the accuracy with which initial intentions predicted actual game behavior.

Other evidence regarding the disruptive effects of unanticipated events comes from studies that have varied the amount of time between assessment of intentions and observation of behavior. Since the likelihood of unforeseen events will tend to increase as time passes, we would expect to find stronger intention–behavior correlations with short rather than long periods of delay. Findings in support of this expectation were reported in a study on voting choice (Fishbein and Coombs 1974). Intentions to vote for Goldwater in the 1964 US presidential election correlated 0.80 with self-reported voting choice when the intention was measured one month prior to the election and 0.89 when it was measured during the week preceding the election.

Additional support for the disruptive potential of temporal delay was reported in a study of weight loss (Sejwacz et al. 1980). A sample of college women indicated their intentions to perform eight weight-reducing behaviors (avoid snacking between meals, participate in sports on a regular basis, etc.) at the beginning of a two-month period and again one month later. Correlations were computed between initial intentions and reported behavior over the two-month period, and between subsequent intentions and reported behavior during the final month. As expected, intention–behavior correlations were stronger for the one-month period than for the two-month period. For example, the correlation between intention to avoid long periods of inactivity and performance of this behavior (as recorded by the women in weekly logs) was higher when the time period was one month ($r = 0.72$) than when it was two months ($r = 0.47$). Considering all eight behaviors, the average correlation increased from 0.51 for the two-month period to 0.67 for the one-month period.

Looking at the literature more generally, meta-analyses of intention–behavior correlations show the expected pattern over time, although the effect is not always significant. For example, in the area of condom use, prediction of behavior from intention was found to become significantly less accurate with the passage of time (Sheeran and Orbell 1998, see also Albarracín et al. 2001). The correlation between effect size (i.e. accuracy of prediction) and amount of time in weeks between assessment of intention and behavior was -0.59 in the Sheeran and Orbell (1998) analysis. In a review covering a broader range of behaviors (Randall and Wolff 1994), intention–behavior correlations declined from 0.65 to 0.40 for intervals of less than a day to one or more years, although this effect reached statistical significance only when objective rather than self-report measures of behavior were considered.

Instead of relying on time interval as a proxy for instability, some studies have assessed stability of intentions directly, and these studies have consistently found that the intention–behavior correlation declines substantially when intentions are unstable. In one of these investigations (Sheeran et al. 1999), undergraduate college students twice indicated their intentions to study over the vacation break, five weeks apart. After returning from the winter vacation, they reported on how many days a week they had actually studied. For participants whose intentions remained relatively stable during the five-week period prior to the vacation, the intention–behavior correlation was 0.58 whereas for participants with relatively unstable intentions, it was 0.08. Similar results were reported with respect to attending a health screening appointment and eating a low-fat diet (Conner et al. 2000).

Literal inconsistency   Even when measures of intention and behavior meet the criterion of compatibility and when the measure of intention is relatively stable over time, we sometimes find that some people do not act on their stated intentions. The gap between intentions and behavior in this case is an instance of literal inconsistency: people say they will do one thing yet do something else. Generally speaking, the pattern of literal inconsistency tends to be asymmetric such that people who do not intend to engage in a socially desirable behavior mostly act in accordance with their negative intentions, but people who intend to perform the behavior may or may not do so. For example, in a study of racial prejudice (Linn 1965), female students were asked to indicate whether they would be willing to release photos of themselves with an African American male for a variety of purposes related to improving race relations. Almost without exception, those who were unwilling to do so later signed very few releases. Among the participants who indicated a high level of willingness to release their photographs, however, only about one-half actually followed through on their intentions. Similarly, research in the health domain has found that participants who do not intend to use condoms, to undergo a cancer screening, or to exercise rarely if ever do so, but of those who intend to engage in these health-protective behaviors, between 26 percent and 57 percent fail to carry out their intentions (Sheeran 2002).

Perhaps the most ingenious explanation for literal inconsistency was offered by Donald Campbell (1963), who suggested that observed discrepancies between words and deeds may often be more apparent than real. He argued that verbal and overt responses to an object are both indicators of an underlying hypothetical disposition and that one of these responses may be more difficult to perform than the other. Using the LaPiere (1934) study described in Chapter 2 as an example, Campbell assumed that rejecting a Chinese couple in a face-to-face situation (overt behavior) is more difficult than rejecting a symbolic representation of 'members of the Chinese race' in response to a written inquiry. Individuals strongly prejudiced toward the Chinese would be expected to give a negative response in both situations, whereas individuals who are not at all prejudiced should provide a positive response in both. The apparent inconsistency in the LaPiere study reflects, according to Campbell, a moderate degree of prejudice toward the Chinese, sufficiently strong to produce the relatively easy verbal rejection in a letter (negative intention) but not strong enough to generate the more difficult overt rejection in a face-to-face encounter (overt behavior).

Campbell (1963, see Figure 5.1) argued that literal inconsistency arises because people with moderate dispositions tend to display behaviors consistent with the disposition when the behaviors are easy to perform (e.g. express an intention to exercise) but not when they are difficult to perform (e.g. actually engage in exercise). Although this argument is intuitively compelling, it has rarely been put to empirical test (Sheeran

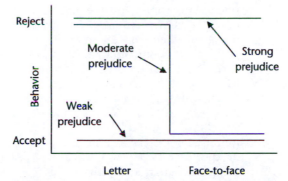

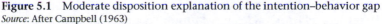

Figure 5.1   Moderate disposition explanation of the intention–behavior gap
Source: After Campbell (1963)

2002; Ajzen et al. 2004). Contrary to Campbell's thesis, research has found that participants who display literal inconsistency do not necessarily hold the expected moderate dispositions. In one experiment (Ajzen et al. 2004), participants could agree to contribute money to a scholarship fund under hypothetical as well as under real payment conditions. Literal inconsistency was shown by participants who agreed to make a contribution when the question was hypothetical but choose not to make a contribution in the real payment situation. The attitudes of these participants toward making a contribution to the scholarship fund were found to be no less favorable than those of participants who agreed to make a contribution under both payment conditions. Similar results were reported by Sheeran (2002) in a re-analysis of data from an earlier study (Sheeran and Orbell 2000) on the prediction of physical exercise.

Implementation intentions

Evidence for literal inconsistency challenges us to explain why some people fail to carry out the intentions they have formed. In some instances, when asked to explain why they failed to act on their intentions, people mention that they simply forgot or that it slipped their minds (Orbell et al. 1997; Sheeran and Orbell 1999). In those instances, a very effective means for closing the intention–behavior gap is to prompt people to form an implementation intention (Gollwitzer 1999). Simply asking people when, where, and how they will carry out their intentions can greatly increase the likelihood that they will do so. This was shown, for example, in a study of breast self-examination among female students and administrative staff (Orbell et al. 1997). Women in the implementation intention condition were asked to write down where and when they would perform breast self-examinations, whereas women in a control group did not formulate such an implementation intention. About one month later, the participants reported their behavior during the preceding month. Formation of an implementation intention was found to be highly effective. At the end of the one-month follow-up, 64 percent of women who had established implementation intentions reported that they had performed the self-examinations as opposed to only 14 percent in the no-intervention control group. All women in the implementation intention group who had indicated clear intentions to perform the examination reported actually doing so, whereas in the control group, of the women who intended to perform the examination, only 53 percent actually did.

The beneficial effects of implementation intentions have been found with respect to such normal, everyday activities as completing a project during Christmas vacation (Gollwitzer and Brandstätter 1997), taking a daily vitamin C pill (Sheeran and Orbell 1999), and eating healthy food (Verplanken and Faes 1999); as well as for disagreeable tasks, such as performing a breast self-examination (Orbell et al. 1997) and resuming functional activities following surgery (Orbell and Sheeran 2000). Formulating an implementation intention has been found of particular benefit for individuals with severe cognitive deficits, such as drug addicts undergoing withdrawal and schizophrenic patients (Gollwitzer and Brandstätter 1997).

According to Gollwitzer (1999; Gollwitzer and Schaal 1998), implementation intentions are effective because they allow people to delegate control of their goal-directed behaviors to the stimulus situation.[2] Formulation of an implementation intention is assumed to activate the mental representation of a specified situation and make it chronically accessible. Consistent with this assumption, implementation intentions are found to enhance vigilance for relevant situational cues which are well remembered and easily detected (Gollwitzer 1996; Orbell et al. 1997; Aarts et al. 1999). As a result, when the situational cues are encountered, initiation of the goal-directed action is expected to be swift, efficient, and to require no conscious intent, the hallmarks of automaticity (Bargh 1996).

Perhaps consistent with this account, implementation intentions may be effective because they improve memory for the behavioral intention. By specifying where, when, and how the behavior will be performed, implementation intentions provide a number of specific cues that can enhance recall of the intention and hence make it more likely that the intention will be carried out. Alternatively, it is possible to attribute the effectiveness of implementation intentions to a sense of commitment they engender. When people state explicitly – and publicly – that they will perform a behavior in a certain situation and at a certain point in time, they arguably make a commitment to carry out their intentions. And there is considerable evidence that making a commitment can greatly increase the likelihood that people will perform the behavior to which they have committed themselves (Kiesler 1971; Braver 1996; Cialdini 2001). Consistent with this interpretation, asking people to make an explicit commitment to return a brief survey concerning TV newscasts was found to be just as effective in helping them carry out their intentions, as was asking them to form an implementation intention (Ajzen et al. 2002). In fact, making a commitment was sufficient to produce a high rate of return, and adding an implementation intention did not further increase intention-consistent behavior. Thus, although there is strong evidence for the power of implementation intentions, more research is needed to determine the mechanism whereby such an intervention achieves its effectiveness.

THE CASE OF INCOMPLETE VOLITIONAL CONTROL

A number of investigators have made a distinction between performing a behavior, such as swimming, and attaining a goal, such as losing weight (Ajzen and Fishbein 1980; Bagozzi and Warshaw 1990; Bandura 1997). As we saw in Chapter 4, a behavioral criterion always contains an action element. In contrast, a goal – whether losing weight or passing a test – involves no specific action, although goal attainment may be attempted by performing a variety of specific behaviors. Thus, to lose weight, people may reduce food intake and work out at the gym; and to pass a test, they may memorize their class notes and take a preparatory course. However, actual goal attainment may also depend on other factors that are not under the person's direct control. The degree of success will thus depend not only on the person's intention, but also on such factors as inherent abilities and physiological dispositions as well as availability of requisite opportunities and resources. To the extent that people have the required opportunities and resources, and intend to perform the behavior, to that extent they should succeed in doing so.

At first glance, the problem of behavioral control may appear to apply only to goal attainment. Closer scrutiny reveals, however, that even behaviors, which can usually be executed (or not executed) at will, are sometimes subject to the influence of factors beyond one's control. Such a simple behavior as driving to the supermarket may be thwarted by mechanical trouble with the car. Conversely, with respect to some goals, such as locating your car in a parking lot, we usually encounter very few problems of control. Volitional control can thus best be viewed as a continuum. On one extreme are behaviors that encounter few if any problems of control. A good case in point is voting choice: once the voter has entered the voting booth, selection among the candidates can be done at will. On the other extreme are events, such as sneezing or lowering one's blood pressure, over which we have very little or no control. Most behaviors and goals fall somewhere in between those extremes. People usually encounter few problems of control when trying to attend a lecture or to read a book, but problems of control are more readily apparent when they try to overcome such powerful habits as smoking or drinking or when they set their sights on such difficult to attain goals as becoming a movie star. Viewed in this light it becomes clear that, strictly speaking, the performance of most intended behaviors, and the attainment of most desired goals, are subject to some degree of uncertainty (see Ajzen 1985).

Control factors

On the following pages we review some of the factors that can influence the degree of control a person has over a given behavior.

Internal factors

Various factors internal to an individual can influence successful performance of an intended action. Some of these factors are readily modified by
training and experience while others are more resistant to change.

Information, skills, and abilities A person who intends to perform a
behavior may, upon trying to do so, discover that he or she lacks the needed
information, skills, or abilities. Everyday life is replete with examples.
We may intend to convert another person to our own political views, to
help a boy with his mathematics, or to repair a malfunctioning video
recorder, but fail in our attempts because we lack the required verbal and
social skills, knowledge of mathematics, or mechanical aptitudes. To be
sure, with experience we tend to acquire some appreciation of our abilities;
yet new situations arise frequently, and failure to perform intended
behaviors or achieve our goals due to lack of requisite skills is the order of
the day.

Lack of ability in an unusual sense is illustrated in a study by Vinokur-
Kaplan (1978) who assessed a couple's intention to have another child next
year. When interviewed 12 months later, actually having given birth to a
child correlated 0.55 with intentions, a correlation which, although significant, is lower than the intention–behavior correlation observed in
many other contexts. Having another child is, of course, only partially
under volitional control since fecundity, miscarriage, and other factors also
mediate attainment of this goal.

Emotions and compulsions Insufficient skills, abilities, and information can
present problems of behavioral control, but it is usually assumed that, at
least in principle, these problems can be overcome. In contrast, some types
of behavior are subject to forces that seem to be largely beyond our control.
People sometimes appear unable to cease thinking or dreaming about
certain events, to stop stuttering, or to hold a tick in check. These com-
pulsive behaviors are performed despite intentions and concerted efforts to
the contrary.

Emotional behaviors seem to share some of the same characteristics.
Individuals are often not held responsible for behaviors performed under
stress or in the presence of strong emotions. We usually attribute little
behavioral control to a person who is 'overcome by emotion.' Violent acts
and poor performance are expected under such conditions, and there seems
to be little we can do about it.

In sum, as we move beyond purely volitional acts, various internal factors
may influence successful performance of intended behavior or attainment of desired goals. It may be fairly easy to gain control over some of
these factors, as when we acquire the requisite information or skills. Other
factors, such as intense emotions, stress, or compulsions, are more difficult
to neutralize.

External factors

Also impinging on a person's control over attainment of behavioral goals
are situational or environmental factors external to the individual. These

factors determine the extent to which circumstances facilitate or interfere with performance of the behavior.

Opportunity It takes little imagination to appreciate the importance of incidental factors or opportunities for successful execution of an intended action. An intention to see a play cannot be carried through if tickets are sold out on a particular night or if the person is involved in a serious accident on the way to the theater. The study of blood donation (Pomazal and Jaccard 1976) mentioned earlier provides relevant examples. When students who had failed to carry out their intentions to donate blood were interviewed, they often indicated that such unforeseen obligations or events as exams, job interviews, and coming down with a cold had prevented them from participating in the blood drive. Given the presence of many disruptive factors, it is hardly surprising that the correlation between intention and behavior was found to be of only moderate magnitude ($r = 0.52$). In some instances, students came to give blood but were turned away because of overcrowding. When these individuals were considered to have performed the behavior, the intention–behavior correlation increased to 0.59.

At first glance, lack of opportunity may appear equivalent to occurrence of unanticipated events that bring about changes in intentions, as discussed previously. While it is true that in the absence of appropriate opportunities people may come to change their intentions, there is an important difference between the two cases. When new information becomes available after intentions have been formed, the person may no longer be interested in carrying out the original intention. By way of contrast, lack of opportunity disrupts an attempted behavior. Here, the person tries to carry out the intention but fails because circumstances prevent it. Although the immediate intention will be affected, the basic desire to perform the behavior need not have changed.

Consider again the intention to see a particular play. Reading a negative review or being told by a friend that the play is not worth seeing may influence intentions such that a person is no longer interested in seeing the play on the night in question or on any other night, unless and until other events again cause a change of mind. Contrast this with the person who intends to see the play, drives to the theater, but is told that there are no more tickets available. The environmental obstacle to performance of the behavior will force a change of plan; but it need not change the person's intention. Instead, it may merely cause the person to try again on a different night.

Note also that lack of opportunity poses a problem only when performance of a behavior on a single occasion is to be predicted. Behavioral tendencies across occasions are relatively unaffected because appropriate opportunities are likely to be present on at least some occasions.

Dependence on others Whenever performance of a behavior depends on the actions of other people, there exists the potential for incomplete control over behaviors or goals. A good example of behavioral interdependence is the case of cooperation. One can cooperate with another person only if that person is also willing to cooperate. Experimental studies of cooperation and competition in laboratory games have provided ample evidence for this interdependence. For example, Ajzen and Fishbein (1970) reported correlations of 0.92 and 0.89 between cooperative strategy choices of the players in two Prisoner's Dilemma games. These high correlations suggest that a person's tendency to make cooperative choices depends on reciprocation by the other player. Similarly, use of a condom during sexual intercourse usually depends on the cooperation of one's partner, one of the factors that can undermine safer sex practices (see Kashima et al. 1993; Sheeran et al. 1999).

As is true of time and opportunity, inability to behave in accordance with intention because of dependence on others need not affect the underlying motivation. Often an individual who encounters difficulties related to interpersonal dependence may be able to perform the desired behavior in cooperation with a different partner. Sometimes, however, this may not be a viable course of action. A wife's adamant refusal to have more children will usually cause the husband eventually to abandon his plan to enlarge the family, rather than shift his effort to a different partner.

In short, lack of opportunity and dependence on others often lead only to temporary changes in intentions. When circumstances prevent performance of a behavior, the person may wait for a better opportunity and when another person fails to cooperate, a more compliant partner may be sought. However, when repeated efforts to perform the behavior result in failure, more fundamental changes in intentions can be expected.

Perceived behavioral control

The above discussion makes clear that many factors can disrupt the intention–behavior relation. Although volitional control is more likely to present a problem for some behaviors than for others, personal deficiencies and external obstacles can interfere with the performance of any behavior. Collectively, these factors represent people's *actual* control or lack of control over the behavior. (See also the discussions of 'facilitating factors' by Triandis, 1977, 'action control' by Kuhl, 1985, 'resources' by Liska, 1984, and 'the context of opportunity' by Sarver, 1983.) Given the problem's ubiquity, a behavioral intention can best be interpreted as an intention to *try* performing a certain behavior. A father's plan to take his children fishing next weekend is best viewed as an intention to try to make time for this activity, to prepare the required equipment, secure a fishing license, and so forth. Successful performance of the intended behavior is contingent on the person's control over the many factors that may prevent it. Of course, the conscious realization that we can only try to perform a given behavior will arise primarily when questions of control over the behavior are salient. Thus, people say that they will try to quit smoking or lose weight, but that they intend to go to church on Sunday. Nevertheless, even the intention to attend Sunday worship services must be viewed as an intention to try performing this behavior since factors beyond the individual's control can prevent its successful execution.

Clearly, then, a measure of intention is likely to predict performance of a behavior or goal attainment only to the extent that these criteria are under volitional control. Some of the relatively low correlations between intentions and behavior reported in the literature may occur when investigators try to predict a criterion over which people have relatively little volitional control. This also implies, however, that we should be able to improve prediction of behavior if we consider not only intention but also the degree to which an individual actually has control over performing the behavior. Volitional control is expected to moderate the intention–behavior relation such that the effect of intention on behavior is stronger when actual control is high rather than low. In fact, when most people actually have control over performance of a behavior, intention by itself should permit good prediction. It is only when people vary in the degree to which they have control can we expect that taking into account control will improve behavioral prediction (Ajzen 1985).

Unfortunately, it is not at all clear what constitutes actual control over a behavior or how to assess it. Although we may be able to measure some aspects of actual control, in most instances we lack sufficient information about all the relevant factors that may facilitate or impede performance of a given behavior. However, it is possible that people's *perceptions* of the extent to which they have control over a behavior quite accurately reflect their actual control. This sense of self-efficacy or *perceived behavioral control*, discussed in Chapter 4, refers to the perceived ease or difficulty of performing the behavior and it is assumed to reflect past experience as well as anticipated impediments and obstacles. To the extent that perceived behavioral control is veridical, it can serve as a proxy for actual control and be used to improve prediction of behavior.

Numerous studies have shown that taking into account perceived behavioral control can indeed improve prediction of behavior. Although, conceptually, perceived control is expected to *moderate* the intention–behavior relation, in practice most investigators have looked at the additive effects of intention and perceptions of control.[3] Meta-analyses that have examined the contribution of perceived behavioral control for a wide variety of behaviors have found that, on average, perceived behavioral control explains approximately an additional 2 percent of the variance in behavior (Cheung and Chan 2000; Armitage and Conner 2001), a small though significant increase. Of course, as noted earlier, we would not expect perceived behavioral control to be an important predictor for every type of behavior. When volitional control is high, intentions are good predictors of behavior, and including a measure of perceived behavioral control accounts for little if any additional variance. When behavior is not under complete volitional control, however, measuring perceptions of control can make a valuable contribution.

In the first phase of a study designed to test this idea (Madden et al. 1992), college students rated their likely control over performance of various common activities, such as exercising regularly, getting a good night's sleep, doing laundry, and going shopping with a friend. Based on these ratings, 10 activities were selected that varied widely in terms of the mean rating of perceived behavioral control. In the second phase, a new student sample indicated their intentions to perform each behavior in the next two weeks as well as their perceived control over doing so. Finally, two weeks later, they were recontacted and asked to report how often they had performed each of the behaviors. Multiple regression analyses were performed to examine the added contribution of perceived behavioral control to the prediction of behavior, over and above the prediction afforded by behavioral intentions. Across all 10 behaviors, accuracy of prediction increased significantly from a correlation of 0.53 to a correlation of 0.62. More importantly, the contribution of perceived behavioral control to the prediction of behavior increased as the mean level of perceived control declined. The correlation between the residual effect of perceived control on behavior (over and above intentions) had a correlation of −0.63 with the mean level of perceived behavioral control.

Consistent with this line of reasoning, it is found that the amount of variance in behavior explained by perceived behavioral control varies significantly across behavioral domains (Notani 1998; Cheung and Chan 2000). For example, in the case of regularly attending an exercise class (Courneya and McAuley 1995), the mean level of perceived behavioral control was relatively high and it explained only 1 percent of additional variance in behavior. In contrast, in a sample of smokers who, on average, perceived that they had relatively little control over not smoking, the measure of perceived behavioral control accounted for an additional 12 percent of the variance in smoking behavior (Godin et al. 1992; see also Madden et al. 1992).

We can gain insight into the prediction of behavior from intentions and perceptions of behavioral control by examining the results of two studies (Schifter and Ajzen 1985; Ajzen and Madden 1986) in which attempts were made to predict attainment of three behavioral goals: attending lectures on a regular basis, getting an 'A' in a course, and losing weight. With respect to regular class attendance, both intentions and perceived control correlated significantly with actual behavior. A hierarchical regression analysis, however, showed that addition of perceived behavioral control did not improve prediction of behavior significantly. This was expected since class attendance is a behavior over which students have considerable volitional control. The addition of a (subjective) measure of control thus added little information of value in the prediction of actual behavior.

In contrast, losing weight does pose greater problems of volitional control. As would therefore be expected, the results with respect to attainment of this goal showed the relevance of perceived behavioral control quite dramatically. Both intentions and perceived control correlated significantly with goal attainment, but perceived control was the better predictor of the two. The addition of perceived behavioral control on the second step of a hierarchical regression analysis improved prediction significantly, raising the multiple correlation with goal attainment from 0.25 to 0.44.

Perhaps the most interesting results, however, emerged in the study on getting an 'A' in a course. The questionnaire assessing the different constructs of the theory of planned behavior was administered twice, once at the beginning of the semester and again toward the end. Perception of control over getting an 'A' should, of course, become more accurate as the end of the semester approaches. As an addition to intentions, the later measure of perceived behavioral control should therefore contribute to the prediction of course grades more than the earlier measure. The data lent support to this hypothesis. Although both measures, intentions and perceived control, gained in predictive accuracy, the more dramatic gain was observed with respect to the latter. Moreover, the hierarchical regression analysis showed that whereas with the data obtained early in the semester, only intention had a significant effect on behavior, with the later data, both intentions and perceived behavioral control had significant regression coefficients. Thus, the addition of perceived behavioral control had no effect on the accuracy of behavioral prediction for the data obtained early in the semester, but it raised the correlation significantly from 0.39 to 0.45 for the data obtained toward the end of the semester.

SPONTANEOUS INTENTIONS

In Chapter 4 we noted that with frequent performance, behaviors tend to become routine or habitual such that they can be performed with little conscious effort. In fact, as we perform our daily routines we are rarely aware of forming an intention to do so. It stands to reason that, for relatively novel behaviors, people engage in a certain amount of deliberation before they form an intention to engage or not engage in the behavior under consideration. After repeated opportunities for performance, however, deliberation is no longer required because the intention is activated spontaneously in the behavior-relevant situation (Ajzen and Fishbein 2000; Ajzen 2002). Thus, once we have become accustomed to taking a certain route to work, we don't have to stop every morning anew to decide how to proceed. Instead, the intention to drive the familiar route is spontaneously activated.

Some theorists (e.g. Ouellette and Wood 1998; Gollwitzer 1999; Aarts and Dijksterhuis 2000) go one step further in their analysis of habitual behavior. They argue that habits are established when people have frequent opportunities to perform a behavior under identical or very similar circumstances. Once a habit has been established under these conditions, initiation of the behavior is said to come under the control of external or internal stimulus cues. In the presence of these cues, the behavior is automatically activated without cognitive intervention. Consider, for example, people's early morning routines to brush their teeth in their bathrooms. The situational cues present in the bathroom (sink, faucet, mirror, etc.) are assumed to automatically elicit the tooth-brushing practice without the intervention of a behavioral intention, even a spontaneously activated one. This analysis implies that intentions become increasingly irrelevant as a behavior habituates. In other words, a measure of intention should be a good predictor of relatively novel or unpracticed behaviors, but it should lose its predictive validity when it comes to routine or habitual responses in familiar situations.

Empirical findings lend little support to this hypothesis. Ouellette and Wood (1998) performed a meta-analysis on 15 data sets from studies that reported intention–behavior correlations. They classified each data set as dealing with a behavior that can be performed frequently (e.g. seat belt use, coffee drinking, class attendance) or infrequently (e.g. flu shots, blood donation, nuclear protest). Contrary to the habit hypothesis, prediction of behavior from intentions was found to be quite accurate for both types of behavior (mean $r = 0.59$ and $r = 0.67$ for high- and low-opportunity behaviors, respectively). The difference between these two correlations is not statistically significant. The same conclusion arose from a similar meta-analysis based on 51 data sets (Sheeran and Sutton, unpublished data).[4] The mean intention–behavior correlation across all 51 studies was 0.49; for behaviors that could be performed infrequently (once or twice a year), the correlation was 0.51; and it was 0.53 for high-opportunity behaviors that could be performed daily or once a week.

A different way of looking at the effect of habit on the predictive validity of intentions is to compare behaviors performed in a stable context to behaviors performed in an unstable context. Because habit formation depends on stable stimulus cues, the intention–behavior correlation would be expected to decline for behaviors performed in a stable context. The meta-analysis by Sheeran and Sutton examined this possibility as well. The investigators rated the behaviors in the 51 data sets as being performed either in a relatively stable context (e.g. study at home) or an unstable context (e.g. get immunized). The results of the meta-analysis showed differences contrary to what would be predicted by the habit hypothesis. For behaviors performed in an unstable context (where intentions should be most relevant), the mean intention–behavior correlation was 0.40, compared to a mean intention–behavior correlation of 0.56 for behaviors performed in a stable context.

It is impossible, however, to derive any definite conclusions from these kinds of meta-analyses because the high-opportunity behaviors differed in substance from the low-opportunity behaviors, as did the behaviors performed in stable and unstable contexts. The behaviors that were compared may thus have differed not only in performance opportunities or context stability but also in degree of importance, familiarity, or other properties that could affect the results.

To address this problem, Ouellette and Wood (1998) conducted an original study that was designed to demonstrate the moderating effect of contextual stability on the prediction of a target behavior from intentions. The behaviors selected were two high-opportunity activities: watching TV and recycling. To estimate stability of the supporting context, participants were asked to list the activities (if any) they always performed prior to engaging in each of these behavior. On the basis of these responses, they were divided into groups of high and low context stability. For such high-opportunity behaviors as watching TV and recycling, a stable context should allow strong habits to be formed, whereas an unstable context should not. The automatic habit perspective therefore suggests that intentions should be relatively good predictors of behavior in an unstable context, but in a stable context, where the behavior is presumably under direct control of stimulus cues, their predictive validity should decline. The results of the study did not support these predictions. With respect to watching TV, the intention–behavior correlation was higher in the unstable context ($r = 0.63$) than in the stable context ($r = 0.46$), but a re-analysis showed that the difference between these two correlations was not statistically significant ($z = 0.96$). Moreover, there was little difference with respect to recycling. Here, the prediction of later behavior from intentions was actually slightly better in the stable context ($r = 0.48$) than in the unstable context ($r = 0.43$). Thus, neither the meta-analyses described earlier nor this primary research provides clear support for the idea that habitual behavior is activated automatically, independent of a spontaneously activated behavioral intention.

SUMMARY AND CONCLUSIONS

We have seen in this chapter that, as a general rule, when people have control over performance of a behavior, they tend to act in accordance with their intentions. Intention–behavior correlations are usually substantial, even though relatively low correlations are sometimes observed. The predictive validity of intentions can suffer when the measure of intention is not perfectly compatible with the observed behavior, as when we try to use intentions to engage in a category of behaviors (e.g. the intention to study) to predict a particular behavior that is a member of the category (e.g. reviewing class notes). We also saw that it is important to take into account the intention's stability over time because changes in intentions tend to lower their predictive validity.

When a behavior is not under complete volitional control, factors internal or external to the individual can prevent performance of an intended behavior. Although objective measures of actual control are usually not available, we can assess perceptions of behavioral control. To the extent that people are reasonably realistic in their assessments of control, such measures can serve as proxies for actual control and help improve prediction of behavior.

Finally, we saw that behavior tends to become routine or habituate with repeated performance. However, research to date suggests that even when this is the case, intentions continue to be good predictors of behavior. This suggests that, rather than coming under the control of stimulus cues, routine behaviors may be controlled by behavioral intentions that are spontaneously activated in the familiar context.

NOTES

1 Note also that, because all participants in this study were enrolled in an exercise program, the measures of exercise intentions and behavior were likely to have suffered from restriction of range.
2 According to Gollwitzer (personal communication), implementation intentions can also transfer control over a behavior to internal cues, such as moods or emotions.
3 The reason for this practice is that empirically, even when an interaction is present in the data, statistical regression analyses often reveal only main effects. To obtain a statistically significant interaction requires that intention and perceived control scores cover the full range of the measurement scale. For most behaviors, however, a majority of respondents fall on one or the other side of these continua.

4 I am grateful to Paschal Sheeran for providing the results of these meta-analyses.

SUGGESTIONS FOR FURTHER READING

Kuhl, J., and Beckmann, J. (eds) (1985) *Action-Control: From Cognition to Behavior*. Heidelberg: Springer. In this book, several theorists present their ideas on the problems of volitional control over behavior and the factors that may interfere with such control.

Sheeran, P. (2002) Intention–behavior relations: a conceptual and empirical review. In W. Stroebe and M. Hewstone (eds), *European Review of Social Psychology* (Vol. 12, pp. 1–36). Chichester: Wiley. This paper reviews empirical research on the relation between intentions and behavior.

SIX

EXPLAINING INTENTIONS AND BEHAVIOR

Reason has always existed, but not always in a reasonable form.

(Karl Marx)

In the previous chapter we saw that intentions are generally good predictors of many different kinds of behavior. However, the fact that intentions often predict behavior quite accurately does not in itself provide much information about the reasons for the behavior. Beyond confirming that the behavior in question is to some extent under volitional control, it is not very illuminating to discover that people do what they intend to do. Because we are interested in *understanding* human behavior, not merely in predicting it, we must try to identify the determinants of behavioral intentions. Ajzen and Fishbein's (1980; Fishbein and Ajzen 1975) theory of reasoned action, mentioned briefly in Chapter 2, was designed to accomplish this goal with respect to volitional behavior; that is, the theory was concerned with the causal antecedents of intentions to perform behaviors over which people have sufficient control. An extension of this model, the *theory of planned behavior* (Ajzen 1985, 1991), addresses the possibility of incomplete volitional control by incorporating the additional construct of perceived behavioral control.

A THEORY OF PLANNED BEHAVIOR

As was true of the theory of reasoned action, the theory of planned behavior is based on the assumption that human beings usually behave in a sensible manner; that they take account of available information and implicitly or explicitly consider the implications of their actions. Consistent with this assumption, and in line with the findings reported in Chapter 5, the theory postulates that a person's intention to perform (or not to perform) a behavior is the most important immediate determinant of that action.

According to the theory of planned behavior, intentions (and behaviors) are a function of three basic determinants, one personal in nature, one reflecting social influence, and a third dealing with issues of control. The personal factor is the individual's *attitude toward the behavior*, first encountered in Chapter 4. Unlike general attitudes toward institutions, people, or objects that have traditionally been studied by social psychologists, this attitude is the individual's positive or negative evaluation of performing the particular behavior of interest. The second determinant of intention is the person's perception of social pressure to perform or not perform the behavior under consideration. Since it deals with perceived normative prescriptions, this factor is termed *subjective norm*. Finally, the third determinant of intentions is the sense of self-efficacy or ability to perform the behavior of interest, termed *perceived behavioral control*. This factor was also discussed in Chapter 4 and, again, in Chapter 5. Generally speaking, people intend to perform a behavior when they evaluate it positively, when they experience social pressure to perform it, and when they believe that they have the means and opportunities to do so.

The theory assumes that the relative importance of attitude toward the behavior, subjective norm, and perceived behavioral control depends in part on the intention under investigation. For some intentions attitudinal considerations are more important than normative considerations, while for other intentions normative considerations predominate. Similarly, as we noted in Chapter 5, perceived behavioral control is more important for some behaviors than for others. In some instances, only one or two of the factors are needed to explain the intention, while in others, all three factors are important determinants. In addition, the relative weights of the three factors may vary from one person to another, or from one population to another. Figure 6.1 is a graphic representation of the theory of planned behavior as described up to this point.

Note that the theory of planned behavior does not deal directly with the amount of control a person actually has in a given situation; instead, it considers the possible effects of *perceived* behavioral control on achievement of behavioral goals. Whereas intentions reflect primarily an individual's willingness to try enacting a given behavior, perceived control is likely to take into account some of the realistic constraints that may exist. To the extent that perceptions of behavioral control correspond reasonably

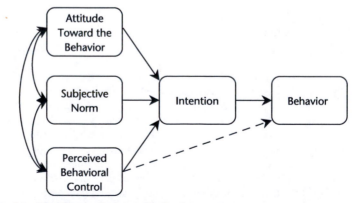

Figure 6.1   The theory of planned behavior

well to actual control, they should provide useful information over and above expressed intentions.

Figure 6.1 shows two important features of the theory of planned behavior. First, the theory assumes that perceived behavioral control has motivational implications for intentions. People who believe that they have neither the resources nor the opportunities to perform a certain behavior are unlikely to form strong behavioral intentions to engage in it even if they hold favorable attitudes toward the behavior and believe that important others would approve of their performing the behavior. We thus expect an association between perceived behavioral control and intention that is not mediated by attitude and subjective norm. In Figure 6.1 this expectation is represented by the arrow linking perceived behavioral control to intention.

The second feature of interest is the possibility of a direct link between perceived behavioral control and behavior. As noted in Chapter 5, in many instances performance of a behavior depends not only on motivation to do so but also on adequate control over the behavior in question. It follows that perceived behavioral control can help predict goal attainment independent of behavioral intention to the extent that it reflects actual control with some degree of accuracy. In other words, perceived behavioral control can influence behavior indirectly, via intentions, and it can also be used to predict behavior directly because it may be considered a proxy or partial substitute for a measure of actual control.

Of course, in some situations perceived behavioral control is not particularly realistic. This is likely to be the case when the individual has little information about the behavior, when requirements or available resources have changed, or when new and unfamiliar elements have entered into the situation. Under those conditions a measure of perceived behavioral control may add little to accuracy of behavioral prediction. The broken arrow in Figure 6.1 indicates that the link between perceived behavioral control and behavior is expected to emerge only when there is some agreement between perceptions of control and the person's actual control over the behavior.

Predicting intentions

Since its inception about 20 years ago, hundreds of studies have applied the theory of planned behavior in a great variety of behavioral domains. (For an on-line list of publications, see Ajzen 2005.) This work has provided considerable support for the theory. In Chapter 5 we saw that, consistent with the theory, behavior can usually be predicted with considerable accuracy from intentions and perceptions of behavioral control. In fact, many of the studies that reported these data were conducted in the context of the theory of planned behavior. In the present chapter we step back to examine the antecedents of intentions, information that will further our understanding of the cognitive underpinnings of human social behavior.

A great number of studies have provided strong support for the proposition that intentions to perform a behavior can be predicted from attitudes toward the behavior, subjective norms, and perceptions of behavioral control. Most of these studies have used multiple linear regression or structural equation analyses to estimate, in terms of a multiple correlation (R), the simultaneous predictive power of the three predictors, as well as their relative contributions to the prediction in terms of standardized regression or path coefficients. Table 6.1 shows the results obtained in a selective sample of investigations. It can be seen that, with respect to a variety of different intentions, consideration of attitudes, subjective norms, and perceived behavioral control permitted highly accurate prediction. The multiple correlations in the studies listed ranged from 0.62 to 0.89. The relative importance of the three predictors is revealed by inspecting columns four, five, and six. With only one exception (subjective norm in the case of leisure activities), all three factors made significant contributions to the prediction of intentions, although their relative importance varied from one intention to another. In some cases (e.g. hunting), attitudes explained most of the variance in intentions, whereas in others, much of the variance was accounted for by perceived behavioral control (e.g. donating blood). Subjective norms generally accounted for less variance than the other two predictors.

Taking a broader perspective, several meta-analyses of the empirical literature provide good support for the theory of planned behavior (see Godin and Kok 1996; Sheeran and Taylor 1999; Albarracín et al. 2001; Armitage and Conner 2001; Hagger et al. 2002b). For a wide range of behaviors, attitudes are found to correlate well with intentions; across the different meta-analyses, the mean correlations range from 0.45 to 0.60. For the prediction of intentions from subjective norms, these correlations range from 0.34 to 0.42, and for the prediction of intention from perceived behavioral control, the range is 0.35 to 0.46. The multiple correlations for the prediction of intentions are found to range from 0.63 to 0.71.

Predicting behavioral goals

The incorporation of perceived behavioral control into the theory of planned behavior permits us to deal not only with volitional behaviors but also with behaviors or behavioral goals over which people have only limited volitional control. For example, in an early test (Schifter and Ajzen 1985), the theory of planned behavior was applied to the prediction of weight loss intentions, and actual weight reduction, among female college students. Attitudes toward losing weight during the next six weeks were assessed by means of several evaluative semantic differential scales. To measure subjective norms, participants were asked to indicate, again on 7-point scales, whether people who were important to them thought they should lose weight over the next six weeks, and whether those people would approve or disapprove of their losing weight. As a measure of perceived behavioral control, participants indicated, on a scale from 0 to 100, the likelihood that if they tried they would manage to lose weight over the next six weeks and their estimates that an attempt on their part to lose weight would be successful. The final measure of interest for present purposes dealt with intentions to lose weight over the next six weeks. Each woman indicated, on several 7-point scales, her intention to try to reduce weight and the intensity of her decision.

Table 6.1 Prediction of intentions from attitude toward the behavior (A_B), subjective norm (SN), and perceived behavioral control (PBC)

Intention	Correlation coefficients			Regression coefficients			
	A_B	SN	PBC	A_B	SN	PBC	R
Physical exercise (Courneya 1995)	0.51	0.47	0.48	0.22	0.17	0.18	0.62
Hunting (Hrubes et al. 2001)	0.91	0.89	0.75	0.58	0.37	0.07	0.93
Recycling of glass (Lüdemann 1997)	0.68	0.62	0.62	0.44	0.17	0.39	0.77
Dropping out of school (Davis et al. 2002)	0.47	0.47	0.62	0.22	0.28	0.44	0.71
Engaging in leisure activities (Ajzen and Driver 1992)	0.61	0.70	0.80	0.28	0.10*	0.66	0.89
Buying stocks (East 1993: Study 1)	0.54	0.54	0.44	0.23	0.29	0.35	0.71
Contributing to a scholarship fund (Ajzen et al. 2004, total sample)	0.51	0.59	0.72	0.13	0.27	0.51	0.77
Donating blood (Giles and Cairns 1995)	0.55	0.22	0.73	0.25	0.11	0.61	0.78
Attending class (Ajzen and Madden 1986)	0.51	0.35	0.57	0.32	0.16	0.44	0.68
Using cannabis (Conner and McMillan 1999)	0.70	0.55	0.69	0.42	0.11	0.43	0.81

Note: * Not significant; all other coefficients $p < 0.05$.

The first row in Table 6.2 shows the correlations of intentions to lose weight with attitudes, subjective norms, and perceived behavioral control. It can be seen that all three predictors correlated significantly with intention. A hierarchical regression analysis was performed on intentions to lose weight in which attitudes and subjective norms were entered on the first step, and perceived behavioral control on the second. This analysis reveals the effect of perceived behavioral control on intentions after the effects of attitude and subjective norm were statistically removed. The results of the analysis confirmed the importance of perceived behavioral control as a determinant of intentions to lose weight. Although the multiple correlation of intentions with attitudes and subjective norms alone was quite high ($R = 0.65$), it increased significantly, to 0.72, with the addition of perceived behavioral control. All three independent variables had significant regression coefficients, indicating that each made an independent contribution to the prediction of weight loss intentions.

The importance of perceived control over a behavioral goal has also been demonstrated in the context of scholastic performance (Ajzen and Madden 1986). In one part of the investigation, undergraduate college students enrolled in upper division courses expressed, at the beginning of the semester, their intentions to attempt getting an 'A' grade in the course, as well as their attitudes, subjective norms, and perceived control over this behavioral goal. The second row in Table 6.2 shows the correlations of intentions to get an 'A' with the direct measures of attitudes, subjective norms, and perceived behavioral control. A hierarchical regression analysis revealed that attitudes and perceived behavioral control each had a significant effect on intention. On the basis of attitude toward the behavior and subjective norm alone, the multiple correlation with intention was 0.48 ($p < 0.01$). The introduction of perceived behavioral control on the second step of the regression analysis raised the multiple correlation significantly, to the level of 0.65.

Losing weight and getting an 'A' in a course are both behavioral goals over which people clearly have only limited volitional control. In addition to the desire to lose weight, people have to be familiar with an appropriate diet or exercise regimen, and they have to be capable of adhering to the diet or exercise program in the face of distractions and temptations. Similarly, getting an 'A' in a course depends not only on strong motivation but also on intellectual ability, availability of sufficient time for study, resisting temptations to engage in activities more attractive than studying, and so

Table 6.2 Correlations of intention (I) with attitude toward the behavior (A_B), subjective norm (SN), and perceived behavioral control (PBC)

Behavioral goal	$A_B - I$	$SN - I$	$PBC - I$
Losing weight	0.62	0.44	0.36
Getting an 'A'	0.48	0.11*	0.44
Attending class	0.51	0.35	0.57

Note: * Not significant; all other correlations $p < 0.05$.
Source: From Schifter and Ajzen (1985) and Ajzen and Madden (1986)

on. It is not surprising, therefore, that in light of these problems, perceived behavioral control is found to influence intentions to pursue or not to pursue the behavioral goal.

There is also evidence, however, that even when problems of volitional control are much less apparent, people's intentions are affected by their control beliefs. In the investigation by Ajzen and Madden (1986) records were kept of students' attendance of eight class lectures following administration of a questionnaire. The questionnaire contained measures of intention to attend classes regularly, attitudes toward this behavior, subjective norms, and perceived behavioral control. In the third row of Table 6.2 it can be seen that perceived behavioral control correlated significantly with intentions, as did attitudes and subjective norms. A hierarchical regression analysis showed that on the basis of attitudes and subjective norms alone, the multiple correlation with intentions was 0.55 ($p < 0.01$). However, addition of perceived behavioral control on the second step improved the prediction significantly, resulting in a multiple correlation of 0.68.

The informational foundation of behavior

For many practical purposes this level of explanation may be sufficient. We can to some extent account for people's intentions and actions by examining their attitudes toward the behavior, their subjective norms, their perceptions of control, and the relative importance of these factors. However, for a more complete understanding it is necessary to explore why people hold certain attitudes, subjective norms, and perceptions of control over a behavior.

Antecedents of attitudes toward the behavior

In Chapter 2 we discussed, in general terms, the formation of attitudes within the framework of the theory of planned behavior. There we showed how evaluation of any object follows reasonably from the beliefs we hold about the object. We can now apply these ideas to the formation of attitudes toward a behavior. According to the theory of planned behavior, attitude toward a behavior is determined by accessible beliefs about the consequences of the behavior, termed *behavioral beliefs*. Each behavioral belief links the behavior to a certain outcome, or to some other attribute such as the cost incurred by performing the behavior. For example, a person may believe that 'going on a low sodium diet' (the behavior) 'reduces blood pressure,' 'leads to a change in life style,' 'severely restricts the range of approved foods,' and so forth (outcomes). The attitude toward the behavior is determined by the person's evaluation of the outcomes associated with the behavior and by the strength of these associations. As we saw in Chapter 2, the evaluation of each salient outcome contributes to the attitude in proportion to the person's subjective probability that the behavior will produce the outcome in question. By multiplying belief strength and outcome evaluation, and summing the resulting products, we obtain an estimate of the attitude toward the behavior, an estimate based on the person's accessible beliefs about the behavior. This expectancy-value model is described symbolically in Equation 6.1, where A_B stands for attitude toward behavior B; b_i is the behavioral belief (subjective probability) that performing behavior B will lead to outcome i; e_i is the evaluation of outcome i; and the sum is over the number of behavioral beliefs accessible at the time. It can be seen that, generally speaking, a person who believes that performing a given behavior will lead to mostly positive outcomes will hold a favorable attitude toward performing the behavior, while a person who believes that performing the behavior will lead to mostly negative outcomes will hold an unfavorable attitude.

$$A_B \propto \sum b_i e_i \qquad\qquad (6.1)$$

Many studies have reported data consistent with the expectancy-value model of attitude described in Equation 6.1. For example, King (1975) assessed behavioral beliefs concerning the advantages and disadvantages of attending church services at least every two weeks as well as evaluations of these outcomes. Responses were used to compute an estimate of attitude toward attending church services in accordance with Equation 6.1. In addition, King used an evaluative semantic differential to obtain a direct measure of the same attitude. The correlation between the direct evaluation of the behavior and the belief-based measure was found to be 0.69. In a meta-analysis of research on condom use (Albarracín et al. 2001), the mean correlation between direct and belief-based measures of attitude was found to be 0.56; and in a meta-analysis of 42 data sets covering a variety of different behaviors (Armitage and Conner 2001), the mean correlation was 0.50.

Antecedents of subjective norms

Subjective norms, the second major determinant of intentions in the theory of planned behavior, are also assumed to be a function of beliefs, but beliefs of a different kind, namely the person's beliefs that specific individuals or groups approve or disapprove of performing the behavior; or that these social referents themselves engage or do not engage in it. For many behaviors, the important referents include a person's parents, spouse, close friends, coworkers, and, depending on the behavior involved, perhaps such experts as physicians or tax accountants. The beliefs that underlie subjective norms are termed *normative beliefs*. Generally speaking, people who believe that most referents with whom they are motivated to comply think they should perform the behavior will perceive social pressure to do so. Conversely, people who believes that most referents with whom they are motivated to comply would disapprove of their performing the behavior will have a subjective norm that puts pressure on them to avoid performing the behavior. The relation between normative beliefs and subjective norm is expressed symbolically in Equation 6.2. Here, SN is the subjective norm; n_i is the normative belief concerning referent i; m_i is the person's motivation to comply with referent i; and the sum is over the number of accessible normative beliefs.

$$SN \propto \sum n_i m_i \tag{6.2}$$

Subjective norms can be assessed in a direct manner by asking respondents to judge how likely it is that most people who are important to them would approve of their performing a given behavior. Such direct measures have been compared with belief-based estimates of subjective norms, computed in accordance with Equation 6.2. Correlations between the two types of measures are found to be of about the same magnitude as those obtained for the relation between behavioral beliefs and attitudes. In their meta-analysis of the literature, Armitage and Conner (2001) reported a correlation of 0.50 between direct and belief-based measures of subjective norm.

Antecedents of perceived behavioral control

The final major predictor in the theory of planned behavior, perceived behavioral control, is also assumed to be a function of beliefs, this time beliefs about the presence or absence of factors that facilitate or impede performance of the behavior. These beliefs may be based in part on past experience with the behavior, but they will usually also be influenced by second-hand information about the behavior, by observing the experiences of acquaintances and friends, and by other factors that increase or reduce the perceived difficulty of performing the behavior in question. The more required resources and opportunities individuals think they possess, and the fewer obstacles or impediments they anticipate, the greater should be their perceived control over the behavior. As with behavioral and normative beliefs, it is possible to separate out these control beliefs and treat them as partially independent determinants of intentions. Just as behavioral beliefs concerning consequences of a behavior are viewed as determining attitudes, and normative beliefs are viewed as determining subjective norms, so beliefs about resources and opportunities may be viewed as underlying perceived behavioral control.

In their totality, these *control beliefs* lead to the perception that one has or does not have the capacity to carry out the behavior, i.e. perceived behavioral control. Equation 6.3 shows the relation between control beliefs and perceived behavioral control in symbolic form. In this equation, *PBC* is perceived behavioral control; c_i is the control belief that a given factor i will be present; p_i is the power of factor i to facilitate or inhibit performance of the behavior; and the sum is over the number of accessible control beliefs.

$$PBC \propto \sum c_i p_i \tag{6.3}$$

It is possible to obtain a direct measure of perceived behavioral control by asking people whether they believe that they are capable of performing a behavior of interest, whether they believe that doing so is completely under their control, and so forth. In support of the model shown in Equation 6.3, such direct measures tend to correlate quite well with belief-based measures of perceived behavioral control. In a meta-analysis of 34 relevant data sets (Armitage and Conner 2001), the mean correlation was found to be 0.52.

The discussion up to this point has shown how behavior can be explained in terms of a limited number of concepts. Through a series of intervening steps the theory of planned behavior traces the causes of behavior to the person's accessible beliefs. Each successive step in this sequence from behavior to beliefs provides a more comprehensive account of the factors that determine the behavior. At the initial level behavior is assumed to be determined by intention and behavioral control. At the next level the intentions are themselves explained in terms of attitudes toward the behavior, subjective norms, and perceptions of behavioral control. The third level accounts for attitudes, subjective norms, and perceptions of control in terms of beliefs about the consequences of performing the behavior, about the normative expectations of important referents, and about the presence of factors that can facilitate or impede performance of the behavior. In the final analysis, then, a person's behavior is explained by considering his or her beliefs. The theory of planned behavior with the addition of beliefs is depicted in Figure 6.2.

The process described above whereby people arrive at their intentions represents a 'reasoned' approach to the explanation and prediction of social behavior in the sense that people's behavioral intentions are assumed to follow from their beliefs about performing the behavior. These beliefs need not be veridical; they may be inaccurate, biased, or even irrational. However, once a set of beliefs is formed it provides the cognitive foundation from which attitudes, subjective norms, and perceptions of control – and, ultimately, intentions and behaviors – are assumed to follow in a reasonable and consistent fashion. However, this should not be taken to mean that people consciously review every step in the chain each time they engage in a behavior. Once formed, attitudes, norms, perceptions of control, and intentions can be highly accessible and readily available to guide performance of the behavior. That is, people do not have to review their behavioral, normative, or control beliefs for these constructs to be activated. For example, a previously formed attitude toward lifting weights is

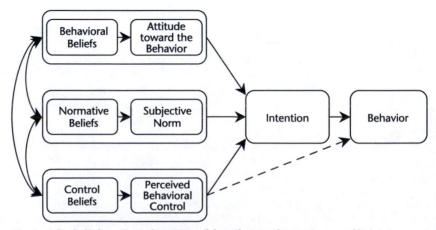

Figure 6.2   Beliefs as the informational foundation of intentions and behavior

automatically activated and can be readily available in the future without having to consider all the likely advantages and disadvantages of this behavior (see Ajzen and Fishbein 2000, for a discussion of automatic processes in reasoned action).

Illustrations

A few concrete examples may help clarify the role of beliefs in determining the intention to perform a specific behavior and thus its actual performance.

Behavioral beliefs and attitudes A good illustration of the explanatory role of behavioral beliefs comes from a study on dropout among African American students in an inner-city high school (Davis et al. 2002). The students completed a theory of planned behavior questionnaire at the beginning of their second year in high school, and their eventual graduation was recorded three years later. A pilot study had identified 14 accessible outcomes of dropping out of school (see Table 6.3). In the questionnaire, the participants first evaluated each of the 14 outcomes (e.g. preparation for college) on a 7-point *good–bad* scale and later rated, again on a 7-point scale, the likelihood that completing the current school year would help them achieve the different outcomes.

Table 6.3 shows the mean belief strength and mean evaluation for each of the 14 outcomes of completing the current school year, as well as the prediction of intentions and behavior from the product of the belief strength and outcome evaluation measures. Inspection of the results provides information about some of the major considerations that guided the students' decisions to stay in school or drop out. Overall, the second-year students held relatively favorable beliefs about the consequences of completing the school year. They believed strongly that doing so would prepare them for college, give them job training, allow them to learn new things, give them new challenges, require hard work, give them a sense of accomplishment or success, and help them to do something positive with their lives. They also valued all of these consequences quite positively.

When we examine the correlations of the belief strength by outcome evaluation products with intentions and actual graduation, we find that the behavioral beliefs listed above correlated strongly with intentions and, most interestingly, were among the best predictors of actual high school graduation. What these beliefs have in common is that they all deal with long-term achievement-related outcomes of graduating from high school. Short-term outcomes of staying in school, such as wasting time, being able to join clubs or participating in sports, keeping out of trouble, and having less time for fun and leisure, correlated with intentions to complete the current school year, but they had little effect on eventual high school graduation.

As a second example, consider a study of hunting attitudes and behavior (Hrubes et al. 2001; Daigle et al. 2002) in which a large sample of registered hunters and visitors to a national forest completed a questionnaire that assessed their beliefs, attitudes, and intentions with respect to hunting, as well as the extent to which they engaged in this behavior. Based on prior

Table 6.3 Mean behavioral belief strength and outcome evaluation, and correlations of belief × evaluation product with intention to complete sophomore year and high school graduation (behavior)

	Belief strength (b)	Outcome evaluation (e)	Correlations	
			b_ie_i with intention	b_ie_i with behavior
Completing the current school year will . . .				
prepare me for college	1.99	1.24	0.37*	0.28*
give me job training	1.48	1.55	0.39*	0.25*
allow me to see my friends on a regular basis	0.97	0.86	0.17	0.20*
waste my time	−2.32	−3.03	0.42*	0.09
allow me to learn new things	2.32	1.62	0.60*	0.21*
give me new challenges	2.14	1.45	0.44*	0.25*
allow me to join clubs or participate in sports	1.54	1.22	0.32*	0.15
keep me out of trouble	1.22	1.44	0.28*	0.11
require hard work	2.27	1.45	0.27*	0.17
mean I will be told by others what to do	0.52	−1.24	0.19	0.07
help me acquire material goods	1.51	1.03	0.21*	0.10
give me a sense of accomplishment or success	2.42	1.82	0.44*	0.13
reduce the amount of time I have for fun or leisure	0.38	−1.71	0.05	0.01
help me to do something positive with my life	2.55	1.92	0.57*	0.24*

Notes: Behavioral belief strength and outcome evaluation scored from −3 to +3;
b_ie_i = behavioral belief × outcome evaluation.
* $p < 0.01$.
Source: From Davis et al. (2002)

research in the field, the investigators selected 12 frequently cited beliefs regarding the benefits and costs of hunting (see Table 6.4 for a list of the beliefs). With respect to each of these 12 accessible behavioral beliefs, the participants were asked to provide two ratings: their subjective probabilities that hunting produces the cited consequence, and their evaluations of that consequence. The first rating was made using an 11-point scale ranging from −5 (*extremely unlikely*) to +5 (*extremely likely*). After completing all of

Table 6.4 Hunting: mean belief strength, mean outcome evaluation, and correlations of belief-evaluation product with intention and behavior

Behavioral belief	Belief strength (b)		Outcome evaluation (e)		Correlation $b_i e_i$ with	
	Hunters	Others	Hunters	Others	Intention	Behavior
Viewing scenery and enjoying nature	4.54	−0.15	2.50	2.80	0.54	0.52
Observing and learning about wildlife	4.31	1.09	2.58	2.21	0.46	0.44
Feeling tired and exhausted	1.07	−1.90	−0.34	0.25	0.12*	0.10*
Creating or maintaining significant relationships with family or friends	3.69	−1.06	2.58	2.73	0.61	0.58
Relaxing and relieving stress	4.20	−1.03	2.61	2.74	0.68	0.65
Getting exercise and staying in shape	3.92	−0.63	2.41	2.74	0.62	0.59
Feeling a sense of competence	3.62	−0.59	2.39	2.50	0.59	0.56
Experiencing solitude, time to think	4.36	0.26	2.51	2.59	0.56	0.52
Getting dirty, wet, or cold	3.25	1.22	−0.24	0.12	0.04*	0.03*
Feeling a sense of belonging and familiarity with nature	4.12	−0.44	2.46	2.45	0.60	0.57
Experiencing excitement	4.56	0.51	2.65	2.16	0.60	0.58
Seeing wounded or dead animals	1.86	2.17	−0.52	−1.99	0.40	0.39

Notes: Belief strength measured on a scale of −5 to +5; outcome evaluation on a scale of −3 to +3; $b_i e_i$ = behavioral belief × outcome evaluation.
* Not significant; all other correlations significant at $p < 0.01$.
Source: from Daigle et al. (2002)

the likelihood ratings, participants indicated their evaluations of the 12 outcomes by rating the desirability of each on a 7-point scale from −3 (*extremely undesirable*) to +3 (*extremely desirable*).

Table 6.4 shows the mean behavioral belief strength (likelihood ratings) and outcome evaluations associated with the perceived outcomes of hunting. In addition, 12 belief-evaluation products were calculated for each respondent and the product terms were correlated with hunting intentions and self-reported hunting over a 12-month period. These correlations are also displayed in Table 6.4. Examination of the results offers a detailed view of the considerations that tend to guide hunting intentions and behavior. It can be seen that the outcomes believed mostly likely to result from hunting were observing wildlife, seeing dead or wounded animals, experiencing excitement, and getting dirty, wet, or cold. The beliefs that these outcomes would occur were moderate in strength, ranging from 2.1 to 2.56 on the −5 to +5 scale. The desirability of these outcomes was mixed, with observing wildlife and experiencing excitement rated as desirable and seeing dead animals and getting dirty, wet, or cold rated as undesirable.

More importantly, all but two of the 12 belief-evaluation products correlated significantly and strongly with intentions and behaviors, suggesting that these beliefs can help explain why some individuals decide to go hunting while others do not. Of particular importance were beliefs that hunting allows you to view scenery and enjoy nature, to create or maintain significant relationships with family or friends, to relax and relieve stress, to get exercise and stay in shape, to feel a sense of competence, to have a sense of belonging and familiarity with nature and to experience excitement. Individuals who held these favorable beliefs about hunting were likely to form intentions to go hunting and to actually engage in this behavior.

Normative beliefs and subjective norms The study on high school dropout (Davis et al. 2002) discussed earlier also provides data concerning the effects of normative beliefs on intentions and behavior. Eight normative referents important with respect to dropout decisions had been identified in pilot work: mother, father, close relatives, boyfriend or girlfriend, school counselor, teachers, classmates, and close friends. With respect to each of these eight referents, two items assessed normative belief strength and motivation to comply. For example, the statement, 'My mother thinks that I should complete the current school year' was rated on a 7-point *unlikely–likely* scale to produce a measure of normative beliefs strength; and to assess motivation to comply, students rated, on the same likelihood scale, the statement, 'Generally speaking, I want to do what my mother thinks I should do.'

Inspection of Table 6.5 shows that students generally felt strong social pressure to complete the school year; this social pressure was perceived to come from all important referents. Parents, family, counselor and teachers, as well as classmates were all viewed as strongly in support of a student's completing the school year, and students were generally motivated to comply with these referents. However, there was sufficient variability in normative beliefs and motivations to comply to permit prediction of intentions and behavior. The stronger the combination (product) of normative belief and motivation to comply, the more students intended to stay in school, and the more likely they were to graduate three years later.

Interesting data concerning the role of normative beliefs was also obtained in a study by Manstead, Proffitt, and Smart (1983) who compared the beliefs of mothers who breast-fed their babies with mothers who used the bottle-feeding method. The accessible normative referents identified in this context were the baby's father, the mother's own mother, her closest female friend, and her medical adviser (usually a gynecologist). With respect to each referent, normative beliefs about breast-feeding and about

Table 6.5 Mean normative belief strength and motivation to comply, and correlations of belief × motivation product with intention to complete sophomore year and high school graduation (behavior)

Normative referent	Belief strength (n)	Motivation to comply (m)	Correlation	
			$n_i m_i$ with intention	$n_i m_i$ with behavior
My mother	6.81	6.01	0.38*	0.25*
My father	6.63	5.48	0.33*	0.28*
Other close relatives	6.80	5.46	0.40*	0.32*
My boyfriend / girlfriend	6.53	4.88	0.34*	0.20
My school counselor	6.64	5.50	0.30*	0.26*
My teachers	6.46	5.26	0.40*	0.25*
My classmates	6.01	4.16	0.23*	0.17
My close friends	6.52	5.08	0.37*	0.27*

Notes: Normative belief strength and motivation to comply scored from 1 to 7;
$n_i m_i$ = normative belief x motivation to comply.
* $p < 0.01$.
Source: From Davis et al. (2002)

bottle-feeding were assessed prior to delivery, as was motivation to comply with each referent. To measure normative beliefs, the mothers were asked to indicate, on 7-point scales, their perception that a given referent thought they should breast-feed or bottle-feed their babies. They then indicated, again on 7-point scales, how much they cared what the referent thought they should do. The products of these two ratings were summed over the four referents to obtain a belief-based measure of subjective norm.

Six weeks following delivery, the mothers' feeding method was recorded. Examination of the differences between mothers who breast-fed their babies and mothers who used the bottle showed first that there was little difference in their motivation to comply with their important referents. Most of the women were highly motivated to comply with the expectations of the baby's father and somewhat less so in relation to the expectations of their mothers, close female friends, and medical advisers. However, there were considerable differences in their normative beliefs regarding the two methods, as can be seen in Table 6.6. The differences between mothers who breast-fed their babies and mothers who used the bottle are statistically significant for each normative belief. Inspection of the normative beliefs for mothers who used the breast-feeding method reveals that, in their opinions, important referents strongly preferred this method over the alternative bottle-feeding method. In contrast, women who believed that their referents had no strong preferences for either method were more likely to feed their babies by means of a bottle.

Control beliefs and perceived behavioral control The role of control beliefs is illustrated in a study that dealt with eating a low-fat diet (Armitage and Conner 1999). Seven factors that could help or hinder consumption of a low-fat diet were identified (see Table 6.7). For each factor, measures were

Table 6.6   Mean normative beliefs about breast- and bottle-feeding

Normative beliefs	Mothers who breast-fed	Mothers who bottle-fed
About breast-feeding		
Baby's father	6.15	4.45
Own mother	5.57	4.45
Closest female friend	5.39	4.47
Medical adviser	6.20	5.25
About bottle-feeding		
Baby's father	2.89	4.16
Own mother	3.24	3.99
Closest female friend	3.43	3.98
Medical adviser	2.96	3.55

Note: Normative beliefs scored from 1 to 7. All differences between breast-feeding and bottle-feeding mothers are statistically significant ($p < 0.05$).
Source: From Manstead et al. (1983)

Table 6.7   Mean control belief strength and power of control factors for people intending and not intending to eat a low-fat diet

Control factors	Belief strength		Facilitating power	
	Intenders	Non-intenders	Intenders	Non-intenders
Time-consuming	3.44	3.67	3.78	3.48
Expensive	3.73	4.19*	3.73	3.54
Temptation of high-fat foods	4.53	4.88	3.50	2.85**
Requires strong motivation	4.86	5.20	4.53	3.85**
Inconvenient	5.22	5.38	3.36	3.01
Lack of knowledge of fat content	3.30	4.05**	4.80	3.74**
Low availability	4.67	5.04	3.40	3.36

Notes: Control belief strength and power scored 1 to 7.
* Difference between intenders and non-intenders $p < 0.05$.
** Difference between intenders and non-intenders $p < 0.01$.
Source: Armitage and Conner (1999)

obtained of control belief strength and of the factor's power to facilitate or inhibit eating a low-fat diet. Specifically, participants indicated, on 7-point scales, the likelihood that the factor would be present (present *never* to *frequently*) and the extent to which its presence would make successful performance of the behavior more or less likely. Participants were divided into two groups, depending on whether they did or did not intend to adhere to a low-fat diet. A comparison of these two groups in terms of their control beliefs is shown in Table 6.7.

Examining only the significant differences, it can be seen that participants who believed that eating a low-fat diet is often expensive and that they frequently lacked knowledge about the fat content of foods did not intend to observe this diet. In addition, intentions to adhere to a low-fat diet were also undermined by perceptions that temptation of high-fat foods, need for strong motivation, and lack of knowledge about fat content made successful performance of the behavior unlikely.

For another example we can return to the investigation of regular class attendance (Ajzen and Madden 1986). In a pilot study conducted prior to the main experiment, college students were asked to list any factors that could help them get an 'A' in a course and any factors that might make it difficult for them to get an 'A.' Four potential facilitating factors mentioned frequently were stimulating subject matter, clear and organized lectures, possession of required skills and background, and availability of help from the instructor. Four frequently mentioned factors whose presence would hamper attaining a good grade were taking other demanding classes, extra-curricular activities, arduous text and reading materials, and difficult exams and course requirements. In the main experiment, toward the end of the semester, college students were asked to judge, with respect to each of these eight factors, how much the factor was likely to influence their ability to get an 'A' in a particular course they were taking at the time.[1]

Table 6.8 shows the average control beliefs, scored in the direction of facilitation (1 = factor hinders attaining a good grade, 7 = factor facilitates attaining a good grade) as well as the correlation of each belief with intention to get an 'A' and with actual grades attained. Inspection of the mean control beliefs reveals that the students who took part in the experiment thought they would be helped by the subject matter of the course which was stimulating enough to motivate them, by the lectures which they considered to be sufficiently clear and organized, by their possessing the required skills and background, and by the ready availability of help from the instructor. On the other hand, the students also believed that they would encounter certain obstacles, especially in the form of demands on

Table 6.8 Mean control beliefs and correlations of control beliefs with intentions to get an 'A' and attained grade

Control beliefs	Mean control belief	Correlation with	
		intention	grade
Facilitating factors			
Stimulating subject matter	5.19	0.50	0.37
Clear and organized lectures	5.37	0.33	0.35
Possession of skills and background	5.11	0.44	0.45
Availability of help	6.17	0.21	0.31
Inhibiting factors			
Other demanding classes	2.41	0.24	0.27
Extracurricular activities	2.67	0.19	0.19
Arduous test and reading materials	4.17	0.11*	0.16*
Exams and course requirements	3.16	0.33	0.35

Notes: Control beliefs scored from 1 (inhibition) to 7 (facilitation).
* Not significant; all other correlations $p < 0.05$.
Source: Ajzen and Madden (1986)

their time and energy imposed by other classes they were taking and in the form of extracurricular activities.

The correlations displayed in Table 6.8 demonstrate the impact of these different control beliefs on intentions to make an effort to get an 'A' in the course and on actual grades attained. Of special importance were perceptions concerning the course's subject matter, lecture organization, possession of required skills and background, and the nature of the exams and other course requirements. The more that students saw these factors as facilitating their performance in the course, the stronger were their intentions to try for an 'A' and the higher were the grades they actually attained.

Background factors

According to the theory of planned behavior, the major determinants of intentions and behavior follow reasonably from – and can be understood in terms of – behavioral, normative, and control beliefs. A multitude of variables may be related to or influence the beliefs people hold: age, gender, ethnicity, socio-economic status, education, nationality, religious affiliation, personality, mood, emotion, general attitudes and values, intelligence, group membership, past experiences, exposure to information, social support, coping skills, and so forth. Clearly, people growing up in different social environments can acquire different information about a variety of issues, information that provides the basis for their beliefs about the consequences of a behavior, about the normative expectations of important others, and about the obstacles that may prevent them from performing a behavior. Similarly, men can have experiences that differ in important ways from the experiences of women, older people acquire information that differs from the information among younger people, and temporary moods can influence the way we perceive things. All of these factors can therefore affect our behavioral, normative, and control beliefs and, as a result, influence our intentions and actions.

In Figure 6.3, these *background factors* are divided into personal, social, and informational categories. It can now be seen that the research reviewed in the first three chapters of this book focused on two major personal factors: general attitudes and personality dispositions. The theory of planned behavior recognizes the potential importance of such background factors. However, the dotted arrows in Figure 6.3 indicate that, although a given background factor may in fact influence behavioral, normative, or control beliefs, there is no necessary connection between background factors and beliefs. Whether a given belief is or is not affected by a particular background factor is an empirical question. In light of the vast number of potentially relevant background factors, it is difficult to know which should be considered without a theory to guide selection in the behavioral domain of interest. Theories of this kind are not part of the planned behavior model but can complement it by identifying relevant background factors and thereby deepen our understanding of a behavior's determinants.

For example, in our discussion of the MODE model in Chapter 3, we noted that general attitudes toward objects can influence performance

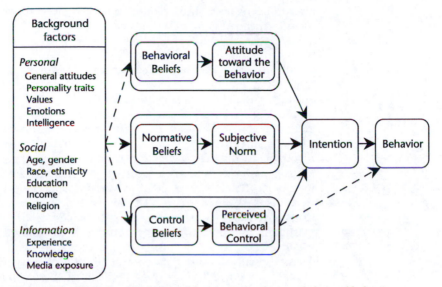

Figure 6.3   The role of background factors in the theory of planned behavior

of a specific behavior by biasing perception of the behavior's likely consequences, i.e. behavioral beliefs. As a result, they can affect attitude toward the behavior and, eventually, intentions and actions. In a similar fashion, general attitudes may also sometimes be found to exert an effect on normative or control beliefs and thus again influence behavior indirectly by changing subjective norms or perceptions of behavioral control. This discussion implies that such background factors as general attitudes influence intentions and behavior indirectly by their effects on behavioral, normative, or control beliefs and, through these beliefs, their effects on attitudes, subjective norms, or perceptions of control. Many studies have obtained patterns of results consistent with this expectation. Although investigators occasionally report significant direct effects of certain background factors after controlling for the theory of planned behavior variables, for the most part the influence of background factors can be traced to their impact on the proximal determinants of intentions.

Consider, for example, the study on hunting reported earlier in this chapter (Hrubes et al. 2001). The questionnaire administered in this study contained not only measures of the theory of planned behavior variables but also two scales designed to assess wildlife-related values (Fulton et al. 1996) and general values to life (Schwartz 1992). The wildlife-related values represented wildlife enjoyment and animal rights (vs. management), and the general life values were the two higher-order dimensions of self-transcendence (vs. self-enhancement) and openness to change (vs. conservatism). Each of these four values was found to correlate significantly with the extent to which the participants engaged in hunting. The correlations ranged from 0.25 for openness to change to 0.52 for animal rights. However, as expected, when the value measures were added to the prediction equation after intentions and perceptions of behavioral control had already been taken into account, they produced no significant improvement in the prediction of hunting behavior.

Similarly, in a study of physical activity (Hagger et al. 2002a), an individual difference measure of intrinsic motivation predicted adolescents' intentions to engage in physical activity. However, the effect of intrinsic motivation on intentions was completely mediated by its impacts on attitudes and perceived behavioral control.

Studying the effect of gender on sexual behavior (Conner and Flesch 2001), it was found that compared to women, men had significantly stronger intentions to have casual sex, but after controlling for the predictors in the theory of planned behavior, the effect of gender was no longer significant. And in an investigation of adolescents' intentions to use marijuana (Fishbein et al. 2002), a variety of different background factors were assessed, including time spent with friends who tend to get into trouble, sensation seeking, and parental supervision. Intentions to smoke marijuana increased with the amount of time spent in the company of friends who tend to get in trouble and with sensation seeking, and decreased with amount of parental supervision. Consistent with the theory of planned behavior, however, the effects of these variables on intentions could be traced to their influence on one or more of the proximal determinants of intentions (i.e. attitudes, subjective norms, and perceived behavioral control). When these determinants were statistically controlled, the background factors no longer correlated significantly with intentions.

In short, general background factors of various kinds can influence intentions and behavior, but this influence is usually mediated by more specific beliefs and attitudes concerning the behavior of interest. By examining the effect of a given background factor on behavioral, normative, and control beliefs, we can gain further insight into the determinants of human behavior.

BEHAVIORAL INTERVENTIONS

The theory of planned behavior has, thus far, been used primarily to explain and predict behavior in various domains. The theory, however, also has important implications for behavioral interventions, that is, for interventions designed to change intentions and behavior. It is beyond the scope of this book to discuss the voluminous literature on persuasion and social influence. The purpose of the present discussion is merely to highlight some of the implications for change that can be derived from the theory of planned behavior, and to describe a few illustrative examples.

Theoretical considerations

According to the theory of planned behavior, interventions can be directed at one or more of a behavior's theoretical determinants: attitudes, subjective norms, or perceptions of behavioral control. Changes in these factors should produce changes in behavioral intentions and, given adequate control over the behavior, the new intentions should be carried out under appropriate circumstances. Thus, if we wanted college students to attend their lectures regularly, we could devise a persuasive campaign to make their attitudes toward this behavior more favorable, to increase the perceived social pressure to attend lectures regularly, and/or to raise their perceived control over performing this behavior. Because attitudes, subjective norms, and perceived behavioral control are assumed to be based on corresponding sets of beliefs, behavioral interventions must try to change the beliefs that, according to the theory, ultimately guide performance of the behavior. It is important to realize, however, that this explanatory function is associated only with beliefs that are readily accessible in memory. Pilot work is required to identify accessible behavioral, normative, and control beliefs. These beliefs provide us with insight into the underlying cognitive foundation of the behavior, i.e. they tell us why people hold certain attitudes, subjective norms, and perceptions of behavioral control and, therefore, why they intend to perform the behavior in question. To produce changes in these variables, we would have to either change some of the behavioral, normative, or control beliefs or make accessible new beliefs supportive of the desired behavior.

Once it has been decided which beliefs the intervention will attempt to change, an effective intervention method must be developed. The theory of planned behavior can provide general guidelines, but it does not tell us what kind of intervention will be most effective. We could consider persuasive communications, perhaps in the form of newspaper ads, flyers distributed in certain neighborhoods, or TV service messages. Alternatively, we might want to try face-to-face discussions, observational modeling, or any other viable method so long as it can be demonstrated that the intervention does indeed influence the beliefs it is designed to change (see Fishbein and Ajzen 2005).

In designing an intervention, it is important to distinguish between two stages that require different approaches. In the first stage, we would try to change the antecedents of intentions to motivate people to engage in the desired behavior. The considerations described above apply at this stage of the intervention. Once favorable intentions have been formed, we need to ensure that these intentions are carried out. Any obstacles that could impede actual control over the behavior must be removed, and specific plans or implementation intentions must be develop to maximize the intervention's effectiveness.

Illustrations

Over the past few years, a number of attempts have been made to examine the effects of interventions in the context of the theory of planned behavior (see Hardeman et al. 2002). Most of these applications have used the theory as a general conceptual framework without careful attention to all of the considerations outlined above. In particular, interventions are usually not designed in such a way as to attack particular beliefs identified as important in a pilot study. Instead, participants are often exposed to information or are engaged in discussion relevant to the behavior of interest, and the effects of this experience on beliefs, attitudes, intentions, and behavior is assessed. Nevertheless, the results are quite encouraging.

Consider, for example, the effects of an intervention that was designed to increase bus use among college students (Bamberg et al. 2003). The major feature of the intervention was the introduction of a pre-paid 'semester ticket' that permitted unlimited rides on the local bus system by presentation of a valid student identification. Initiation of the semester ticket plan was preceded by considerable discussion and publicity beginning about one year prior to the first wave of data collection. Articles concerning the proposed policy appeared in the student newspaper, and student representatives organized several informational meetings. A theory of planned behavior questionnaire was administered to a sample of students about two months prior to introduction of the new plan and, again, about eight months after its introduction. Actual use of the bus to get to the campus was also assessed at these two points in time.

Based on the theory of planned behavior, it was predicted that introduction of the semester ticket plan, if effective, would change students' beliefs about using the bus to go to the campus; make attitudes, subjective norms, and perceptions of control with regard to riding the bus more favorable; and thus modify intentions and raise the rate of bus use. The results displayed in Table 6.9 confirm these expectations. Introduction of the semester bus ticket significantly increased students' attitudes to use the bus to get to the campus; it raised perceived social pressure (subjective norms) to do so as well as perceptions of control over this behavior; it led to more favorable intentions; and it more than doubled the proportion of bus users from 15 percent prior to the intervention to 36 percent afterwards.

An intervention to encourage men to perform testicular self-examination (TSE) for early detection of testicular cancer (Brubaker and Fowler 1990) provided information about changes in some of the underlying beliefs about the behavior. Male college students were exposed to a 10-minute tape-recorded message designed to change their beliefs about the consequences of performing TSE. Participants in a second condition of the experiment were exposed to a message of equal length that provided general information about testicular cancer, and participants in a control condition received no message at all. About four weeks later, all participants

Table 6.9   Mean bus use before and after intervention

	Pre-test	Post-test
Attitude toward using bus	2.31	2.60
Subjective norm	2.24	2.46
Perceived behavioral control	2.57	2.99
Intention to use bus	1.65	2.11
Bus use (percent)	0.15	0.36

Note: Attitude, subjective norm, perceived behavioral control, and intention can range from 1 to 5. Bus use is the proportion of participants who used the bus. All differences between pre- and post-test are significant at $p < 0.01$.
Source: Bamberg et al. (2003)

completed a theory of planned behavior questionnaire and reported whether they had performed TSE in the interim.

The results of the study showed the effectiveness of a theory-based intervention. In the no-message control group, about 19 percent of the participants reported having performed TSE at the end of the four-week period. This compares with about 44 percent in the general information group and fully 71 percent in the theory-based message condition. A structural equation analysis showed that exposure to the messages influenced behavioral, normative, and control beliefs with respect to performing TSE; that these changes in beliefs affected attitudes toward the behavior, subjective norms, and perceptions of behavioral control; that changes in these three factors raised intentions to perform TSE which, in turn, led to the observed increase in reported testicular self-examination.

The results of these studies show that changing intentions can have a marked impact on actual behavior, but there are instances where producing a favorable intention may not be sufficient. In those cases, getting participants to formulate a specific plan or implementation intention can further increase the intervention's effectiveness. An illustration is provided by an investigation of the use of vitamin C supplements among college students (Sheeran and Orbell 1999: Experiment 2). On initial contact in their homes, participants were given a bottle of 50 vitamin C tablets and were encouraged to take one each day. After two weeks, the investigators returned, counted the remaining pills, and encouraged the students to continue taking a tablet each day for another three weeks. At this point, the participants completed a theory of planned behavior questionnaire in which they expressed their attitudes toward taking a vitamin C pill each day, as well as their subjective norms, perceptions of behavioral control, and intentions regarding this behavior. Finally, participants in an implementation intention group were asked to specify where and at what time they would take a vitamin C pill every day for the next three weeks. Participants in a control group underwent identical procedures, but they were not asked to form an implementation intention. Three weeks later, the investigators returned once more, counted the remaining pills in the bottle, and also asked the participants to indicate how many vitamin C pills they had taken.

The questionnaire responses indicated that participants in both experimental conditions were highly motivated to take a vitamin C pill every day. They had very favorable attitudes toward this behavior, they perceived social pressure to take vitamin C pills, they thought that they had a high level of control, and most importantly, they intended to take a pill every day. On the 7-point intention scale, the average response was 6.75 in the implementation intention condition and 6.70 in the control condition. Consistent with these strong behavioral intentions, participants in both conditions took most of their vitamin C pills. Nevertheless, in the control group, 61 percent missed taking at least one pill over the three-week period and, on average, missed taking 2.5 pills. When fortified with an implementation intention, only 26 percent missed taking a pill, for an average of less than one missed pill.

SUMMARY AND CONCLUSIONS

This chapter discussed a theoretical framework, the theory of planned behavior, that can help us predict and understand performance of specific action tendencies. We examined some of the factors that influence deliberate performance of willful actions as well as additional factors that must be taken into account when we are dealing with behaviors or behavioral goals over which people have only limited volitional control. We saw that volitional control is best defined as a continuum, where the ideal case at one extreme is represented by purely volitional acts and the ideal case at the other extreme are behavioral events which are completely beyond volitional control. Most behaviors, however, fall somewhere between these extremes. Toward the volitional side of the continuum, it is possible to predict behavior with a great deal of accuracy on the basis of intentions to perform the behavior in question. Intentions also contribute to the attainment of behavioral goals that are only partly under volitional control; here, however, their predictive validity is attenuated and we must take account of factors that can interfere with or facilitate performance of the intended behavior. Perceived behavioral control can reflect the presence of such factors and, to the extent that it does so accurately, contributes to the prediction of behavioral achievement.

Perceived behavioral control can also have motivational implications, influencing the formation of behavioral intentions. When resources or opportunities are seen as inadequate, motivation to try performing the behavior is likely to suffer. In addition to being affected by perceived behavioral control, intentions are also influenced by attitudes toward the behavior and by subjective norms. Generally speaking, then, people intend to perform a behavior if their personal evaluations of it are favorable, if they think that important others would approve of it, and if they believe that the requisite resources and opportunities will be available. To some extent, strength in one factor can compensate for weakness in another. People who doubt their ability to carry out a certain behavioral plan may nevertheless intend to make a serious effort if they place a high positive value on performing the behavior or if they experience strong social pressure to do so.

Substantive knowledge about the determinants of specific action tendencies is obtained by examining the informational foundation of attitudes, subjective norms, and perceived behavioral control. Beliefs concerning the likely outcomes of a behavior, and subjective evaluations of those outcomes, reveal why a person holds a favorable or unfavorable attitude toward performing the behavior; beliefs about the normative expectations of salient referent individuals or groups, and motivations to comply with these referents, provide an understanding of perceived social pressure to perform or not perform the behavior; and beliefs concerning factors that can prevent or facilitate goal attainment disclose the considerations that produce perceptions of high or low behavioral control. Taken together, this informational base provides us with a detailed explanation of a person's tendency to perform, or not to perform, a particular behavior.

General attitudes and personality dispositions are two of the many background factors that can help account for differences in behavioral, normative, and control beliefs. Among other background factors are various individual difference variables, social and demographic characteristics, as well as past experience and exposure to other sources of information. In fact, behavioral interventions generally expose people to new information designed to change their behavioral, normative, and control beliefs. We saw that such interventions performed in the context of the theory of planned behavior can have a substantial impact on intentions and behavior, and that it is possible to help people carry out their intentions by asking them to form a specific behavioral plan or implementation intention.

NOTE

1 Separate measures of control belief strength and the power of the control factors were not obtained in this study.

SUGGESTIONS FOR FURTHER READING

Ajzen, I. (1991) The theory of planned behavior. *Organizational Behavior and Human Decision Processes*, 50, 179–211. This article describes the theory of planned behavior and some of the early research generated by the theory.

Ajzen, I. (2005) *The Theory of Planned Behavior*. Available: http://www.people.umass.edu/aizen/tpbrefs.html (accessed March 3 2005). Practical guidance regarding research with the theory of planned behavior is available at this web site.

Armitage, C. J., and Conner, M. (2001) Efficacy of the theory of planned behavior: A meta-analytic review. *British Journal of Social Psychology*, 40, 471–499. In this article, the authors review and evaluative empirical evidence for the theory of planned behavior.

SEVEN

CONCLUSION

People carry within them the accumulated experiences of countless prior generations handed down in the form of genetic endowment, as well as the outcomes of their own unique life histories. Genetic differences and divergent personal experiences ensure that no two individuals are exactly alike. It is hardly surprising that attempts to understand human behavior have proved to be as frustrating as they are challenging. The historical processes and events that have shaped a person's complex makeup can never be fully unraveled. Nevertheless, our task is not hopeless. A person's current behavior must be determined by factors that exert their effects right here and now. Past events are important only to the extent that they have left an enduring mark on the person, a mark that continues to wield its impact. As Campbell (1963) has noted, attitudes and personality traits are meant to capture these residues of past experience. By assessing attitudes or personality traits we attempt to unveil the hidden factors that, as a result of past events, have come to predispose an individual to act in certain ways.

We have learned a great deal in the past three decades about the nature of these behavioral dispositions. No longer do we hear calls for abandoning the trait approach in personality or for dispensing with the attitude construct. It is now generally understood that there is no magic about trait or attitude measures. We cannot construct a broad personality inventory or attitude scale and hope to use it as a basis for the prediction and explanation of any conceivable behavioral criterion. In fact, the very distinction between, on the one hand, attitudes and personality traits assessed by means of a questionnaire, and, on the other hand, 'overt' or objective behavior must be discarded. Even so-called overt actions, observed and recorded by trained investigators, are usually of little interest in and of themselves. We rarely attempt to predict or explain single acts performed under a unique set of circumstances. Instead, behavioral observations normally serve as indicators of people's more general response tendencies; that is, of their behavioral dispositions. Whether responses used to infer a disposition are verbal or nonverbal, obtained by means of a questionnaire, observation of behavior, self-reports, or peer reports is largely immaterial. Depending on circumstances, one means of data collection may produce more valid measures than another, but there is no difference in principle. Each of these methods can be used to infer the underlying disposition of interest.

It has also become very clear that response dispositions can be defined and measured at various levels of generality or specificity. Aggregation of responses across time, contexts, targets, or actions – or across a combination of these elements – permits inferences of dispositions at varying levels of generality. Inferred dispositions can range from the tendency to perform a single action (over time) to the tendency to engage in a broad range of actions, as reflected in a multiple-act aggregate. Even when they address the same content domain, two measures can be considered indicators of the same disposition only if they correspond in their levels of generality. And it is only in the presence of such compatibility that behavioral consistencies manifest themselves reliably. The realization that measures of global attitudes and personality traits, obtained by means of responses to questionnaires, are compatible only with equally general, broadly aggregated measures of other types of responses has helped to clarify much of the initially baffling lack of predictive validity.

It is no longer very meaningful to ask whether attitudes and personality traits predict behavior – they clearly do. Nor does the crucial issue have to do with the conditions under which attitudes and personality traits are related to behavior. Instead, the literature poses and provides answers to three interrelated questions. First, is there consistency between different observations of behavior? Second, do verbal responses predict nonverbal behavior? Finally, are general behavioral dispositions related to specific response tendencies?

BEHAVIORAL CONSISTENCY

The answer to the question of behavioral consistency across observations is closely tied to the principle of aggregation. Generally speaking, observations of single actions on individual occasions do not correlate well with each other. Too many factors unique to a given occasion prevent emergence of a clear response tendency. However, by aggregating observations of a given behavior across occasions we obtain a stable measure of the disposition to perform the behavior in question. Temporal stability is in fact found to become quite high with aggregation over a sufficient number of observations.

There is also evidence for consistency between behavioral measures that aggregate across different actions, so long as each aggregate assesses the same broad underlying disposition. We can infer broad dispositions from representative samples of behaviors performed in a variety of situations, and multiple measures of this kind tend to correlate highly with each other.

The aggregation solution to the consistency dilemma of course limits the explanatory and predictive utilities of traits and attitudes to broad classes of responses; it does not provide a means for the prediction of tendencies to engage in specific behaviors. This limitation, however, is perhaps of more concern in applied attitude research, where the aim often is to predict specific actions, than it is in personality research, which deals largely with broad response tendencies. The principle of compatibility overcomes the limitation in the attitude domain by permitting attitudes to be reduced to the level of individual behaviors.

GENERAL DISPOSITIONS AND SPECIFIC ACTIONS

As a general rule, broad response dispositions are poor predictors of specific actions. This is perhaps the most important lesson to be learned from the prolonged consistency controversy, but also perhaps the most difficult to accept. It would indeed be very convenient if we could measure general attitudes or personality traits and use the resulting scores to predict any behavior that appears relevant to the disposition in question. Unfortunately, both theory and empirical findings negate this possibility.

The attempt to link broad behavioral dispositions to specific response tendencies by means of moderating variables has produced some interesting studies, but future progress along these lines faces serious difficulties. One drawback of this approach is the sheer number of personal and situational factors that can potentially moderate the effect of attitudes or personality on behavior, as well as the complications introduced by higher-order interactions among these factors. In the attitudes domain, this problem was alleviated in part by development of the MODE model (Fazio 1990a; Fazio and Towles-Schwen 1999) which links the effects of many moderating variables to the concept of attitude strength or accessibility in memory. According to this view, only strong, highly accessible attitudes are likely to be guide behavior. Variables such as self-monitoring tendency, need for cognition, involvement with the attitude object, confidence in one's attitude, and direct experience with the attitude object are assumed to moderate the relation between attitudes and behavior because they influence the attitude's accessibility in memory.

The MODE model offers a useful conceptual framework to think about the effects of general attitudes on specific behaviors and about the role of moderating variables. However, the moderating variables approach must ultimately end in failure because it leads to the unavoidable conclusion that behavior can be predicted from attitudes or personality traits only for some individuals under a limited set of circumstances. The multitude of conditions that moderating variables place on prediction of specific responses from broad dispositions severely limits the practical utility of this approach.

VERBAL AND NONVERBAL RESPONSES

What people say and what they do are not always the same (Deutscher 1966, 1973). In part, this is a problem of measurement validity. The validity of verbal responses has often been questioned because of the possible presence of social desirability biases, acquiescence tendencies, strategic biases, and so forth. The current popularity of implicit measurement techniques, such as the Implicit Association Test and sequential priming (Fazio and Olson 2003) attest to the continuing concern with measurement validity. Somewhat less attention has been given to the measurement implications of the fact that observed actions may be equally biased to create favorable impressions, to avoid conflict, or to gain an advantage by means of ingratiation. The consequence of such biases is to invalidate the measures from which behavioral dispositions are inferred. If the biases associated with a verbal response differ greatly from the biases operating on the physical action, correlations between the two measures will necessarily deteriorate.

The potential for biased responding does not, however, doom efforts to predict nonverbal from verbal behaviors. Many situations provide little incentive for strong biases, and tendencies toward biased responding can be further reduced by careful application of appropriate measurement procedures. The question therefore remains, what is the relation between valid, relatively unbiased verbal and nonverbal responses? The answer to this question is related to the principle of compatibility, and it has nothing to do with the fact that one indicator of the disposition is verbal and the other nonverbal. Instead, the answer revolves around the generality or specificity of the measures involved. As noted above, verbal measures of broad attitudes or personality traits have been shown to predict equally broad, multiple-act measures of overt behavior. However, as a general rule, they do not predict specific responses, whether nonverbal or verbal. To predict single actions, we must turn to dispositional measures that deal specifically with those actions. The concept of intention appears to be a useful starting point. Intentions represent behavioral dispositions that conceptually are very closely tied to the corresponding behavior, and there is good evidence to show that many behaviors are sufficiently under volitional control to be predictable from people's intentions. Barring unforeseen events, people tend to carry out their behavioral plans. Added difficulties arise when achievement of a behavioral goal is at least partly determined by internal or external factors over which a person has only limited control. The theory of planned behavior described in Chapter 6 represents an attempt to account for the formation of intentions and the achievement of behavioral goals. Attitudes toward the behavior, subjective norms, and perceived behavioral control are the three primary deter-minants of intentions. Their formation is traced, respectively, to beliefs about the behavior's likely outcomes, beliefs about the expectations of important others, and beliefs about factors that may facilitate or hinder performance of the behavior. When people are aware of potential diffi-culties, they are assumed to plan their actions accordingly. The theory of planned behavior is thus designed to permit prediction and explanation of behavioral achievement by taking into account motivational antecedents, reflected in intentions, as well as other factors that are only partly under volitional control, factors that are reflected in perceived behavioral control. A great deal of research over the past 20 years has provided good support for the theory.

This book ends the way it began, with the dispositional prediction of human behavior. It should be clear by now that dispositional concepts are not only useful, they are indispensable tools at the disposal of the behavioral scientist. While measures of behavioral dispositions cannot be used indiscriminately, when appropriately employed they yield highly valuable information. As intuitive observation would suggest, people are quite consistent in the patterns of behavior they exhibit. They act in ways that cannot be described as capricious, nor would it be accurate to claim that their behavior is controlled by external forces. Instead, human action is found to follow reasonably and consistently from relevant behavioral dispositions.

REFERENCES

Aarts, H., and Dijksterhuis, A. (2000) Habits as knowledge structures: Automaticity in goal-directed behavior. *Journal of Personality and Social Psychology*, 78, 53–63.

Aarts, H., Dijksterhuis, A., and Midden, C. (1999) To plan or not to plan? Goal achievement of interrupting the performance of mundane behaviors. *European Journal of Social Psychology*, 29, 971–9.

Abelson, R. P., Aronson, E., McGuire, W. J., Newcomb, T. M., Rosenberg, M. J., and Tannenbaum, P. H. (1968) *Theories of Cognitive Consistency: A Sourcebook*. Chicago: Rand-McNally.

Ajzen, I. (1971) Attitudinal vs. normative messages: An investigation of the differential effects of persuasive communications on behavior. *Sociometry*, 34, 263–80.

Ajzen, I. (1982) On behaving in accordance with one's attitudes. In M. P. Zanna, E. T. Higgins and C. P. Herman (eds), *Attitude Structure and Function. The Third Ohio State University Volume on Attitudes and Persuasion* (Vol. 2, pp. 3–15). Hillsdale, NJ: Erlbaum.

Ajzen, I. (1985) From intentions to actions: A theory of planned behavior. In J. Kuhl and J. Beckman (eds), *Action-Control: From Cognition to Behavior* (pp. 11–39). Heidelberg: Springer.

Ajzen, I. (1987) Attitudes, traits, and actions: Dispositional prediction of behavior in personality and social psychology. In L. Berkowitz (ed.), *Advances in Experimental Social Psychology* (Vol. 20, pp. 1–63). San Diego, CA: Academic Press, Inc.

Ajzen, I. (1991) The theory of planned behavior. *Organizational Behavior and Human Decision Processes*, 50, 179–211.

Ajzen, I. (2002) Residual effects of past on later behavior: Habituation and reasoned action perspectives. *Personality and Social Psychology Review*, 6, 107–22.

Ajzen, I. (2005) *The Theory of Planned Behavior: A Bibliography*. Available: http://www.people.umass.edu/aizen/tpbrefs.html [accessed March 3 2005].

Ajzen, I., Brown, T. C., and Carvajal, F. (2004) Explaining the discrepancy between intentions and actions: The case of hypothetical bias in contingent valuation. *Personality and Social Psychology Bulletin*, 30, 1108–21.

Ajzen, I., Czasch, C., and Flood, M. G. (2002) From intentions to behavior: Implementation intention, commitment, and conscientiousness. Unpublished manuscript. University of Massachusetts.

Ajzen, I., and Driver, B. L. (1992) Application of the theory of planned behavior to leisure choice. *Journal of Leisure Research*, 24, 207–24.

Ajzen, I., and Fishbein, M. (1970) The prediction of behavior from attitudinal and normative variables. *Journal of Experimental Social Psychology*, 6, 466–87.

Ajzen, I., and Fishbein, M. (1977) Attitude-behavior relations: A theoretical analysis and review of empirical research. *Psychological Bulletin*, 84, 888–918.

Ajzen, I., and Fishbein, M. (1980) *Understanding Attitudes and Predicting Social Behavior*. Englewood-Cliffs, NJ: Prentice-Hall.

Ajzen, I., and Fishbein, M. (2000) Attitudes and the attitude-behavior relation: Reasoned and automatic processes. In W. Stroebe and M. Hewstone (eds), *European Review of Social Psychology* (Vol. 11, pp. 1–33). Chichester: Wiley.

Ajzen, I., and Fishbein, M. (2005) The influence of attitudes on behavior. In D. Albarracín, B. T. Johnson and M. P. Zanna (eds), *Handbook of Attitudes and Attitude Change: Basic Principles*. Mahwah, NJ: Lawrence Erlbaum Associates.

Ajzen, I., and Madden, T. J. (1986) Prediction of goal-directed behavior: Attitudes, intentions, and perceived behavioral control. *Journal of Experimental Social Psychology*, 22, 453–74.

Ajzen, I., and Timko, C. (1986) Correspondence between health attitudes and behavior. *Basic and Applied Social Psychology*, 7, 259–76.

Ajzen, I., Timko, C., and White, J. B. (1982) Self-monitoring and the attitude-behavior relation. *Journal of Personality and Social Psychology*, 42, 426–35.

Alagna, S. W., and Reddy, D. M. (1984) Predictors of proficient technique and successful lesion detection in breast self-examination. *Health Psychology*, 3, 113–27.

Albarracín, D., Johnson, B. T., Fishbein, M., and Muellerleile, P. A. (2001) Theories of reasoned action and planned behavior as models of condom use: A meta-analysis. *Psychological Bulletin*, 127, 142–61.

Allport, G. W. (1935) Attitudes. In C. Murchison (ed.), *Handbook of Social Psychology* (pp. 798–844). Worcester, MA: Clark University Press.

Allport, G. W. (1937) *Personality: A Psychological Interpretation*. New York: Holt, Reinhart and Winston.

Allport, G. W. (1954) *The Nature of Prejudice*. Oxford: Addison-Wesley.

Allport, G. W. (1961) *Pattern and Growth in Personality*. New York: Holt, Reinhart and Winston.

Armitage, C. J., and Conner, M. (1999) Distinguishing perceptions of control from self-efficacy: Predicting consumption of a low-fat diet using the theory of planned behavior. *Journal of Applied Social Psychology*, 29, 72–90.

Armitage, C. J., and Conner, M. (2001) Efficacy of the theory of planned behavior: A meta-analytic review. *British Journal of Social Psychology*, 40, 471–99.

Asendorpf, J. B., Banse, R., and Muecke, D. (2002) Double dissociation between implicit and explicit personality self-concept: The case of shy behavior. *Journal of Personality and Social Psychology*, 83, 380–93.

Bagozzi, R. P. (1978) The construct validity of the affective, behavioral, and cognitive components of attitude by analysis of covariance structures. *Multivariate Behavioral Research*, 13, 9–31.

Bagozzi, R. P., and Burnkrant, R. E. (1979) Attitude organization and the attitude-behavior relationship. *Journal of Personality and Social Psychology*, 37, 913–29.

Bagozzi, R. P., and Burnkrant, R. E. (1985) Attitude organization and the attitude-behavior relation: A reply to Dillon and Kumar. *Journal of Personality and Social Psychology*, 49, 47–57.

Bagozzi, R. P., and Warshaw, P. R. (1990) Trying to consume. *Journal of Consumer Research*, 17, 127–40.

Bamberg, S., Ajzen, I., and Schmidt, P. (2003) Choice of travel mode in the theory of planned behavior: The roles of past behavior, habit, and reasoned action. *Basic and Applied Social Psychology*, 25, 175–88.

Bandura, A. (1977) Self-efficacy: Toward a unifying theory of behavioral change. *Psychological Review*, 84, 191–215.

Bandura, A. (1982) Self-efficacy mechanism in human agency. *American Psychologist*, 37, 122–47.

Bandura, A. (1997) *Self-Efficacy: The Exercise of Control*. New York: Freeman.

Bandura, A., Adams, N. E., and Beyer, J. (1977) Cognitive processes mediating behavioral change. *Journal of Personality and Social Psychology*, 35, 125–39.

Bandura, A., Blanchard, E. B., and Ritter, B. (1969) Relative efficacy of desensitization and modeling approaches for inducing behavioral, affective, and attitudinal changes. *Journal of Personality and Social Psychology*, 13, 173–99.

Bargh, J. A. (1996) Automaticity in social psychology. In E. T. Higgins and A. W. Kruglanski (eds), *Social Psychology: Handbook of Basic Principles*. (pp. 169–83). New York: Guilford Press.

Baron, R. M., and Kenny, D. A. (1986) The moderator-mediator variable distinction in social psychological research: Conceptual, strategic, and statistical considerations. *Journal of Personality and Social Psychology*, 51, 1173–82.

Bar-Tal, D., and Bar-Zohar, Y. (1977) The relationship between perception of locus of control and academic achievement: Review and some educational implications. *Contemporary Educational Psychology*, 2, 181–99.

Bassett, J. F., and Dabbs, J. M. Jr. (2003) Evaluating explicit and implicit death attitudes in funeral and university students. *Mortality*, 8, 352–71.

Baumeister, R. F., and Tice, D. M. (1988) Metatraits. *Journal of Personality*, 56, 571–98.

Becherer, R. C., and Richard, L. M. (1978) Self-monitoring as a moderating variable in consumer behavior. *Journal of Consumer Research*, 5, 159–62.

Bem, D. J. (1965) An experimental analysis of self-persuasion. *Journal of Experimental Social Psychology*, 1, 199–218.

Bem, D. J. (1970) *Beliefs, Attitudes, and Human Affairs*. Oxford: Brooks/Cole.

Bem, D. J., and Allen, A. (1974) On predicting some of the people some of the time: The search for cross-situational consistencies in behavior. *Psychological Review*, 81, 506–20.

Berger, I. E., and Mitchell, A. A. (1989) The effect of advertising on attitude accessibility, attitude confidence, and the attitude-behavior relationship. *Journal of Consumer Research*, 16, 269–79.

Bernberg, R. E. (1952) Socio-psychological factors in industrial morale: I. The prediction of specific indicators. *Journal of Social Psychology*, 36, 73–82.

Bernreuter, R. (1933) Validity of the personality inventory. *Personnel Journal*, 11, 383–6.

Bizer, G. Y., and Krosnick, J. A. (2001) Exploring the structure of strength-related attitude features: The relation between attitude importance and attitude accessibility. *Journal of Personality and Social Psychology*, 81, 566–86.

Blass, T. (1984) Social psychology and personality: Toward a convergence. *Journal of Personality and Social Psychology*, 47, 1013–27.

Bowers, K. S. (1973) Situationism in psychology: An analysis and a critique. *Psychological Review*, 80, 307–36.

Braver, S. (1996) Social contracts and the provision of public goods. In D. Schroeder (ed.), *Social Dilemmas: Perspectives on Individuals and Groups* (pp. 69–86). Westport, CT: Praeger.

Breckler, S. J. (1984) Empirical validation of affect, behavior, and cognition as distinct components of attitude. *Journal of Personality and Social Psychology*, 47, 1191–205.

Brown, D. W. (1974) Adolescent attitudes and lawful behavior. *Public Opinion Quarterly*, 38, 98–106.

Brubaker, R. G., and Fowler, C. (1990) Encouraging college males to perform testicular self-examination: Evaluation of a persuasive message based on the revised theory of reasoned action. *Journal of Applied Social Psychology*, 20, 1411–22.

Buss, A. H. (1961) *The Psychology of Aggression*. New York: Wiley.

Buss, A. H. (1980) *Self-Consciousness and Social Anxiety*. San Francisco: W. H. Freeman.

Buss, D. M., and Craik, K. H. (1980) The frequency concept of disposition: Dominance and prototypically dominant acts. *Journal of Personality*, 48, 379–92.

Buss, D. M., and Craik, K. H. (1981) The act frequency analysis of interpersonal dispositions: Aloofness, gregariousness, dominance and submissiveness. *Journal of Personality*, 49, 175–92.

Buss, D. M., and Craik, K. H. (1984) Acts, dispositions, and personality. In B. A. Maher and W. B. Maher (eds), *Progress in Experimental Personality Research* (pp. 241–301). San Diego: Academic Press.

Cacioppo, J. T., Crites, S. L., Berntson, G. G., and Coles, M. G. (1993) If attitudes affect how stimuli are processed, should they not affect the event-related brain potential? *Psychological Science*, 4, 108–12.

Cacioppo, J. T., Petty, R. E., Kao, C. F., and Rodriguez, R. (1986) Central and peripheral routes to persuasion: An individual difference perspective. *Journal of Personality and Social Psychology*, 51, 1032–43.

Cacioppo, J. T., Petty, R. E., Losch, M. E., and Kim, H. S. (1986) Electromyographic activity over facial muscle regions can differentiate the valence and intensity of affective reactions. *Journal of Personality and Social Psychology*, 50, 260–8.

Campbell, A., Converse, P. E., Miller, W. E., and Stokes, D. E. (1960) *The American Voter*. New York: Wiley.

Campbell, D. T. (1950) The indirect assessment of social attitudes. *Psychological Bulletin*, 47, 15–38.

Campbell, D. T. (1963) Social attitudes and other acquired behavioral dispositions. In S. Koch (ed.), *Psychology: A Study of a Science* (Vol. 6, pp. 94–172). New York: McGraw-Hill.

Carver, C. S. (1975) Physical aggression as a function of objective self-awareness and attitudes toward punishment. *Journal of Experimental Social Psychology*, 11, 510–19.

Carver, C. S., and Scheier, M. F. (1981) *Attention and Self-Regulation: A Control-Theory Approach to Human Behavior*. New York: Springer.

Cattell, R. B. (1946) *Description and Measurement of Personality*. Oxford: World Books.

Cattell, R. B. (1947) Confirmation and clarification of primary personality factors. *Psychometrika*, 12, 197–220.

Chaiken, S., and Trope, Y. (eds) (1999) *Dual-Process Theories in Social Psychology*. New York: Guilford Press.

Chaiken, S., and Yates, S. (1985) Affective-cognitive consistency and thought-induced attitude polarization. *Journal of Personality and Social Psychology*, 49, 1470–81.

Chaplin, W. F., and Goldberg, L. R. (1984) A failure to replicate the Bem and Allen study of individual differences in cross-situational consistency. *Journal of Personality and Social Psychology*, 47, 1074–90.

Cheung, S.-F., and Chan, D. K.-S. (2000) The role of perceived behavioral control in predicting human behavior: A meta-analytic review of studies on the theory of planned behavior. Unpublished manuscript, Chinese University of Hong Kong.

Cialdini, R. B. (2001) *Influence: Science and Practice* (4th edn.). Boston, MA: Allyn and Bacon.

Clarke, N. E. C., and Nancy M. (2000) Stakeholder attitudes toward ADA Title I: Development of an indirect measurement method. *Rehabilitation Counseling Bulletin*, 43, 58–65.

Cohen, J. (1978) Partialed products are interactions; partialed powers are curve components. *Psychological Bulletin*, 85, 858–66.

Cohen, J. (1983) The cost of dichotomization. *Applied Psychological Measurement*, 7, 249–53.

Conner, M., and Flesch, D. (2001) Having casual sex: Additive and interactive effects of alcohol and condom availability on the determinants of intentions. *Journal of Applied Social Psychology*, 31, 89–112.

Conner, M., and McMillan, B. (1999) Interaction effects in the theory of planned behavior: Studying cannabis use. *British Journal of Social Psychology*, 38, 195–222.

Conner, M., Sheeran, P., Norman, P., and Armitage, C. J. (2000) Temporal stability as a moderator of relationships in the Theory of Planned Behaviour. *British Journal of Social Psychology*, 39, 469–93.

Cook, S. W., and Selltiz, C. (1964) A multiple-indicator approach to attitude measurement. *Psychological Bulletin*, 62, 36–55.

Corey, S. M. (1937) Professed attitudes and actual behavior. *Journal of Educational Psychology*, 28, 271–80.

Courneya, K. S. (1995) Understanding readiness for regular physical activity in older individuals: An application of the theory of planned behavior. *Health Psychology*, 14, 80–7.

Courneya, K. S., and McAuley, E. (1995) Cognitive mediators of the social influence-exercise adherence relationship: A test of the theory of planned behavior. *Journal of Behavioral Medicine*, 18, 499–515.

Crandall, V. C., Katkovsky, W., and Crandall, V. J. (1965) Children's belief in their own control of reinforcements in intellectual-academic achievement situations. *Child Development*, 36, 91–109.

Cronbach, L. J. (1975) Beyond the two disciplines of scientific psychology. *American Psychologist*, 30, 116–27.

Cunningham, W. A., Preacher, K. J., and Banaji, M. R. (2001) Implicit attitude measures: Consistency, stability, and convergent validity. *Psychological Science*, 121, 163–70.

Daigle, J. J., Hrubes, D., and Ajzen, I. (2002) A comparative study of beliefs, attitudes, and values among hunters, wildlife viewers, and other outdoor recreationists. *Human Dimensions of Wildlife*, 7, 1–19.

Davis, L. E., Ajzen, I., Saunders, J., and Williams, T. (2002) The decision of African American students to complete high school: An application of the theory of planned behavior. *Journal of Educational Psychology*, 94, 810–19.

De Fleur, M. L., and Westie, F. R. (1958) Verbal attitudes and overt acts: An experiment on the salience of attitudes. *American Sociological Review*, 23, 667–73.

Dean, L. R. (1958) Interaction, reported and observed: The case of one local union. *Human Organization*, 17, 36–44.

Deutscher, I. (1966) Words and deeds: Social science and social policy. *Social Problems*, 13, 235–54.

Deutscher, I. (1973) *What We Say/What We Do: Sentiments and Acts.* Glenview, IL: Scott, Foresman.

Devine, P. G. (1989) Stereotypes and prejudice: Their automatic and controlled components. *Journal of Personality and Social Psychology*, 56, 5–18.

Digman, J. M., and Inouye, J. (1986) Further specification of the five robust factors of personality. *Journal of Personality and Social Psychology*, 50, 116–23.

Dillon, W. R., and Kumar, A. (1985) Attitude organization and the attitude-behavior relation: A critique of Bagozzi and Burnkrant's reanalysis of Fishbein and Ajzen. *Journal of Personality and Social Psychology*, 49, 33–46.

Doll, J., and Ajzen, I. (1992) Accessibility and stability of predictors in the theory of planned behavior. *Journal of Personality and Social Psychology*, 63, 754–65.

Dovidio, J. F., Brigham, J. C., Johnson, B. T., and Gaertner, S. L. (1996) Stereotyping, prejudice, and discrimination: Another look. In N. Macrae, C. Stangor and M. Hewstone (eds), *Stereotypes and Stereotyping* (pp. 276–319). New York: Guilford.

Dovidio, J. F., Kawakami, K., Johnson, C., Johnson, B., and Howard, A. (1997) On the nature of prejudice: automatic and controlled processes. *Journal of Experimental Social Psychology*, 33, 510–40.

Duckitt, J. H. (1992) *The Social Psychology of Prejudice.* Westport, CT: Praeger.

Dudycha, G. J. (1936) An objective study of punctuality in relation to personality and achievement. *Archives of Psychology*, 29, 1–53.

Dulany, D. E. (1968) Awareness, rules, and propositional control: A confrontation with S-R behavior theory. In D. Hornton and T. Dixon (eds), *Verbal Behavior and S-R Behavior Theory* (pp. 340–87). Englewood Cliffs: NJ: Prentice-Hall.

Duval, S., and Wicklund, R. A. (1972) *A Theory of Objective Self-Awareness.* San Diego: Academic Press.

Eagly, A. H. (1974) Comprehensibility of persuasive arguments as a determinant of opinion change. *Journal of Personality and Social Psychology*, 29, 758–73.

Eagly, A. H. (1998) Attitudes and the processing of attitude-relevant information. In J. G. Adair and D. Belanger (eds), *Advances in Psychological Science*, Vol. 1: *Social, Personal, and Cultural Aspects* (pp. 185–201). Hove: Psychology Press/Erlbaum (UK) Taylor and Francis.

Eagly, A. H., and Chaiken, S. (1993) *The Psychology of Attitudes.* Fort Worth, TX: Harcourt Brace.

Eagly, A. H., and Chaiken, S. (1998) Attitude structure and function. In

D. T. Gilbert and S. T. Fiske (eds), *The Handbook of Social Psychology* (4th edn., Vol. 1, pp. 269–322). Boston, MA: McGraw-Hill.

East, R. (1993) Investment decisions and the theory of planned behavior. *Journal of Economic Psychology*, 14, 337–75.

Edwards, A. L. (1957) *Techniques of Attitude Scale Construction*. East Norwalk, CT: Appleton-Century-Crofts.

Edwards, A. L., and Abbott, R. D. (1973a) Relationships among the Edwards Personality Inventory Scales, the Edwards Personality Preference Schedule, and the Personality Research Form Scales. *Journal of Consulting and Clinical Psychology*, 40, 27–32.

Edwards, A. L., and Abbott, R. D. (1973b) Relationships between the EPI Scales and the 16 PF, CPI, and EPPS Scales. *Educational and Psychological Measurement*, 33, 231–8.

Edwards, A. L., and Kenney, K. C. (1946) A comparison of the Thurstone and Likert techniques of attitude scale construction. *Journal of Applied Psychology*, 30, 72–83.

Eichstaedt, J., and Silvia, P. J. (2003) Noticing the self: Implicit assessment of self-focused attention using word recognition latencies. *Social Cognition*, 21, 349–61.

Ekehammar, B. (1974) Interactionism in personality from a historical perspective. *Psychological Bulletin* 81, 1026–48.

Elliott, M. A., Armitage, C. J., and Baughan, C. J. (2003) Drivers' compliance with speed limits: An application of the theory of planned behavior. *Journal of Applied Psychology*, 88, 964–72.

Endler, N. S., and Magnusson, D. (1976) Toward an interactional psychology of personality. *Psychological Bulletin*, 83, 956–74.

Epstein, S. (1979) The stability of behavior: I. On predicting most of the people much of the time. *Journal of Personality and Social Psychology*, 37, 1097–126.

Epstein, S. (1980a) The self-concept: A review and the proposal of an integrated theory of personality. In E. Staub (ed.), *Personality: Basic Aspects and Current Research* (pp. 81–132). Englewood Cliffs, NJ: Prentice-Hall.

Epstein, S. (1980b) The stability of behavior: II. Implications for psychological research. *American Psychologist*, 35, 790–806.

Epstein, S. (1983a) Aggregation and beyond: Some basic issues on the prediction of behavior. *Journal of Personality*, 51, 360–92.

Epstein, S. (1983b) The unconscious, the preconscious, and the self-concept. In J. Suls and A. G. Greenwald (eds), *Psychological Perspectives on the Self* (Vol. 2, pp. 219–47). Hillsdale, NJ: Lawrence Erlbaum Associates.

Epstein, S., and O'Brien, E. J. (1985) The person-situation debate in historical and current perspective. *Psychological Bulletin*, 98, 513–37.

Estabrooks, P., and Courneya, K. S. (1997) Relationships among self-schema, intention, and exercise behavior. *Journal of Sport and Exercise Psychology*, 19, 156–68.

Evans, D. A., and Alexander, S. (1970) Some psychological correlates of civil rights activity. *Psychological Reports*, 26, 899–906.

Eysenck, H. J. (1947) *Dimensions of Personality*. Oxford: Kegan Paul.

Eysenck, H. J. (1953) *The Structure of Human Personality*. New York: Methuen.

Eysenck, H. J. (1956) The questionnaire measurement of neuroticism and extraversion. *Revista de Psicologia*, 50, 113–40.

Eysenck, H. J. (1967) *The Biological Basis of Personality*. Springfield, IL: Thomas.

Fazio, R. H. (1986) How do attitudes guide behavior? In R. M. H. Sorrentino and

Edward Tory (eds), *Handbook of Motivation and Cognition: Foundations of Social Behavior* (pp. 204–43). New York: Guilford Press.

Fazio, R. H. (1990a) Multiple processes by which attitudes guide behavior: The MODE model as an integrative framework. In M. P. Zanna (ed.), *Advances in Experimental Social Psychology* (Vol. 23, pp. 75–109). San Diego, CA: Academic Press.

Fazio, R. H. (1990b) A practical guide to the use of response latency in social psychological research. In C. Hendrick and M. S. Clark (eds), *Research Methods in Personality and Social Psychology: Review of Personality and Social Psychology* (Vol. 11, pp. 74–97). Newbury Park, CA: Sage.

Fazio, R. H. (1995) Attitudes as object-evaluation associations: Determinants, consequences, and correlates of attitude accessibility. In R. E. Petty and J. A. Krosnick (eds), *Attitude Strength: Antecedents and Consequences* (pp. 247–82). Mahwah, NJ: Erlbaum.

Fazio, R. H., Chen, J., McDonel, E. C., and Sherman, S. J. (1982) Attitude accessibility, attitude-behavior consistency, and the strength of the object-evaluation association. *Journal of Experimental Social Psychology*, 18, 339–57.

Fazio, R. H., and Dunton, B. C. (1997) Categorization by race: The impact of automatic and controlled components of racial prejudice. *Journal of Experimental Social Psychology*, 33, 451–70.

Fazio, R. H., Jackson, J. R., Dunton, B. C., and Williams, C. J. (1995) Variability in automatic activation as an unobstrusive measure of racial attitudes: A bona fide pipeline? *Journal of Personality and Social Psychology*, 69, 1013–27.

Fazio, R. H., and Olson, M. A. (2003) Implicit measures in social cognition research: Their meaning and uses. *Annual Review of Psychology*, 54, 297–327.

Fazio, R. H., Powell, M. C., and Herr, P. M. (1983) Toward a process model of the attitude-behavior relation: Accessing one's attitude upon mere observation of the attitude object. *Journal of Personality and Social Psychology*, 44, 723–35.

Fazio, R. H., Powell, M. C., and Williams, C. J. (1989) The role of attitude accessibility in the attitude-to-behavior process. *Journal of Consumer Research*, 16, 280–8.

Fazio, R. H., and Towles-Schwen, T. (1999) The MODE model of attitude-behavior processes. In S. Chaiken and Y. Trope (eds), *Dual-Process Theories in Social Psychology* (pp. 97–116). New York: Guilford.

Fazio, R. H., and Williams, C. J. (1986) Attitude accessibility as a moderator of the attitude-perception and attitude-behavior relations: An investigation of the 1984 presidential election. *Journal of Personality and Social Psychology*, 51, 505–14.

Fazio, R. H., and Zanna, M. P. (1978a) Attitudinal qualities relating to the strength of the attitude-behavior relationship. *Journal of Experimental Social Psychology*, 14, 398–408.

Fazio, R. H., and Zanna, M. P. (1978b) On the predictive validity of attitudes: The roles of direct experience and confidence. *Journal of Personality*, 46, 228–43.

Fazio, R. H., and Zanna, M. P. (1981) Direct experience and attitude-behavior consistency. In L. Berkowitz (ed.), *Advances in Experimental Social Psychology* (Vol. 14, pp. 161–202). New York: Academic Press.

Fenigstein, A., Scheier, M. F., and Buss, A. H. (1975) Public and private self-consciousness: Assessment and theory. *Journal of Consulting and Clinical Psychology*, 43, 522–7.

Festinger, L. (1957) *A Theory of Cognitive Dissonance*. Oxford: Row, Peterson.

Fishbein, M. (1963) An investigation of the relationships between beliefs about an object and the attitude toward that object. *Human Relations*, 16, 233–40.

Fishbein, M., and Ajzen, I. (1974) Attitudes towards objects as predictors of single and multiple behavioral criteria. *Psychological Review*, 81, 59–74.

Fishbein, M., and Ajzen, I. (1975) *Belief, Attitude, Intention, and Behavior: An Introduction to Theory and Research*. Reading, MA: Addison-Wesley.

Fishbein, M., and Ajzen, I. (1981) Attitudes and voting behavior: An application of the theory of reasoned action. In G. M. Stephenson and J. M. Davis (eds), *Progress in Applied Social Psychology* (Vol. 1, pp. 95–125). London: Wiley.

Fishbein, M., and Ajzen, I. (2005) Theory-based behavior change interventions: Comments on Hobbis and Sutton. *Journal of Health Psychology*, 10, 27–31.

Fishbein, M., Cappella, J., Hornik, R., Sayeed, S., Yzer, M., and Ahern, R. K. (2002) The role of theory in developing effective antidrug public service announcements. In W. D. Crano and M. Burgoon (eds), *Mass Media and Drug Prevention: Classic and Contemporary Theories and Research* (pp. 89–117). Mahwah, NJ: Lawrence Erlbaum Associates, Publishers.

Fishbein, M., and Coombs, F. S. (1974) Basis for decision: An attitudinal analysis of voting behavior. *Journal of Applied Social Psychology*, 4, 95–124.

Fishbein, M., Thomas, K., and Jaccard, J. J. (1976) *Voting Behavior in Britain: An Attitudinal Analysis*. London: SSRC Survey Unit.

Fisher, J. D., and Fisher, W. A. (1992) Changing AIDS-risk behavior. *Psychological Bulletin*, 111, 455–74.

Fiske, D. W. (1949) Consistency of the factorial structures of personality ratings from different sources. *Journal of Abnormal and Social Psychology*, 44, 329–44.

Freeman, L. C., and Ataoev, T. (1960) Invalidity of indirect and direct measures of attitude toward cheating. *Journal of Personality*, 28, 443–7.

Froming, W. J., Walker, G. R., and Lopyan, K. J. (1982) Public and private self-awareness: When personal attitudes conflict with societal expectations. *Journal of Experimental Social Psychology*, 18, 476–87.

Fulton, D. C., Manfredo, M. J., and Lipscomb, J. (1996) Wildlife value orientations: A conceptual and measurement approach. *Human Dimensions of Wildlife*, 1, 24–47.

Funder, D. C., Block, J. H., and Block, J. (1983) Delay of gratification: Some longitudinal personality correlates. *Journal of Personality and Social Psychology*, 44, 1198–213.

Furnham, A., and Lovett, J. (2001) Predicting the use of complementary medicine: A test of the theories of reasoned action and planned behavior. *Journal of Applied Social Psychology*, 31, 2588–620.

Gaertner, S. L., and Dovidio, J. F. (1986) The aversive form of racism. In J. F. Dovidio and S. L. Gaertner (eds), *Prejudice, Discrimination, and Racism*. (pp. 61–89). Orlando, FL: Academic Press.

Gibb, C. A. (1969) Leadership. In G. Lindzey and E. Aronson (eds), *Handbook of Social Psychology* (2 edn., Vol. 4, pp. 205–82). Reading, MA: Addison-Wesley.

Giles, M., and Cairns, E. (1995) Blood donation and Ajzen's theory of planned behaviour: An examination of perceived behavioural control. *British Journal of Social Psychology*, 34, 173–88.

Godin, G., and Kok, G. (1996) The theory of planned behavior: A review of its applications to health-related behaviors. *American Journal of Health Promotion*, 11, 87–98.

Godin, G., Valois, P., Lepage, L., and Desharnais, R. (1992) Predictors of smoking behaviour: An application of Ajzen's theory of planned behaviour. *British Journal of Addiction*, 87, 1335–43.

Godin, G., Valois, P., Shephard, R. J., and Desharnais, R. (1987) Prediction of leisure-time exercise behavior: A path analysis (LISREL V) model. *Journal of Behavioral Medicine*, 10, 145–58.

Gollwitzer, P. M. (1993) Goal achievement: The role of intentions. In W. Stroebe and M. Hewstone (eds), *European Review of Social Psychology* (Vol. 4, pp. 141–85). Chichester, England: Wiley.

Gollwitzer, P. M. (1996) The volitional benefits of planning. In P. M. Gollwitzer and J. A. Bargh (eds), *The Psychology of Action: Linking Cognition and Motivation to Behavior* (pp. 287–312). New York: Guilford.

Gollwitzer, P. M. (1999) Implementation intentions: Strong effects of simple plans. *American Psychologist*, 54, 493–503.

Gollwitzer, P. M., and Brandstätter, V. (1997) Implementation intentions and effective goal pursuit. *Journal of Personality and Social Psychology*, 73, 186–99.

Gollwitzer, P. M., and Schaal, B. (1998) Metacognition in action: The importance of implementation intentions. *Personality and Social Psychology Review*, 2, 124–36.

Gore, P. M., and Rotter, J. B. (1963) A personality correlate of social action. *Journal of Personality*, 31, 58–64.

Gough, H. G. (1957) *Manual for the California Psychological Inventory*. Palo Alto, CA: Consulting Psychologists Press.

Green, B. F. (1954) Attitude measurement. In G. Lindzey (ed.), *Handbook of Social Psychology* (Vol. 1, pp. 335–69). Reading, MA: Addison-Wesley.

Greenwald, A. G., and Farnham, S. D. (2000) Using the Implicit Association Test to measure self-esteem and self-concept. *Journal of Personality and Social Psychology*, 79, 1022–38.

Greenwald, A. G., McGhee, D. E., and Schwartz, J. L. K. (1998) Measuring individual differences in implicit cognition: The implicit association test. *Journal of Personality and Social Psychology*, 74, 1464–80.

Guilford, J. P. (1954) *Psychometric Methods* (2nd edn.). New York: McGraw-Hill.

Guttman, L. (1957) Introduction to facet design and analysis. Paper presented at the Fifteenth International Congress of Psychology, Brussels.

Guttman, L. (1959) A structural theory for intergroup beliefs and action. *American Sociological Review*, 24, 318–28.

Hagger, M. S., Chatzisarantis, N. L. D., and Biddle, S. J. H. (2002a) The influence of autonomous and controlling motives on physical activity intentions within the Theory of Planned Behaviour. *British Journal of Health Psychology*, 7, 283–97.

Hagger, M. S., Chatzisarantis, N. L. D., and Biddle, S. J. H. (2002b) A meta-analytic review of the theories of reasoned action and planned behavior in physical activity: Predictive validity and the contribution of additional variables. *Journal of Sport and Exercise Psychology*, 24, 3–32.

Hall, S. M., and Hall, R. G. (1974) Outcome and methodological considerations in behavioral treatment of obesity. *Behavior Therapy*, 5, 352–64.

Hammond, K. R. (1948) Measuring attitudes by error choice: An indirect method. *Journal of Abnormal and Social Psychology*, 43, 38–48.

Hardeman, W., Johnston, M., Johnston, D. W., Bonetti, D., Wareham, N. J., and Kinmonth, A. L. (2002) Application of the Theory of Planned Behaviour in behaviour change interventions: A systematic review. *Psychology and Health*, 17, 123–58.

Hartshorne, H., and May, M. A. (1928) *Studies in the Nature of Character:* Vol. 1. *Studies in Deceit.* New York: Macmillan.

Hartshorne, H., May, M. A., and Maller, J. B. (1929) *Studies in the Nature of Character:* Vol. 2. *Studies in Self-Control*. New York: Macmillan.

Hartshorne, H., May, M. A., and Shuttleworth, F. K. (1930) *Studies in the Nature of Character:* Vol. 3. *Studies in the Organization of Character*. New York: Macmillan.

Haugtvedt, C. P., and Petty, R. E. (1992) Personality and persuasion: Need for cognition moderates the persistence and resistance of attitude changes. *Journal of Personality and Social Psychology*, 63, 308–19.

Hausenblas, H. A., Carron, A. V., and Mack, D. E. (1997) Application of the theories of reasoned action and planned behavior to exercise behavior: A meta-analysis. *Journal of Sport and Exercise Psychology*, 19, 36–51.

Heider, F. (1944) Social perception and phenomenal causality. *Psychological Review*, 51, 358–74.

Heider, F. (1958) *The Psychology of Interpersonal Relations*. Oxford: Wiley.

Hilgard, E. R. (1980) The trilogy of mind: Cognition, affection, and conation. *Journal of the History of the Behavioral Sciences*, 16, 107–17.

Hill, R. J. (1981) Attitudes and behavior. In M. Rosenberg and R. H. Turner (eds), *Social Psychology: Sociological Perspectives* (pp. 347–77). New York: Basic Books.

Himelstein, P., and Moore, J. (1963) Racial attitudes and the action of Negro and white background figures as factors in petition-signing. *Journal of Social Psychology*, 61, 267–72.

Hovland, C. I., Janis, I. L., and Kelley, H. H. (1953) *Communication and Persuasion: Psychological Studies of Opinion Change*. New Haven, CT: Yale University Press.

Hrubes, D., Ajzen, I., and Daigle, J. (2001) Predicting hunting intentions and behavior: An application of the theory of planned behavior. *Leisure Sciences*, 23, 165–78.

Isen, A. M., and Levin, P. F. (1972) Effect of feeling good on helping: Cookies and kindness. *Journal of Personality and Social Psychology*, 21, 384–8.

Jaccard, J. J. (1974) Predicting social behavior from personality traits. *Journal of Research in Personality*, 7, 358–67.

Jackson, D. N. (1967) *Personality Research Form Manual*. Goshen, NY: Research Psychologists Press.

Jackson, D. N. (1971) The dynamics of structured personality tests: 1971. *Psychological Review*, 78, 229–48.

Jackson, D. N., and Paunonen, S. V. (1985) Construct validity and the predictability of behavior. *Journal of Personality and Social Psychology*, 49, 554–70.

Jessor, R., and Jessor, S. (1977) *Problem Behavior and Psychosocial Development*. San Diego: Academic Press.

Jones, E. E., and Davis, K. E. (1965) From acts to dispositions: The attribution process in person perception. In L. Berkowitz (ed.), *Advances in Experimental Social Psychology* (Vol. 2, pp. 219–66). San Diego: Academic Press.

Kardes, F. R., Sanbonmatsu, D. M., Voss, R. T., and Fazio, R. H. (1986) Self-monitoring and attitude accessibility. *Personality and Social Psychology Bulletin*, 12, 468–74.

Karpinski, A. (2004) Measuring self-esteem using the Implicit Association Test: The role of the other. *Personality and Social Psychology Bulletin*, 30, 22–34.

Karpinski, A., and Hilton, J. L. (2001) Attitudes and the Implicit Association Test. *Journal of Personality and Social Psychology*, 81, 774–88.

Kashima, Y., Gallois, C., and McCamish, M. (1993) The theory of reasoned action and cooperative behaviour: It takes two to use a condom. *British Journal of Social Psychology*, 32, 227–39.

Katz, D., and Stotland, E. (1959) A preliminary statement to a theory of attitude structure and change. In S. Koch (ed.), *Psychology: A Study of a Science*. Vol. 3. *Formulations of the Person and the Social Context* (pp. 423–75). New York: McGraw-Hill.

Kawakami, K., and Dovidio, J. F. (2001) The reliability of implicit stereotyping. *Personality and Social Psychology Bulletin*, 27, 212–25.

Kelley, H. H. (1971) *Attribution in Social Interaction*. New York: General Learning Press.

Kelly, G. A. (1955) *The Psychology of Personal Constructs*. Oxford: Norton.

Kendzierski, D. (1988) Self-schemata and exercise. *Basic and Applied Social Psychology*, 9, 45–59.

Kendzierski, D., and Costello, M. C. (2004) Healthy eating self-schema and nutrition behavior. *Jounal of Applied Social Psychology*, 34, 2437–51.

Kerner, M. S., and Grossman, A. H. (1998) Attitudinal, social, and practical correlates to fitness behavior: A test of the theory of planned behavior. *Perceptual and Motor Skills*, 87, 1139–54.

Kidder, L. H., and Campbell, D. T. (1970) The indirect testing of attitudes. In G. F. Summers (ed.), *Attitude Measurement* (pp. 333–85). Chicago: Rand-McNally.

Kiesler, C. A. (1971) *The Psychology of Commitment: Experiments Linking Behavior to Belief*. San Diego, CA: Academic Press.

King, G. W. (1975) An analysis of attitudinal and normative variables as predictors of intentions and behavior. *Speech Monographs*, 42, 237–44.

Kirkpatrick, C. (1949) Religion and humanitarianism: A study of institutional implications. *Psychological Monographs*, 63, 191 (Whole No. 304).

Kleinmuntz, B. (1967) *Personality Measurement: An Introduction*. Homewood, IL: Dorsey.

Kline, S. L. (1987) Self-monitoring and attitude-behavior correspondence in cable television subscription. *Journal of Social Psychology*, 127, 605–9.

Knapper, C. K., and Cropley, A. J. (1981) Social and interpersonal factors in driving. In G. M. Stephenson and J. H. Davis (eds), *Progress in Applied Social Psychology* (Vol. 1, pp. 191–220). New York: Wiley.

Kokkinaki, F., and Lunt, P. (1997) The relationship between involvement, attitude accessibility and attitude-behaviour consistency. *British Journal of Social Psychology*, 36, 497–509.

Kothandapani, V. (1971) Validation of feeling, belief, and intention to act as three components of attitude and their contribution to prediction of contraceptive behavior. *Journal of Personality and Social Psychology*, 19, 321–33.

Kraus, S. J. (1995) Attitudes and the prediction of behavior: A meta-analysis of the empirical literature. *Personality and Social Psychology Bulletin*, 21, 58–75.

Krosnick, J. A. (1988) The role of attitude importance in social evaluation: A study of policy preferences, presidential candidate evaluations, and voting behavior. *Journal of Personality and Social Psychology*, 55, 196–210.

Krosnick, J. A., Boninger, D. S., Chuang, Y. C., Berent, M. K., and Carnot, C. G. (1993) Attitude strength: One construct or many related constructs? *Journal of Personality and Social Psychology*, 65, 1132–51.

Kuhl, J. (1985) Volitional aspects of achievement motivation and learned helplessness: Toward a comprehensive theory of action control. In

B. A. Maher (ed.), *Progress in Experimental Personality Research* (Vol. 13, pp. 99–171). San Diego: Academic Press.

Kuhl, J. and Beckmann, J. (eds) (1985) *Action-Control: From Cognition to Behavior*. Heidelberg; Springer.

LaPiere, R. T. (1934) Attitudes vs. actions. *Social Forces*, 13, 230–7.

Lefcourt, H. M. (1981a) Overview. In H. M. Lefcourt (ed.), *Research with the Locus of Control Construct*. Vol. 1: *Assessment Methods* (pp. 1–11). San Diego: Academic Press.

Lefcourt, H. M. (ed.) (1981b) *Research with the Locus of Control Construct*. Vol. 1: *Assessment Methods*. San Diego: Academic Press.

Lefcourt, H. M. (1982) *Locus of Control: Current Trends in Theory and Research* (2nd edn.). Hillsdale, NJ: Lawrence Erlbaum Associates.

Lefcourt, H. M. (ed.) (1983) *Research with the Locus of Control Construct*. Vol. 2: *Developments and Social Problems*. San Diego: Academic Press.

Lenski, G. E., and Leggett, J. C. (1960) Caste, class, and deference in the research interview. *American Journal of Sociology*, 65, 463–7.

Leon, G. R., and Roth, L. (1977) Obesity: Psychological causes, correlations, and speculations. *Psychological Bulletin*, 84, 117–39.

Levenson, H. (1981) Differentiating among internality, powerful others, and chance. In H. M. Lefcourt (ed.), *Research with the Locus of Control Construct*. Vol. 1: *Assessment Methods* (pp. 15–63). San Diego: Academic Press.

Likert, R. (1932) A technique for the measurement of attitudes. *Archives of Psychology*, 140, 5–53.

Lilienfeld, S. O., Wood, J. M., and Garb, H. N. (2000) The scientific status of projective techniques. *Psychological Science in the Public Interest*, 1, 27–66.

Linn, L. S. (1965) Verbal attitudes and overt behavior: A study of racial discrimination. *Social Forces*, 43, 353–64.

Liska, A. E. (1984) A critical examination of the causal structure of the Fishbein/Ajzen attitude-behavior model. *Social Psychology Quarterly*, 47, 61–74.

Locke, E. A., Frederick, E., Lee, C., and Bobko, P. (1984) Effect of self-efficacy, goals, and task strategies on task performance. *Journal of Applied Psychology*, 69, 241–51.

Lord, C. G., Lepper, M. R., and Mackie, D. (1984) Attitude prototypes as determinants of attitude-behavior consistency. *Journal of Personality and Social Psychology*, 46, 1254–66.

Lorr, M., O'Connor, J. P., and Seifert, R. F. (1977) A comparison of four personality inventories. *Journal of Personality Assessment*, 41, 520–6.

Lüdemann, C. (1997) *Rationalität und Umweltverhalten*. Wiesbaden: Deutscher Universitäts-Verlag.

Madden, T. J., Ellen, P. S., and Ajzen, I. (1992) A comparison of the theory of planned behavior and the theory of reasoned action. *Personality and Social Psychology Bulletin*, 18, 3–9.

Mann, R. D. (1959) A review of the relationships between personality and performance in small groups. *Psychological Bulletin*, 56, 241–70.

Manstead, A. S. R., Proffitt, C., and Smart, J. (1983) Predicting and understanding mothers' infant-feeding intentions and behavior: Testing the theory of reasoned action. *Journal of Personality and Social Psychology*, 44, 657–71.

Markey, P. M., Markey, C. N., and Tinsley, B. J. (2004) Children's behavioral manifestations of the five-factor model of personality. *Personality and Social Psychology Bulletin*, 30, 423–32.

Markus, H. (1977) Self-schemata and processing information about the self. *Journal of Personality and Social Psychology*, 35, 63–78.

Matthews, G., Deary, I. J., and Whiteman, M. C. (2003) *Personality Traits* (2nd edn.). Cambridge: Cambridge University Press.

McConahay, J. B. (1986) Modern racism, ambivalence, and the Modern Racism Scale. In J. F. Dovidio and S. L. Gaertner (eds), *Prejudice, Discrimination, and Racism* (pp. 91–125). San Diego, CA: Academic Press, Inc.

McCrae, R. R., and John, O. P. (1992) An introduction to the five-factor model and its applications. *Journal of Personality*, 60, 175–215.

McGowan, J., and Gormly, J. (1976) Validation of personality traits: A multicriteria approach. *Journal of Personality and Social Psychology*, 34, 791–95.

McGuire, W. J. (1960a) Cognitive consistency and attitude change. *Journal of Abnormal and Social Psychology*, 60, 345–53.

McGuire, W. J. (1960b) A syllogistic analysis of cognitive relationships. In M. J. Rosenberg, C. I. Hovland, W. J. McGuire, R. P. Abelson and J. W. Brehm (eds), *Attitude Organization and Change: An Analysis of Consistency among Attitude Components* (pp. 65–111). New Haven, CT: Yale University Press.

McGuire, W. J. (1969) The nature of attitudes and attitude change. In G. Lindzey and E. Aronson (eds), *The Handbook of Social Psychology* (2nd edn., Vol. 3, pp. 136–314). Reading, MA: Addison-Wesley.

McGuire, W. J. (1985) The nature of attitudes and attitude change. In G. Lindzey and E. Aronson (eds), *Handbook of Social Psychology* (3rd edn., Vol. 2, pp. 223–346). New York: Random House.

McMillan, B., and Conner, M. (2003) Applying an extended version of the theory of planned behavior to illicit drug use among students. *Jounal of Applied Social Psychology*, 33, 1662–83.

Merton, R. K. (1940) Fact and factitiousness in ethnic opinionnaires. *American Sociological Review*, 5, 13–28.

Millar, M. G., and Millar, K. U. (1998) The effects of prior experience and thought on the attitude-behavior relation. *Social Behavior and Personality*, 26, 105–14.

Millar, M. G., and Tesser, A. (1986) Effects of affective and cognitive focus on the attitude-behavior relation. *Journal of Personality and Social Psychology*, 51, 270–6.

Miller, G. A. (1956) The magical number seven, plus or minus two: some limits on our capacity for processing information. *Psychological Review*, 63, 81–97.

Miller, L. E., and Grush, J. E. (1986) Individual differences in attitudinal versus normative determination of behavior. *Journal of Experimental Social Psychology*, 22, 190–202.

Minard, R. D. (1952) Race relations in the Pocahontas coal field. *Journal of Social Issues*, 8, 29–44.

Mischel, W. (1968) *Personality and Assessment*. New York: Wiley.

Mischel, W. (1969) Continuity and change in personality. *American Psychologist*, 24, 1012–18.

Mischel, W. (1983) Alternatives in the pursuit of the predictability and consistency of persons: Stable data that yield unstable interpretations. *Journal of Personality*, 51, 578–604.

Mischel, W. (1984) Convergences and challenges in the search for consistency. *American Psychologist*, 39, 351–64.

Mischel, W., and Peake, P. K. (1982a) Beyond déjà vu in the search for cross-situational consistency. *Psychological Review*, 89, 730–55.

Mischel, W., and Peake, P. K. (1982b) In search of consistency: Measure for measure. In M. P. Zanna, E. T. Higgins and C. P. Herman (eds), *Consistency in Social Behavior: The Ontario Symposium* (Vol. 2, pp. 187–207). Hillsdale, NJ: Lawrence Erlbaum Associates.

Monson, T. C., Hesley, J. W., and Chernick, L. (1982) Specifying when personality traits can and cannot predict behavior: An alternative to abandoning the attempt to predict single-act criteria. *Journal of Personality and Social Psychology*, 43, 385–99.

Nisbett, R. (1977) Interaction versus main effects as goals of personality research. In D. Magnusson and N. S. Endler (eds), *Personality at the Crossroads: Current Issues in International Psychology* (pp. 235–41). New York: Wiley.

Nisbett, R., and Ross, L. (1980) *Human Inference: Strategies and Shortcomings of Social Judgment*. Englewood Cliffs, NJ: Prentice-Hall.

Norman, P., and Smith, L. (1995) The theory of planned behaviour and exercise: An investigation into the role of prior behaviour, behavioural intentions and attitude variability. *European Journal of Social Psychology*, 25, 403–15.

Norman, R. (1975) Affective-cognitive consistency, attitudes, conformity, and behavior. *Journal of Personality and Social Psychology*, 32, 83–91.

Norman, W. T. (1963) Toward an adequate taxonomy of personality attributes: Replicated factor structure in peer nomination personality ratings. *Journal of Abnormal and Social Psychology*, 66, 574–83.

Notani, A. S. (1998) Moderators of perceived behavioral control's predictiveness in the theory of planned behavior: A meta-analysis. *Journal of Consumer Psychology*, 7, 247–71.

Olweus, D. (1979) Stability of aggressive reaction patterns in males: A review. *Psychological Bulletin*, 86, 852–75.

Orbell, S., Blair, C., Sherlock, K., and Conner, M. (2001) The theory of planned behavior and ecstasy use: Roles for habit and perceived control over taking versus obtaining substances. *Journal of Applied Social Psychology*, 31, 31–47.

Orbell, S., Hodgkins, S., and Sheeran, P. (1997) Implementation intentions and the theory of planned behavior. *Personality and Social Psychology Bulletin*, 23, 945–54.

Orbell, S., and Sheeran, P. (2000) Motivational and volitional processes in action initiation: A field study of the role of implementation intentions. *Journal of Applied Social Psychology*, 30, 780–97.

Osgood, C. E., Suci, G. J., and Tannenbaum, P. H. (1957) *The Measurement of Meaning*. Urbana, IL: University of Illinois Press.

Oskamp, S. (1991) *Attitudes and Opinions* (2nd edn.). Upper Saddle River, NJ: Prentice-Hall, Inc.

Ostrom, T. M. (1969) The relationship between the affective, behavioral, and cognitive components of attitude. *Journal of Experimental Social Psychology*, 5, 12–30.

Ouellette, J. A., and Wood, W. (1998) Habit and intention in everyday life: The multiple processes by which past behavior predicts future behavior. *Psychological Bulletin*, 124, 54–74.

Paulhus, D. L. (1991) Measurement and control of response bias. In J. P. Robinson, P. R. Shaver and L. S. Wrightsman (eds), *Measures of Personality and Social Psychological Attitudes* (pp. 17–59). San Diego, CA: Academic Press.

Paunonen, S. V. (2003) Big Five factors of personality and replicated predictions of behavior. *Journal of Personality and Social Psychology*, 84, 411–22.

Peterson, D. R. (1968) *The Clinical Study of Social Behavior*. East Norwalk, CT: Appleton-Century-Crofts.

Petty, R. E., and Cacioppo, J. T. (1981) *Attitudes and Persuasion: Classic and Contemporary Approaches*. Dubuque, IA: Wm. C. Brown.

Petty, R. E., and Cacioppo, J. T. (1986) *Communication and Persuasion: Central and Peripheral Routes to Attitude Change*. New York: Springer Verlag.

Petty, R. E., and Cacioppo, J. T. (1986) The elaboration likelihood model of persuasion. In L. Berkowitz (ed.), *Advances in Experimental Social Psychology* (Vol. 19, pp. 123–205). New York: Academic Press.

Petty, R. E., and Krosnick, J. A. (eds) (1995) *Attitude Strength: Antecedents and Consequences*. Mahwah, NJ: Erlbaum.

Pomazal, R. J., and Jaccard, J. J. (1976) An informational approach to altruistic behavior. *Journal of Personality and Social Psychology*, 33, 317–26.

Pryor, J. B., Gibbons, F. X., Wicklund, R. A., Fazio, R. H., and Hood, R. (1977) Self-focused attention and self-report validity. *Journal of Personality*, 45, 513–27.

Raden, D. (1985) Strength-related attitude dimensions. *Social Psychology Quarterly*, 48, 312–30.

Randall, D. M., and Wolff, J. A. (1994) The time interval in the intention-behaviour relationship: Meta-analysis. *British Journal of Social Psychology*, 33, 405–18.

Regan, D. T., and Fazio, R. H. (1977) On the consistency between attitudes and behavior: Look to the method of attitude formation. *Journal of Experimental Social Psychology*, 13, 28–45.

Rosenberg, M. J. (1956) Cognitive structure and attitudinal affect. *Journal of Abnormal and Social Psychology*, 53, 367–72.

Rosenberg, M. J. (1965) Inconsistency arousal and reduction in attitude change. In I. D. Steiner and M. Fishbein (eds), *Current Studies in Social Psychology* (pp. 121–34). New York: Holt, Reinhart, and Winston.

Rosenberg, M. J. (1968) Hedonism, inauthenticity, and other goals toward expansion of a consistency theory. In R. P. Abelson, E. Aronson, W. J. McGuire, T. M. Newcomb, M. J. Rosenberg and P. H. Tannenbaum (eds), *Theories of Cognitive Consistency* (pp. 73–111). Chicago: Rand McNally.

Rosenberg, M. J., and Hovland, C. I. (1960) Cognitive, affective, and behavioral components of attitudes. In C. I. Hovland and M. J. Rosenberg (eds), *Attitude Organization and Change: An Analysis of Consistency among Attitude Components* (pp. 1–14). New Haven, CT: Yale University Press.

Roth, H. G., and Upmeyer, A. (1985) Matching attitudes towards cartoons across evaluative judgments and nonverbal evaluative behavior. *Psychological Research*, 47, 173–83.

Rotter, J. B. (1954) *Social Learning and Clinical Psychology*. Oxford: Prentice-Hall.

Rotter, J. B. (1966) Generalized expectancies for internal versus external control of reinforcement. *Psychological Monographs (General and Applied)*, 80, 1–28.

Rundquist, E. A., and Sletto, R. F. (1936) *Personality in the Depression*. Minneapolis, MN: University of Minnesota Press.

Rushton, J. P., Brainerd, C. J., and Pressley, M. (1983) Behavioral development and construct validity: The principle of aggregation. *Psychological Bulletin*, 94, 18–38.

Sample, J., and Warland, R. (1973) Attitude and prediction of behavior. *Social Forces* (Vol. 51, pp. 292–304): University of North Carolina Press.

Sanger, S. P., and Alker, H. A. (1972) Dimensions of internal-external locus of control and the women's liberation movement. *Journal of Social Issues*, 28, 115–29.

Sarver, V. T. (1983) Ajzen and Fishbein's 'theory of reasoned action': A critical assessment. *Journal for the Theory of Social Behaviour*, 13, 155–63.

Saucier, D. A., and Miller, C. T. (2003) The persuasiveness of racial arguments as a subtle measure of racism. *Personality and Social Psychology Bulletin*, 29, 1303–15.

Scheier, M. F., Buss, A. H., and Buss, D. M. (1978) Self-consciousness, self-report of aggressiveness, and aggression. *Journal of Research in Personality*, 12, 133–40.

Schifter, D. E., and Ajzen, I. (1985) Intention, perceived control, and weight loss: An application of the theory of planned behavior. *Journal of Personality and Social Psychology*, 49, 843–51.

Schlegel, R. P. (1975) Multidimensional measurement of attitude towards smoking marijuana. *Canadian Journal of Behavioural Science*, 7, 387–96.

Schlegel, R. P., D'Avernas, J. R., Zanna, M. P., DeCourville, N. H., et al. (1992) Problem drinking: A problem for the theory of reasoned action? *Journal of Applied Social Psychology*, 22, 358–85.

Schlegel, R. P., and DiTecco, D. (1982) Attitudinal structures and the attitude-behavior relation. In M. P. Zanna, E. T. Higgins and C. P. Herman (eds), *Consistency in Social Behavior: The Ontario Symposium* (Vol. 2, pp. 17–49). Hillsdale, NJ: Erlbaum.

Schneider, W., and Shiffrin, R. M. (1977) Controlled and automatic human information processing: I. Detection, search, and attention. *Psychological Review*, 84, 1–66.

Schultz, P. W., Shriver, C., Tabanico, J. J., and Khazian, A. M. (2004) Implicit connections with nature. *Journal of Environmental Psychology*, 24, 31–42.

Schuman, H., and Johnson, M. P. (1976) Attitudes and behavior. *Annual Review of Sociology*, 2, 161–207.

Schwartz, S. H. (1977) Normative influences on altruism. In L. Berkowitz (ed.), *Advances in Experimental Social Psychology* (Vol. 10, pp. 221–79). San Diego: Academic Press.

Schwartz, S. H. (1992) Universals in the content and structure of values: Theoretical advances and empirical tests in 20 countries. In M. P. Zanna (ed.), *Advances in Experimental Social Psychology* (Vol. 25, pp. 1–65). San Diego, CA: Academic Press.

Sears, D. O. (1988) Symbolic racism. In P. A. Katz and D. A. Taylor (eds), *Eliminating Racism: Profiles in Controversy. Perspectives in Social Psychology* (pp. 53–84). New York: Plenum Press.

Sejwacz, D., Ajzen, I., and Fishbein, M. (1980) Predicting and understanding weight loss: Intentions, behaviors, and outcomes. In I. Ajzen and M. Fishbein (eds), *Understanding Attitudes and Predicting Social Behavior* (pp. 101–12). Englewood-Cliffs, NJ: Prentice-Hall.

Sekaquaptewa, D., Espinoza, P., Thompson, M., Vargas, P., and von Hippel, W. (2003) Stereotypic explanatory bias: Implicit stereotyping as a predictor of discrimination. *Journal of Experimental Social Psychology*, 39, 75–82.

Sengupta, J., and Fitzsimons, G. J. (2000) The effects of analyzing reasons for brand preferences: Disruption or reinforcement? *Journal of Marketing Research*, 37, 318–30.

Sheeran, P. (2002) Intention-behavior relations: A conceptual and empirical review. In W. Stroebe and M. Hewstone (eds), *European Review of Social Psychology* (Vol. 12, pp. 1–36). Chichester: Wiley.

Sheeran, P., Abraham, C., and Orbell, S. (1999) Psychosocial correlates of hetero-sexual condom use: A meta-analysis. *Psychological Bulletin*, 125, 90–132.

Sheeran, P., and Orbell, S. (1998) Do intentions predict condom use? Meta-analysis and examination of six moderator variables. *British Journal of Social Psychology*, 37, 231–50.

Sheeran, P., and Orbell, S. (1999) Implementation intentions and repeated behaviour: Augmenting the predictive validity of the theory of planned behaviour. *European Journal of Social Psychology*, 29, 349–69.

Sheeran, P., and Orbell, S. (2000) Self-schemas and the theory of planned behaviour. *European Journal of Social Psychology*, 30, 533–50.

Sheeran, P., Orbell, S., and Trafimow, D. (1999) Does the temporal stability of behavioral intentions moderate intention-behavior and past behavior-future behavior relations? *Personality and Social Psychology Bulletin*, 25, 721–30.

Sheeran, P., and Taylor, S. (1999) Predicting intentions to use condoms: A meta-analysis and comparison of the theories of reasoned action and planned behavior. *Journal of Applied Social Psychology*, 29, 1624–75.

Shepherd, B. H., Hartwick, J., and Warshaw, P. R. (1988) The theory of reasoned action: A meta-analysis of past research with recommendations for modifications and future research. *Journal of Consumer Research*, 15, 325–42.

Sherif, M., and Hovland, C. I. (1961) *Social Judgment: Assimilation and Contrast Effects in Communication and Attitude Change*. New Haven, CT: Yale University Press.

Sherman, S. J., and Fazio, R. H. (1983) Parallels between attitudes and traits as predictors of behavior. *Journal of Personality*, 51, 308–45.

Shestowsky, D., Wegener, D. T., and Fabrigar, L. R. (1998) Need for cognition and interpersonal influence: Individual differences in impact on dyadic decisions. *Journal of Personality and Social Psychology*, 74, 1317–28.

Shiffrin, R. M., and Schneider, W. (1977) Controlled and automatic human information processing: II. Perceptual learning, automatic attending and a general theory. *Psychological Review*, 84, 127–90.

Shweder, R. A. (1975) How relevant is an individual difference theory of personality? *Journal of Personality*, 43, 455–84.

Siem, F. M. (1998) Metatraits and self-schemata: Same or different? *Journal of Personality*, 66, 783–803.

Sivacek, J., and Crano, W. D. (1982) Vested interest as a moderator of attitude-behavior consistency. *Journal of Personality and Social Psychology*, 43, 210–21.

Sjöberg, L. (1982) Attitude-behavior correlation, social desirability and perceived diagnostic value. *British Journal of Social Psychology*, 21, 283–92.

Small, S. A., Zeldin, S., and Savin-Williams, R. (1983) In search of personality traits: A multimethod analysis of naturally occurring prosocial and dominance behavior. *Journal of Personality*, 51, 1–16.

Smetana, J. G., and Adler, N. E. (1980) Fishbein's Value x Expectancy model: An examination of some assumptions. *Personality and Social Psychology Bulletin*, 6, 89–96.

Smith, M. B. (1947) The personal setting of public opinions: A study of attitudes toward Russia. *Public Opinion Quarterly*, 11, 507–23.

Snyder, M. (1974) Self-monitoring of expressive behavior. *Journal of Personality and Social Psychology*, 30, 526–37.

Snyder, M. (1979) Self-monitoring processes. In L. Berkowitz (ed.), *Advances in Experimental Social Psychology* (Vol. 12, pp. 85–128). San Diego: Academic Press.

Snyder, M. (1982) When believing means doing: Creating links between attitudes and behavior. In M. P. Zanna, E. T. Higgins and C. P. Herman (eds), *Consistency in Social Behavior: The Ontario Symposium* (Vol. 2, pp. 105–30). Hillsdale, NJ: Erlbaum.

Snyder, M., and Kendzierski, D. (1982a) Acting on one's attitudes: Procedures for linking attitude and behavior. *Journal of Experimental Social Psychology*, 18, 165–83.

Snyder, M., and Kendzierski, D. (1982b) Choosing social situations: Investigating the origins of correspondence between attitudes and behavior. *Journal of Personality*, 50, 280–95.

Snyder, M., and Swann, B. W., Jr. (1976) When actions reflect attitudes: The politics of impression management. *Journal of Personality and Social Psychology*, 34, 1034–42.

Songer-Nocks, E. (1976) Situational factors affecting the weighting of predictor components in the Fishbein model. *Journal of Experimental Social Psychology*, 12, 56–69.

Sroufe, L. A. (1979) The coherence of individual development: Early care, attachment, and subsequent developmental issues. *American Psychologist*, 34, 834–41.

Sroufe, L. A., and Waters, E. (1977) Attachment as an organizational construct. *Child Development* (Vol. 48, pp. 1184–99): Blackwell Publishing Limited.

Staub, E. (1974) Helping a distressed person: Social, personality, and stimulus determinants. In L. Berkowitz (ed.), *Advances in Experimental Social Psychology* (Vol. 7, pp. 293–341). San Diego: Academic Press.

Stiff, J. B., and Mongeau, P. A. (2003) *Persuasive Communication* (2nd edn.). New York: Guilford Press.

Tedeschi, J. T., Schlenker, B. R., and Bonoma, T. V. (1971) Cognitive dissonance: Private ratiocination or public spectacle? *American Psychologist*, 26, 685–95.

Tellegen, A., Kamp, J., and Watson, D. (1982) Recognizing individual differences in predictive structure. *Psychological Review*, 89, 95–105.

Terry, D. J., and O'Leary, J. E. (1995) The theory of planned behaviour: The effects of perceived behavioural control and self-efficacy. *British Journal of Social Psychology*, 34, 199–220.

Thurstone, L. L. (1931) The measurement of social attitudes. *Journal of Abnormal and Social Psychology*, 26, 249–69.

Thurstone, L. L., and Chave, E. J. (1929) *The Measurement of Attitude: A Psychological Method and Some Experiments with a Scale for Measuring Attitude Toward the Church*. Chicago: University of Chicago Press.

Tittle, C. R., and Hill, R. J. (1967) Attitude measurement and prediction of behavior: An evaluation of conditions and measurement techniques. *Sociometry*, 30, 199–213.

Triandis, H. C. (1977) *Interpersonal Behavior*. Monterey, CA: Brooks/Cole.

Uhlmann, E., and Swanson, J. (2004) Exposure to violent video games increases automatic aggressiveness. *Journal of Adolescence*, 27, 41–52.

Underwood, B., and Moore, B. S. (1981) Sources of behavioral consistency. *Journal of Personality and Social Psychology*, 40, 780–5.

Upmeyer, A. (1981) Perceptual and judgmental processes in social contexts. In L. Berkowitz (ed.), *Advances in Experimental Social Psychology* (Vol. 14, pp. 257–308). San Diego: Academic Press.

van den Putte, B. (1993) On the theory of reasoned action. Unpublished dissertation, University of Amsterdam.

Veevers, J. E. (1971) Drinking attitudes and drinking behavior: An exploratory study. *Journal of Social Psychology*, 85, 103–9.

Vernon, P. E. (1964) *Personality Assessment: A Critical Survey*. Oxford: John Wiley and Sons.

Verplanken, B., and Faes, S. (1999) Good intentions, bad habits, and effects of forming implementation intentions on healthy eating. *European Journal of Social Psychology*, 29, 591–604.

Verplanken, B., and Orbell, S. (2003) Reflections on past behavior: A self-report index of habit strength. *Jounal of Applied Social Psychology*, 33, 1313–30.

Vinokur, A., and Caplan, R. D. (1987) Attitudes and social support: Determinants of job-seeking behavior and well-being among the unemployed. *Journal of Applied Social Psychology*, 17, 1007–24.

Vinokur, A., Caplan, R. D., and Williams, C. C. (1987) Effects of recent and past stress on mental health: Coping with unemployment among Vietnam veterans and nonveterans. *Journal of Applied Social Psychology*, 17, 710–30.

Vinokur-Kaplan, D. (1978) To have – or not to have – another child: Family planning attitudes, intentions, and behavior. *Journal of Applied Social Psychology*, 8, 29–46.

Vroom, V. H. (1964) *Work and Motivation*. New York: Wiley.

Wallston, B. S., Wallston, K. A., Kaplan, G. D., and Maides, S. A. (1976) Development and validation of the Health Locus of Control (HLC) Scale. *Journal of Consulting and Clinical Psychology*, 44, 580–5.

Wallston, K. A., and Wallston, B. S. (1981) Health locus of control scales. In H. M. Lefcourt (ed.), *Research with the Locus of Control Construct*. Vol. 1: *Assessment Methods* (pp. 189–243). San Diego: Academic Press.

Wallston, K. A., Wallston, B. S., and DeVellis, R. (1978) Development of the Multidimensional Health Locus of Control (MHLC) scales. *Health Education Monographs* (Vol. 6, pp. 160–70).

Waly, P., and Cook, S. W. (1965) Effect of attitude on judgments of plausibility. *Journal of Personality and Social Psychology*, 2, 745–9.

Warehime, R. G. (1972) Generalized expectancy for locus of control and academic performance. *Psychological Reports*, 30, 314.

Warland, R. H., and Sample, J. (1973) Response certainty as a moderator variable in attitude measurement. *Rural Sociology*, 38, 174–86.

Warner, L. G., and DeFleur, M. L. (1969) Attitude as an interactional concept: Social constraint and social distance as intervening variables between attitudes and action. *American Sociological Review*, 34, 153–69.

Waters, E. (1978) The reliability and stability of individual differences in infant-mother attachment. *Child Development*, 49, 483–94.

Weigel, R. H., and Newman, L. S. (1976) Increasing attitude-behavior correspondence by broadening the scope of the behavioral measure. *Journal of Personality and Social Psychology*, 33, 793–802.

Weigel, R. H., Vernon, D. T., and Tognacci, L. N. (1974) Specificity of the attitude as a determinant of attitude-behavior congruence. *Journal of Personality and Social Psychology*, 30, 724–8.

Werner, P. D. (1978) Personality and attitude-activism correspondence. *Journal of Personality and Social Psychology*, 36, 1375–90.

Wicker, A. W. (1969) Attitudes versus actions: The relationship of verbal and overt behavioral responses to attitude objects. *Journal of Social Issues*, 25, 41–78.

Wicker, A. W., and Pomazal, R. J. (1971) The relationship between attitudes and behavior as a function of specificity of attitude object and presence of a significant person during assessment conditions. *Representative Research in Social Psychology*, 2, 26–31.

Wicklund, R. A. (1975) Objective self awareness. In L. Berkowitz (ed.), *Advances in Experimental Social Psychology* (Vol. 8, pp. 233–75). San Diego, CA: Academic Press.

Widaman, K. F. (1985) Hierarchically nested covariance structure models for multitrait-multimethod data. *Applied Psychological Measurement*, 9, 1–26.

Wiggins, J. S. (1973) *Personality and Prediction: Principles of Personality Assessment*. Reading, MA: Addison-Wesley.

Wilde, G. J., and de Wit, O. E. (1970) Self-report and error choice: Inter-individual differences in the operation of the error-choice principle and their validity in personality questionnaire tests. *British Journal of Psychology*, 61, 219–28.

Wilde, G. J., and Fortuin, S. (1969) Self-report and error choice: An application of the error-choice principle to the construction of personality test items. *British Journal of Psychology*, 60, 101–8.

Wilson, T. D., and Dunn, D. S. (1986) Effects of introspection on attitude-behavior consistency: Analyzing reasons versus focusing on feelings. *Journal of Experimental Social Psychology*, 22, 249–63.

Wilson, T. D., Dunn, D. S., Bybee, J. A., Hyman, D. B., and Rotondo, J. A. (1984) Effects of analyzing reasons on attitude-behavior consistency. *Journal of Personality and Social Psychology*, 47, 5–16.

Wilson, T. D., Lindsey, S., and Schooler, T. Y. (2000) A model of dual attitudes. *Psychological Review*, 107, 101–26.

Wright, J. C. (1983) The structure and perception of behavioral consistency. Unpublished doctoral dissertation, Stanford University, Stanford, CA.

Yin, Z., and Boyd, M. P. (2000) Behavioral and cognitive correlates of exercise self-schemata. *Journal of Psychology: Interdisciplinary and Applied*, 134, 269–82.

Zajonc, R. B. (1968) Cognitive theories in social psychology. In G. Lindzey and E. Aronson (eds), *The Handbook of Social Psychology* (2nd edn., Vol. 1, pp. 320–441). Reading, MA: Addison-Wesley.

Zanna, M. P., Olson, J. M., and Fazio, R. H. (1980) Attitude-behavior consistency: An individual difference perspective. *Journal of Personality and Social Psychology*, 38, 432–40.

Zedeck, S. (1971) Problems with the use of 'moderator' variables. *Psychological Bulletin*, 76, 295–310.

Zuckerman, M., and Reis, H. T. (1978) Comparison of three models for predicting altruistic behavior. *Journal of Personality and Social Psychology*, 36, 498–510.

AUTHOR INDEX

SUBJECT INDEX